ARTISANS AND ARCHITECTS

By the same author

HOMES FIT FOR HEROES: The Politics and Architecture of Early
State Housing in Britain

Artisans and Architects

The Ruskinian Tradition in
Architectural Thought

Mark Swenarton

St. Martin's Press   New York

All rights reserved. For information, write:
Scholarly and Reference Division,
St. Martin's Press, Inc., 175 Fifth Avenue, New York, NY 10010

First published in the United States of America in 1988

Printed in Hong Kong

ISBN 0-312-02375-8

Library of Congress Cataloging-in-Publication Data
Swenarton, Mark.
Artisans and architects: The Ruskinian tradition in architectural
thought/Mark Swenarton.
   p.   cm.
Bibliography: p.
Includes index.
ISBN 0-312-02375-8: $35.00 (est.)
1. Architecture, Modern—19th century—Great Britain.
2. Architecture—Great Britain.   3. Ruskin, John, 1819–1900—
Influence.   4. Architecture—Philosophy.   I. Title.
NA967.S94   1989
720'.1—dc19   88–14853
                                             CIP

To the memory of
Maggie Scruton

Contents

List of Illustrations

Acknowledgements

I would like to thank the many individuals who have helped in various ways with this work, including John Brandon-Jones, Bridie Diamond and Bruce Hanson, David Dunster, Brigid Grafton Green, Alan and Hilary Graham, Sheila Kirk, Mervyn Miller, Francis Milsom, Michael Penty, Ruth Richardson, Godfrey Rubens, Sir John Summerson, David Thistlewood, F. M. L. Thompson, William Vaughan and above all Martin O'Doherty and Adrian Forty. I should also like to thank collectively the staff of the libraries and archives that I consulted.

The publication of this book has been assisted by a grant from the Twenty-Seven Foundation.

Introduction

This book is a study of what has been arguably the major British contribution to architectural thought in the past 150 years: the tradition based on the chapter entitled 'The Nature of Gothic' in Ruskin's *Stones of Venice* of 1853. This way of thinking about architecture was most fully expounded by William Morris in the 1880s, and was further developed by associates and disciples of Ruskin and Morris – including Philip Webb, W. R. Lethaby, Raymond Unwin and A. J. Penty – in the period up to the First World War.

The central notion in this tradition was that architecture should be the expression of the character of the worker. Gothic was seen as the great exemplar from the past of an architecture in which the worker had been not a 'slave', but a free artist, able to put his soul and feelings into the work. Against the division of labour involved in industrial production, thinkers of this persuasion sought to reunite the 'heart' with the 'hand', and regarded medieval guilds as models of integrated labour. This idea led directly to the building guild experiment of the early 1920s, an episode which marked both the culmination and, in the event, the termination of this tradition.

Why should we be interested in the Ruskinian tradition today? One obvious consideration is the crisis into which architecture has been thrown by the collapse of modernism. After fifty years' intellectual hegemony, and at least thirty years' dominance over the practice of architecture, modernism, or the 'Modern Movement' as it was called when still a credo, became in the 1970s subject to general review and quite frequent attack. If nothing else, this has focused historical attention on to strands and traditions in architecture other than modernism and makes the Ruskinian tradition an obvious candidate for reappraisal – all the more so because hitherto no full-scale historical study of it has been made.[1]

There are in addition more specific reasons for a reappraisal of the Ruskinian tradition. During the period of political consensus that lasted roughly from the Second World War to the oil crisis of 1973, the relationship between architecture and social democracy was not generally seen as problematic within western architectural thought. To a substantial extent architectural practice and education was oriented around the welfare state and the provision of social services, in the form of housing, hospitals, schools and so on. But in the 1970s in a number of western countries there emerged a powerful demand for the 'rolling back' of the welfare state, which brought into question the assumption that architecture should be directed to social welfare goals. In their very different ways the writings of the New Right in Cambridge and of the Venetian marxist school bear witness to this change of focus.[2] Political events of the 1980s, notably the sustained electoral success of governments antagonistic to welfare provision, have made this question of the relationship between architecture and the goals of social democracy even more pressing.

The main response of architectural historians to these developments has been to re-examine the relationship between architecture and social welfare in modernism. Recent years have seen a number of studies which have substantially changed our understanding of the social ambitions of architectural modernism, especially in the key periods after the two world wars.[3] To advance this discussion further it is necessary to move into different territory. The Ruskinian tradition, which is widely regarded as the major socialist tradition in architecture prior to the advent of modernism, offers a fruitful ground for the further exploration of these issues.

Another factor of a more academic nature that points in the same direction is the current concern with the role of idealism in architectural thought. Idealism in this context (and indeed throughout this book) refers to the philosophical system, most fully developed in Germany in the early nineteenth century, which holds that ideas exist prior to and independently of material conditions; the notion of 'the spirit of the age' as a determining force in history is its most obvious manifestation. The role of idealism in art and art history was identified as a major issue by Ernst Gombrich in the 1960s and 1970s.[4] Within architecture the dependence of modernist thought and modernist history on idealist notions had long been apparent, but it was only in the 1970s that the process of charting it in a precise way was begun.[5] An examination of the relationship between idealism and architectural thought in the period prior to modernism therefore seems in order.

In the case of the Ruskinian tradition, this twin interest in social democracy and idealism as issues in architecture raises as a key question the relationship between Ruskinian thought and the historical materialism of Marx and Engels. Marx's theory of history and of society was conceived explicitly as a counter to the historical idealism of Hegel: as Engels said of Marx,

> now idealism was driven from its last refuge, the philosophy of history; now a materialistic treatment of history was propounded, and a method found of explaining man's 'knowing' by his being, instead of, as heretofore, his 'being' by his 'knowing'.[6]

Marx's ideas, moreover, constituted the intellectual platform for the socialist movement and for social democratic politics in many European countries (although not, it must be said, in Britain). They were the product of the same period of social crisis as the ideas that Ruskin presented in 'The Nature of Gothic'; and although never read by Ruskin, Marx was known to Webb and Penty and studied attentively by Morris and Unwin. The question of how much the thinkers in the Ruskinian tradition learned from this source becomes, in the light of the concerns outlined above, an historical issue of some importance.

On the methodological level, this book belongs to an established specialism of architectural history: the history of architectural thought. That is to say, the concern is less with what was designed or built than with the ideas about architecture and building held by architects and critics of architecture – whom for convenience I have termed 'architectural thinkers'. This however immediately raises a problem in that, as a genre, the history of architectural thought has been dominated by the idealist notions described above. For the most part, in existing studies architectural ideas are treated as though they were self-generated and as though they existed on a different plane from the everyday world of material life.[7] Against this I have attempted to develop a different and, I hope, a more realistic approach, treating developments in architectural ideas partly as a response to other ideas but partly as a response to changing economic and political conditions. Economic crises and political movements figure alongside the play of ideas and argument in the explanation of the intellectual developments studied in these pages. In that this approach posits ideas as existing on the basis of, and in some sort of relation to, material conditions, and sees both as undergoing a process of development over time, it takes its general inspiration from historical materialism.

The book is organised as a series of studies of six individual thinkers: Ruskin, Webb, Morris, Lethaby, Unwin and Penty. Others doubtless might have been added (Edward Prior, or C. R. Ashbee, or the architects of the London County Council housing division) but without substantially changing the overall picture.[8] Although the chapters are generally chronological in arrangement they are not biographical or synoptic; rather in each case they focus on a key episode and period (for example Ruskin's thought in the 1840s, or Lethaby's educational work in the 1890s). In some cases (Ruskin, Morris) the subject is architectural thought in the 'pure' state of writings on architecture; in the others (Webb, Lethaby, Unwin, Penty) it is architectural thought as 'applied' in the fields of art architecture, design education, city planning, and guild socialism.

At the outset a couple of points of a geographical nature should be made. Although the book deals primarily with architectural thought in Britain, necessarily it cannot ignore what was happening elsewhere: the British tradition formed part of the European Romantic movement and fed both on and into intellectual developments on a world scale. One of the recurrent themes in the book is the part played in the development of British thought by non-British thinkers such as Goethe, Viollet-le-Duc and the American transcendentalists. As a complement to this, the final chapter takes the form of an epilogue surveying the impact of Ruskinian ideas on architectural thought in France, Germany and the USA.

Within Britain, the Ruskinian tradition had a distinctive geography: it was the product of the south of England, particularly Oxford and London. It was in the ancient university town of Oxford that Ruskin studied and taught, and that Morris, Webb and Unwin spent formative periods of their youth; and it was in London – the centre of government and luxury consumption – that all six of our thinkers, with one significant exception, lived. It is a curiosity that the process of industrialisation, which figured so large within the architectural thought of these people, was largely absent from the region in which they lived and worked: in the south production was still artisanal and the organisation of the labour movement, in both industrial and political terms, was correspondingly weak. As Morris noted, 'the London workmen are blasé of politics & have none of the solidarity which the workmen of the big industries have'.[9] This was to have significant effects on attitudes both to work and to the potential of organised labour in the southern tradition. Of our six thinkers, Unwin alone stood outside this southern affiliation, living and working in the socialist movement of the industrial north. In this sense the chapter on Unwin, which traces the major differences between his thought and Ruskinian orthodoxy, provides the counterpoint to the rest of the study.

Finally a point should be made on sources. There are considerable differences in the availability in readily accessible form of the works and papers of the six authors: at one extreme is Ruskin, with the magnificent 39 volumes of the collected works, plus further published diaries and letters; at the other is Philip Webb, who did not publish any books and whose letters and diaries are to be found only in archives and scattered periodicals. In general my principle has been to work from the original sources, both published and unpublished, except where the availability of reliable published collections makes it unnecessary. A list of the main archives consulted can be found with the references.

1

Ruskin and 'The Nature of Gothic'

Although Ruskin's life was long (1819–1900), and even his publishing career extended for more than half a century, his architectural output belongs almost entirely to two relatively circumscribed periods: the period 1848–53, in which he became preoccupied with architecture as an aside from *Modern Painters* and produced his most famous architectural works, *The Seven Lamps of Architecture* and *The Stones of Venice*; and the period of the 1870s and early 1880s, in which his interest in architecture was reawakened by a plan for a new edition of *The Stones of Venice*, but which instead led to new work, including *St Mark's Rest* and *The Bible of Amiens*. Although the products of Ruskin's second architectural period are by no means without interest or importance, our concern here is with the first: the period that opened with his notebook scheme for *The Seven Lamps of Architecture* in the spring of 1848 and closed with the publication of the third and final volume of *The Stones of Venice* in October 1853. This has often been described as a period of transition in Ruskin's life, with Ruskin the critic of art turning into Ruskin the critic of society. In his architectural studies, we see Ruskin developing the ideas about art and architecture that he had inherited from the Romantics in the light of the current concerns about work and industrial production generated by the social crisis of 'the hungry forties'.

RUSKIN AND GERMAN ROMANTIC THOUGHT

Ruskin's art criticism of the 1840s and 1850s was to a large extent informed by the ideas and values of the Romantic movement. Above all, Ruskin shared the Romantics' belief that art was the product of, and addressed to, the full creative powers of the human spirit. In this he followed Wordsworth (whom Ruskin regarded as a major influence), who had written in 1815 in a sonnet dedicated to the painter B. R. Haydon:

1.1 'The Author of Modern Painters': portrait of John Ruskin by George Richmond (1843)

High is our calling, Friend! – Creative Art
(Whether the instrument of words she use,
Or pencil pregnant with ethereal hues,)
Demands the service of a mind and heart. . . .[1]

While Romanticism was a phenomenon of Europe as a whole, many of these ideas about art had first been developed in Germany, by Goethe, Schiller, *et al.*, during the last quarter of the eighteenth century and in particular in the turbulent decade that followed the French Revolution of 1789. Following Ruskin's own persistent denigration of German art and German thought, Ruskin scholarship has tended to overlook the extent to which his thought drew on this German Romantic tradition. To get into proper perspective therefore both the ideas that Ruskin himself presented in 'The Nature of Gothic', and the intellectual tradition that subsequently developed with 'The Nature of Gothic' at its centre, it is necessary at the outset to look briefly at the concept of art developed by the German writers.[2]

The Romantic notion of art as a vehicle of spiritual communication between the artist and the observer was first set out by Goethe in his youthful essay *Von Deutscher Baukunst* of 1772–3. In this key text of the *Sturm und Drang*, Goethe offered up a hymn of praise to Strasburg cathedral, dramatically recreating the impression made on him by the sight of the Gothic cathedral and hailing its purported architect, Master Erwin, as a great artist and a great spirit.

> With what unexpected emotion did the sight surprise me as I stopped before it. A complete and total impression filled my soul. . . . And how often did I return to enjoy this heavenly-earthly joy, to embrace the gigantic spirit of our older brothers in their works![3]

Goethe here presented the idealist notion that art was the expression of the creative human spirit and the work of art was matter endowed with spirit. In the course of the essay Goethe developed his theory of the 'characteristic' in art: true art was not (as classical theory held) a matter of formal beauty so much as a matter of 'character', the expression in the object of the God-given urge in man to 'find material in which to breathe his spirit'.[4] Against neo-classical notions of 'good taste', Goethe saw art as the expression of the primitive, and he exalted Gothic, and Strasburg in particular, as its supreme example:

> No-one will push Erwin from the level to which he has climbed. Here is his work: approach and recognise the deepest feeling of truth and beauty of proportion emanating from a strong, vigorous German soul . . . .[5]

Goethe saw Gothic as analogous to nature and thereby in a special relationship with the divinity. Art was 'another Nature':[6] as the divine spirit had created nature, Goethe implied, so the spirit in man had created Gothic. The cathedral 'rises like a tall, sublime, wide-spreading tree of God, which, with a thousand branches, millions of twigs and leaves as the sands of the sea, proclaims to the country round about the glory of the Lord, its Master'.[7] Returning to Strasburg a few years later (1776), Goethe was struck by the cathedral's resemblance to the landscape of Switzerland and the Rhine: the peaks and lakes, the towering cliffs and wild ravines.[8]

The new status given by Goethe to art, as the link between the here-and-now and the eternal, was reproduced by Kant in his philosophical treatment of the aesthetic. If Kant's *Critique of Pure Reason* of 1781 constituted the foundation of modern philosophy, his *Critique of Judgement* of 1790, by establishing the particularity of the aesthetic, marked the beginning of modern philosophical aesthetics. In Kant's system of 'transcendental idealism', a correlation was posited between the capacities of the knower and the nature of the known; it was the faculty of judgement, primarily moral but also aesthetic, that demonstrated this harmony between our faculties and the external world. Kant's *Critique of Judgement* suggested that the aesthetic formed a bridge between the sensuous and the transcendental,

> between the territory of the conception of Nature, that is, the sensuous, and the territory of the conception of Freedom, that is, the supra-sensuous . . . making possible a transition from the mode of thinking dictated by the principles of the one world to that dictated by the principles of the other world.[9]

Looking back from the standpoint of the 1820s, Hegel declared that Kant's work had constituted 'the starting point for the true comprehension of the beauty of art', but that it was others who broke through the limitations of Kant's system to make aesthetics into a 'science'.[10] The 1790s – which saw the French Revolution spill beyond its national frontiers and drag the German principalities into a war between revolution and conservatism – was a decade of intellectual as well as political ferment in Germany, in the course of which, proceeding from the ideas of Kant and the young Goethe, the main tenets of Romantic art theory were established. In his *Letters on Aesthetic Culture* of 1794, Schiller explicitly took Kant as his starting-point but further elevated the sensuous against the rational, declaring that only through the development of the sense of beauty ('aesthetic culture') would humanity reach self-consciousness and, thereby, freedom. In Dresden the Schlegel brothers and the philosopher Schelling proclaimed the doctrine of art as the representation within the material or finite of the spiritual or infinite; as Schelling put it in his *System of Transcendental Idealism* of 1800, 'the infinite represented in finite form is Beauty'.[11]

The contrast between this new concept of art and that of the past was explored both by Schiller, in his essay on 'Naive and Sentimental Poetry' (1795–96), and by August Wilhelm von Schlegel, who held that the artist was the representative of his age, and that art was the expression of the spirit of the age that made it. In his *Lectures on Dramatic Art* of 1808, Schlegel argued that art should be appreciated in relation to its age: there was a basic contrast between the ancient or classical and the modern or romantic; Westminster Abbey was quite different from but as perfect as the Parthenon, just as Shakespeare was different from but as great as Sophocles.

These ideas suggested that Gothic art was the equal of classical; Friedrich von Schlegel regarded Gothic as 'Christian art' and therefore as superior. Following suggestions made by Wackenroder in the evocatively entitled *Heartfelt Effusions of an Art-loving Monk* (1797), Schlegel praised the early painters of Italy and the Netherlands, judging them superior to their Renaissance successors on account of both their piety and their 'childlike' simplicity of expression. Schlegel's *Letters from a Journey* of 1806 (later re-issued as the *Principles of Gothic Architecture* in 1823) contained some of the most powerful evocations of Gothic produced by the Romantic movement. Schlegel presented Gothic not just as the expression of the northern (Germanic) climate and character, but also as the artistic equivalent of nature and the spiritual expression of

Christianity: 'by its imitation of the beauties of nature' Gothic architecture brought 'the idea of the Divinity palpably before our minds'.[12] For Schlegel the apogee of this was Cologne cathedral. The tower was

> like some incomparable production of the vegetable kingdom; while the numerous, wide-spreading, flying buttresses, with their arches, decorations, crockets, finials, and pinnacles, resemble a forest. The Gothic pillars in the interior have not unaptly been compared to a lofty avenue of trees . . . . These columns have been also compared to natural basaltic pillars; and the lofty vaulted arch might almost be likened to the jet of a mighty fountain . . . . And if the exterior, with its countless towers and pinnacles, appears at a distance not unlike a forest, the whole prodigious structure, on a nearer approach, looks like some magnificent crystallisation. It is, in a word, the wonder-work of art; and from the incomparable abundance of its decorations, seems to vie with the inexhaustible variety of nature herself.[13]

The most systematic exposition of the new artistic ideas was provided by Hegel in his lectures on *Aesthetics*, delivered in the 1820s and published posthumously in 1835. With his customary thoroughness Hegel provided both an historical overview (dividing the history of art into three periods, Symbolic, Classical and Romantic) and an analytical classification, ranking the modes of artistic expression (architecture, sculpture, painting, music, poetry) in ascending order of ideality, with architecture, as the most material, at the bottom. In this system he drew heavily on Schiller, A. W. von Schlegel and Schelling. Throughout, the concept of art was the idealist one inherited from Goethe and Kant:

> art and works of art, by springing from and being created by the spirit, are themselves of a spiritual kind . . . . In the products of art, the spirit has to do solely with its own.[14]

Throughout the Romantic period, the German thinkers had taken much of their inspiration from eighteenth-century English and Scottish thought: from David Hume's philosophical scepticism, from Edward Young's paean to genius, from Burke's theory of the sublime, and from Adam Ferguson's comments on the divisive effects of the development of commercial society. During the first half of the nineteenth century the direction was reversed and British thought gradually absorbed the new German ideas. One of the first to be inspired by the Germans (particularly Schiller) was Coleridge, who with Wordsworth made a pilgrimage to Germany in 1798 to study the writers and aestheticians. As the *Biographia Literaria* (1817) showed, this visit had a lasting impact on Coleridge's thought. A major populariser of German thought in Britain was Madame de Staël, the companion of A. W. von Schlegel, whose *Germany* of 1813 surveyed both literature (Goethe, Schiller, the Schlegels *et al.*) and Kantian and post-Kantian philosophy. The other major exponent of German literature and philosophy was Thomas Carlyle, particularly with the *Life of Schilller* (1825; published in German in 1830 with a preface by Goethe, and reprinted in England in 1845), and 'The State of German Literature' of 1827 (reprinted 1840), which emphasised the importance attached by the Germans, poets and philosophers alike, to 'the inmost Spirit of Man'.[15]

In the field of the visual arts, as William Vaughan has shown, German ideas made relatively little impression until the 1830s and 1840s, a period of social and ideological crisis, when they were taken up with a vengeance. In 1836 two books appeared in London that proclaimed the doctrine of 'Christian art' of Wackenroder and Schlegel within the terms of the Catholic revival: Pugin's *Contrasts* and Rio's *De la poésie Chrétienne*. In *Contrasts* Pugin combined two different pairs of contrasts under a single head: while his text, a history of the protestant reformation in England, presented the contrast between the piety of the middle ages and the paganism of the Renaissance postulated by the 'Christian art' writers, his illustrations drew on the contrast between the pre-industrial 'golden age' and early nineteenth-century society postulated by the early critics of industrialism, particularly Cobbett. A.-F. Rio was a former pupil of Schelling and a devotee of Friedrich von Schlegel; his book, a guide to the early Italian painters of Florence, Sienna and Venice, drew its interpretation from Wackenroder and Friedrich von Schlegel and its information from the subsequent researches of Rumohr (1827–30). Rio's book vanished without trace in Paris but in London, supported by the Anglo-Catholic tendency, both the book and its author became celebrities, and soon a flood of English derivatives of the doctrine of 'Christian art' appeared, including William Dyce (1844), Anna Jameson (1845 and 1848), Lord Lindsay (1847) – and, as we will see, Ruskin (1846).

The vogue for 'Christian art' coincided with a renewed interest in German literature which culminated in 'the religion of Schiller' of the 1840s. English translations of German turn-of-the-century writings poured off the presses. Among the Schiller issues was the *Philosophical and Aesthetic Letters* (1845), which included the *Letters on Aesthetic Culture*. The major works of Friedrich von Schlegel appeared in a series of issues (1835; 1841; 1846; 1847; 1849), the last being an edition of *Aesthetic and Miscellaneous Works* that included the *Principles of Gothic Architecture*. Also published in English in these years were Schelling's *Philosophy of Art* (1845), A. W. von Schlegel's *Lectures on Dramatic Art* (1846), and Goethe's *Conversations* (1850). Generally the English interest in German aesthetic thought at this stage was literary rather than philosophical: the major treatises on aesthetics by Kant and Hegel were not translated into English until much later in the century, although for those, like Ruskin, who read French but not German there were French translations available, of both Kant's *Critique of Judgement* (1846) and Hegel's *Aesthetics* (1840–52).

By the time of his architecture studies of 1848–53 Ruskin had encountered these German ideas about art through a variety of sources. First, through English interpreters of German thought: Ruskin knew many of Coleridge's poems by heart and was reading his prose works in the 1840s, which was also the period in which he 'discovered' Carlyle. Second, through the 'Christian art' writers of the 1830s and 1840s: Rio (1836) and Kugler (1842), and the English writers Pugin (1836 and 1841), Anna Jameson (1845 and 1848), Eastlake (1847 and 1848) and Lord Lindsay (1847). All of these were read by Ruskin at this time.[16] Third, by reading the German Romantics direct, in the English translations that became popular in the 1840s. In his discussion of aesthetics in *Modern Painters* II (1846), Ruskin paraded this knowledge of German writing, referring to 'the *Anschauung* of the Germans'.[17] We know for certain of two major works of German Romantic art theory read by Ruskin at this time: the *Letters on Aesthetic Culture* by Schiller, which he read on their appearance in English in 1845, and A. W. von Schlegel's *Lectures on Dramatic Art*, which Ruskin was reading in Venice in February 1852, while working on 'The Nature of Gothic'.[18]

RUSKIN'S INTELLECTUAL DEVELOPMENT UP TO 1848

Ruskin first acquired celebrity in 1843 with the publication of the first volume of *Modern Painters*. The title originally proposed for the book, 'Turner and the Ancients', gave a better idea of its contents. The art criticism presented in this book was based on the worship of nature characteristic of the first generation of the Romantics. All glory was to be found in nature: the role of the painter was to convey this glory to the viewer. Thus Ruskin urged students of painting to

> go to Nature in all singleness of heart, and walk with her laboriously and trustingly, having no other thoughts but how best to penetrate her meaning and remember her instruction; rejecting nothing, selecting nothing, and scorning nothing, believing all things to be right and good and rejoicing always in the truth.[19]

Turner was hailed as the artist who, more than any other, had penetrated and communicated the meaning and power of nature.

What Ruskin meant by 'nature' was not just the elements of the natural world – mountains, rocks, trees and so on – although these were an important part of it. For Ruskin, nature was a theological as well as a physical construct: simply put, nature was the work of God. More than that: nature had been made by God for the enjoyment of humanity. It was therefore not only a pleasure, said Ruskin, to study and observe nature: it was also a Christian duty. In art therefore it was a Christian duty to portray nature as it really was (that is, as God had made it) – not, as the picturesque school would have it, to 'improve' on nature by adjustment and rearrangement. Truth and sincerity were the great values in art: above all the painter had to be truthful to what lay in nature and to the powers of observation that had been given by God. The job of the artist was to convey to the viewer his pleasure in, and understanding of, what God had made for humanity: and the only possible basis for this was truth. Such was the message of *Modern Painters* I.

Ruskin shared the Romantic conception of art as a form of language or communication. 'Painting, or art generally, as such, with all its technicalities, difficulties and particular ends, is nothing but a noble and expressive language'.[20] This meant that it was not the work of art in itself that was important, so much as the communication that it contained; and this in turn was directly dependent on the powers and virtue of the artist who was formulating the 'message'. The emphasis, as with Goethe, was on the person making the work of art rather than on the work of art in itself. What we perceive in a work of art, Ruskin said, was the powers of the artist who made it; and these were 'independent of the nature or worthiness of the object from which they are received'.[21] As Ruskin stated at the end of *The Stones of Venice*, 'art is valuable or otherwise, only as it expresses the personality, activity and living perception of a good and great human soul'.[22]

In *Modern Painters* I Ruskin saw nature and art in religious terms. In *Modern Painters* II, published in 1846, he equated religious virtue in art with a specific period of history: the period before the Renaissance. His hero now was the early-fifteenth-century Florentine painter Fra Angelico, whom he considered 'not an artist properly so-called, but an inspired saint'.[23] As we have seen, this equation of Christian virtue with medieval art had first been made by Wackenroder and Friedrich von Schlegel, but in England was given new emphasis with Rio's book of 1836. For Rio Fra Angelico, the painter-monk, was the archetype of the Christian artist, and medieval Venice, significantly, was 'the prime model of a Christian commonwealth'.[24] Ruskin read Rio in 1844–45; was inspired by it; and when he went to Italy in 1845, saw what he now called the Christian painters in Rio's terms. As he recalled a few years later, 'in 1845 came a total change': having 'read Rio on the old religious painters . . . . I went to Italy with a new perception'.[25] From now on for Ruskin medieval meant Christian and virtuous; Renaissance meant pagan and immoral.

It was in the course of this discovery of 'Christian art' that Ruskin's interest in architecture was rekindled, or, as he subsequently interpreted it in his autobiography *Praeterita*, that his eyes were properly opened to architecture for the first time. One of his first publications (1837–38) had been a series of essays on 'The Poetry of Architecture', in which architecture had been considered 'in its Association with Natural Scenery and National Character' – in other words, in terms of the contribution made by buildings to picturesque scenes in the various countries. Now, fired with enthusiasm for the Christian virtues of medieval art – piety, fidelity, simplicity, naturalism – his attention was drawn to that branch of art in which those qualities were most evident: the ornamental

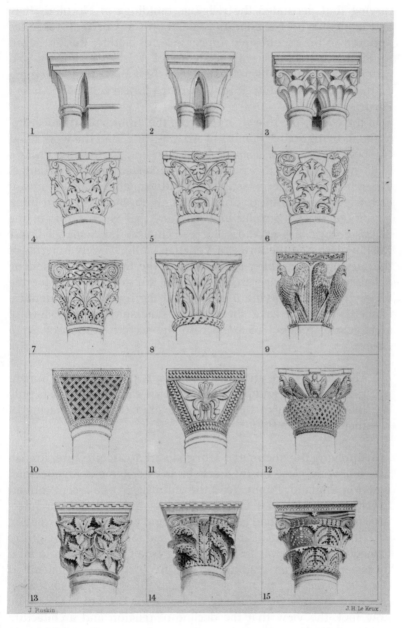

1.2 John Ruskin: Byzantine capitals, concave group (from *The Stones of Venice* II 1853)

carving that decorated the religious buildings of Northern Italy and France. With his mind now fixed on the Christian value, as opposed to the picturesque appearance, of Gothic, Ruskin began to fill his notebooks with sketches of Gothic sculptures and carvings; and during 1846–47, started to think of writing something on the 'Spirits of Architecture' as part of a future volume of *Modern Painters*.

In the event, the title changed from the 'Spirits of Architecture' to the more figurative 'Lamps of Architecture', and the work filled two books – *The Seven Lamps of Architecture* and *The Stones of Venice* – in its own right. But the conception of architecture did not change. When he used the term 'architecture' Ruskin almost always meant architectural sculpture or ornament; only rarely did Ruskin think in a more strictly architectural manner, that is, in terms of the disposition of masses and volumes. Thus in *The Stones of Venice* Ruskin discussed the forms of Venetian Gothic largely in terms of the carving of the thirty-six capitals of the Ducal Palace; and he dismissed Renaissance architecture on the grounds that for the variety of Gothic carving it substituted the repetition of identical elements. Ruskin gave the clearest statement to this view of architecture in the 1855 preface to the second edition of *Seven Lamps*:

> The fact is, there are only two fine arts possible to the human race, sculpture and painting. What we call architecture is only the association of these in noble masses, or the placing of them in fit places.[26]

In applying the doctrine of 'Christian art' to architecture, Ruskin was following close on the heels of another famous architectural writer in England, Pugin. With the enthusiasm of a recent convert to Catholicism, Pugin in *Contrasts* (1836) counterposed the architectural excellence that had existed in England before the Reformation with the architectural degradation that had followed as the country turned from what was in his view the true Catholic faith to false Protestantism. After reading Rio and his associate Montalembert (*De l'état actuel de l'art réligieux en France*, 1839), Pugin somewhat modified the schema for the second edition (1841) of his book: he now took the view that the decline of religion and architecture predated the Henrician Reformation, and was well under way in the fifteenth century. Nonetheless the main point was unchanged:

excellence in architecture was grounded solely in Christian piety, and had come to an end with the demise of that piety.

But while Pugin and Ruskin were at one in the doctrine of Christian art, they were at opposite poles in denominational terms as a Catholic proselytiser and a fierce Evangelical. This at least partly explains the vehemence of the attacks that Ruskin made on Pugin: finding views which to a large extent he shared associated with a cause to which he was antagonistic, Ruskin took refuge in abuse. The first volume of *The Stones of Venice* contained as an appendix an intemperate attack on 'Modern Romanist Art' in general and Pugin in particular ('not a great architect, but one of the smallest possible or conceivable'); and in *Modern Painters* III (1856) Ruskin vehemently denied the charge made by one hostile reviewer 'that I borrow from Pugin'.[27] But however heated Ruskin's denials, the resemblance remained: for Pugin as for Ruskin Gothic architecture was true because Christian; Renaissance architecture was false because pagan.

As noted above, Pugin's thought drew not just on art theory but also on social criticism – specifically, on the backward-looking critique of the new industrial society developed by Cobbett and others. In the 1830s and 1840s the concern of the legislature and intelligentsia over the moral and social consequences of industrialisation came to a head, as the industrial economy experienced its first great crisis. In retrospect, we can recognise this as the first of the cyclical slumps of the industrial economy, which by the 1850s was to turn to boom, but at the time no-one could know this: all that could be stated with confidence at the time was the fact that, as the House of Commons was told in 1842, 'the labouring people of this country were suffering from destitution and misery, to an extent hitherto unknown'.[28] Within intellectual circles the problem was defined as 'the Condition of England' question: in Carlyle's formulation (1839),

> Is the condition of the English working people wrong; so wrong that rational working men cannot, will not, and even should not rest quiet under it?[29]

The sense of crisis lasted throughout the 1840s: with the economic depression, Chartism, the Irish Famine of 1845–46 and the 1848 revolutions in Europe, it was little wonder that at the time of the publication of the *Seven Lamps* in May 1849, as Ruskin's father put it, the 'public mind is in a state of anxiety and agitation about politics and trade'.[30]

In the 1840s Ruskin was increasingly disturbed at the inequity of his own position, as the son of a wealthy merchant living a life of leisure, in the midst of such social deprivation. In 1845 he wrote to his parents from the Continent that, after yet another luxurious meal, he 'felt sad at thinking how few were capable of having such enjoyment, and very doubtful whether it were at all proper in me to have it all to myself'.[31] The 1848 revolutions intensified this sense of anxiety: he wrote to a friend

> I begin to feel all the work I have been doing, and all the loves I have been cherishing, are ineffective and frivolous – that these are not times for watching clouds or dreaming over quiet waters, that more serious work is to be done . . . .[32]

Similar doubts at this time prompted other wealthy English intellectuals, led by F. D. Maurice, to launch the Christian Socialist movement. Ruskin was constrained by his economic and emotional dependence on his father (a staunch Tory) from involving himself in any overtly political activities, but he took a great interest in the activities of the Christian Socialists (of which he was kept informed by his admirer F. J. Furnivall) and his thinking on social issues had a good deal in common with theirs.

It was with this sense of social concern that Ruskin turned for guidance to Thomas Carlyle, the pre-eminent diagnostician of the 'social malady' of the day. In *Past and Present* (1843) Carlyle dismissed as irrelevant all issues other than the 'Condition of England' question, asking how it was that while England was richer than ever before, most of the population suffered from poverty, material and spiritual, unequalled in human history. *Past and Present* contained many of the themes that were to inform Ruskin's social criticism: the antipathy to commercialism and money; the paternalistic concept of a society in which rich and poor were bonded to each other by ties of mutual obligation; and the insistence that, *pace* the political economists, the Bible taught that man was not a commodity and could not be treated as such. The early stages of Ruskin's relationship with Carlyle are unclear, but it seems that Ruskin read *Past and Present* on or soon after its publication in 1843, became interested in Carlyle's ideas between 1843 and 1847 and by, at the latest, 1850 had managed to meet him. Thereafter the two became close friends, with Ruskin publicly adopting the role of disciple to the 'master'.[33]

While working in Venice on 'The Nature of Gothic', Ruskin was reflecting on these social questions. On the grounds that 'the crisis we have reached in England no longer permits the silence of any one who perceives its peril', he composed three letters on political questions for publication in *The Times* – letters that his father refused to pass on.[34] Nonetheless Ruskin's sense of the social crisis was not without issue. On the contrary: by combining the sense of the crisis of industrial society that informed those letters with the notions of art that he had inherited from German Romanticism, Ruskin forged the notion of Gothic architecture 'as involving the liberty of the workman' that he presented in 'The Nature of Gothic'.[35]

THE SEVEN LAMPS OF ARCHITECTURE AND *THE STONES OF VENICE*

In 1847 Ruskin suffered his first breakdown, following the failure of his suit for Charlotte Lockhart, the granddaughter of Sir Walter Scott. Under pressure from his parents he then proposed to Euphemia (Effie) Chalmers Gray, was accepted, and travelled to Scotland in the spring of 1848 for the wedding, which coincided with the great Chartist demonstration of 10 April. On his way north Ruskin had drafted out a schema for *The Seven Lamps of Architecture* and, after a short holiday with his wife, in July was back at work, studying and measuring Salisbury cathedral. The choice of Salisbury was in keeping with the injunction in the schema: 'necessity of universal return to Early English if anything is to be done in England'.[36] But the cold interior of the building threatened the recovery of his health and the work had to be abandoned. Instead in August he and Effie went off to Normandy, returning to London in October via the Paris of the 1848 Revolution. With the material brought back from Normandy, Ruskin set down in the winter of 1848–49 to write *The Seven Lamps of Architecture*.

The book, published in May 1849, reflected his experience and thinking up to that time. Against what he described as the tendency of the age towards a dominance of the material over the spiritual, Ruskin excluded the functional or utilitarian from his definition of the term architecture:

Let us, therefore, at once confine the name to that art which, taking up and admitting, as conditions of its working, the necessities and common uses of the building, impresses on its form certain characters venerable or beautiful, but otherwise unnecessary.[37]

His aim, he said, was to show that virtue in architecture depended on virtue in moral and religious life, and that accordingly 'every form of architecture is in some sort the embodiment of the Polity, Life, History and Religious Faith of Nations' – in other words, the generalised version of the doctrine of 'Christian art' as expounded by Rio, Pugin *et al.*[38] In the first chapter, 'The Lamp of Sacrifice', Ruskin's Calvinist conscience battled with the problem posed by the Catholic splendour of medieval art, and sought to demonstrate that, considered as sacrifice or work, such splendour was not only acceptable but was positively a Christian duty. 'The Lamp of Truth' applied the doctrines of *Modern Painters* I to architecture: truth in construction and ornament was as necessary in architecture as in any other art. In 'The Lamps of Power' and 'The Lamp of Beauty', Burke's theory of the sublime and the beautiful (which had been so important for Kant and Schiller) was recast in Ruskin's moralising terms: 'The Lamp of Power' followed Burke to the extent of actually talking about architectural matters – mass and space – rather than architectural sculpture, but 'The Lamp of Beauty' dealt purely with the laws regarding the representation of nature in architectural ornament. English architecture was now disparaged ('we have built like frogs and mice since the thirteenth century') and contrasted unfavourably with that of Normandy and Italy:

What a contrast between the pitiful little pigeon-holes which stand for doors in the east [sic] front of Salisbury . . . and the soaring arches and kingly crowning of the gates of Abbéville, Rouen, and Rheims . . . or the dark and vaulted porches and writhed pillars of Verona![39]

The fifth lamp, Life, dealt with the role of vitality and variety in architectural ornament; this chapter represented an important development of an idea in *Modern Painters* I, and we must look at it in more detail below. The sixth lamp, Memory, dealt with the value conferred on a building by age or history, and denounced the common practice of 'restoring' Gothic buildings as a betrayal of the spirit that had produced them. The seventh lamp, Obedience, returned to the notion of art as language, and demanded that architects should learn to speak the existing language of Gothic before they thought of inventing a new language of their own.

A note inserted at the back of *The Seven Lamps of Architecture* announced: 'In Preparation, *The Stones of Venice*, by John Ruskin'. From November 1849 to March 1850 Ruskin was in Venice working on this, and a year later, in March 1851, the first volume of *The Stones of Venice* was published, together with a large and expensive folio volume of additional illustrations. After a summer spent in England – taking in the famous controversy over the Pre-Raphaelites at the Royal Academy summer exhibition – Ruskin returned to Venice in September 1851, and stayed there until June 1852 working on and largely completing the two further volumes of *The Stones of Venice*. These were published in July and October 1853.

While on holiday in August 1853, Ruskin realised that, partly due to the incremental way in which the book had been written, nowhere in the three volumes of *The Stones of Venice* was there a clear statement of its aims and scope. He therefore wrote for insertion into volume III an 'Explanatory Note' for all three volumes, stating 'finally and clearly, both what they intend and what they contain'. The 'theorem of these volumes' was the doctrine of Christian art as applied to architecture. Whereas before the birth of Christ various nations had produced arts and architecture of a tolerable standard, it was only with the advent of Christianity that the 'full development of the soul of man, and therefore the full development of the arts of man' became possible; and although it took some time before the full effects of this were realised in architecture, eventually in the thirteenth century a fully Christian architecture was produced. But then in the fifteenth century 'the Christianity of Europe was undermined'; this allowed a pagan architecture to be introduced, based on that of the pre-Christian ancients, and this worthless architecture remained predominant in Europe from that point on. As for the nineteenth century, the message was clear:

> We must give up this style totally, despise it and forget it, and build henceforth only in that perfect and Christian style hitherto called Gothic, which is everlastingly the best'.[40]

Venice, he believed, was the *locus classicus* of this transformation from the absolute purity of Gothic to the absolute paganism of Renaissance: the stones of Venice were therefore the 'touchstones' for both the architecture and the moral condition of Europe as a whole.[41]

Despite their considerable length, the contents of the three volumes of *The Stones of Venice* can be summarised quite briefly. The first volume was given over to establishing the ground-rules of architectural judgement: the rules of good construction (chapters 3–19) and the rules of good ornament (chapters 20–29). The second and third volumes dealt with the history of Venetian architecture. Volume II dealt with the 'Christian' period of Venetian architecture (early Christian, Byzantine, and Gothic), focusing particularly on St Mark's as the exemplar of the Byzantine and the Ducal Palace as the exemplar of Gothic. In between the sections on Byzantine and Gothic stood the chapter explaining 'The Nature of Gothic'. Volume III described 'The Fall' (that is, the Renaissance), in which the collapse of religion and moral virtue was accompanied by the revival of a pagan and worthless architecture. The concluding chapter restated the main themes of the work – Ruskin's 'theorem' of the doctrine of Christian art – and called again for the revival of Gothic as the only Christian architecture.

Overall, then, both *The Seven Lamps of Architecture* and *The Stones of Venice* were conceived on the basis of ideas about art inherited from German Romanticism. Ruskin's 'new' way of thinking about architecture – based on the fusion of these German ideas with the social criticism of industrialism generated by the economic crisis of the 1830s and 1840s – was presented in the chapter on 'The Nature of Gothic' in volume III of *The Stones of Venice* (1853). Before then however it had made an appearance, in equally isolated fashion, in both *The Seven Lamps of Architecture* (1849) and volume I of *The Stones of Venice*.

The starting-point for this development was a notion that Ruskin had already advanced in *Modern Painters* I (1843). There, in talking about the general principles of art, he had defined one of the main ideas that could be conveyed by art as 'the perception or conception of the mental or bodily powers by which the work was produced' – in other words, the Romantic view that the work of art communicated the creative powers of the person that made it.[42] These ideas of power, he wrote, are of the noblest connected with art; but the differences in degree of dignity among themselves are infinite, being correspondent with every order of power – from that of the fingers to that of the most exalted intellect.[43]

In the case of a Turner, the power perceived was of the highest order; in the case of ornamental work, including architectural decoration, the power perceived was of a much lower order – but no less valid for that.

> These are, indeed, powers of a low order, yet the pleasure arising from the conception of them enters very largely into our admiration of all elaborate ornament, architectural decoration, etc. The delight with which we look on the fretted front of Rouen Cathedral depends in no small degree on the simple perception of time employed and labour expended in its production.[44]

It was to this notion – which he now termed the doctrine of 'the value of the appearance of labour upon architecture' – that Ruskin referred in re-opening the subject in *The Seven Lamps of Architecture*.[45] In 'The Lamp of Sacrifice' he cited this passage from *Modern Painters* I, and argued from it that an increase in labour meant an increase in beauty – and therefore (Calvinist misgivings notwithstanding) that lavish ornament was acceptable. Again, in 'The Lamp of Truth', in attacking what he saw as the inherent deceit in the use of machinery to produce ornament, Ruskin harked back to this idea, and stated that the pleasure derived from architecture (that is, architectural sculpture) was a pleasure derived from the impression of the character of the carvers conveyed by the stones:

> all our pleasure in the carved work . . . results from our consciousness of its being the work of poor, clumsy, toilsome men. Its true delightfulness depends on our discovering in it the record of thoughts, and intents, and heart-breakings – of recoveries and joyfulnesses of success . . . .[46]

This idea provided the theme of 'The Lamp of Life'. The notion of life as a central principle of art had been a particular theme of Schelling and Schlegel, and was reiterated in Eastlake's essay 'On

1.3 John Ruskin: South transept, Rouen cathedral (1854)

the Philosophy of the Fine Arts', read by Ruskin on its publication in 1848.[47] Both in nature and in art, Ruskin now stated, beauty depended on vitality; and most of all was this the case with the creations of architecture. These

> being not essentially composed of things pleasant in themselves – as music of sweet sounds, or paintings of fair colours, but of inert substance – depend, for their dignity and pleasurableness in the utmost degree, upon the vivid expression of intellectual life which has been concerned in their production.[48]

Such vitality Ruskin found in the scorn for accurate measurement displayed in the west front of the Duomo at Pisa, in the infinite variation in the proportions and arrangement of the west front of St Mark's, and in the endless inventiveness of the carving of the north door of Rouen cathedral. From here Ruskin arrived at his famous question:

> I believe the right question to ask, respecting all ornament, is simply this: was it done with enjoyment – was the carver happy while he was about it?

Only if the carver was happy would his work express vitality; and only then would it meet this basic requirement of art. Ruskin was aware of the portentousness of the formulation: 'How much of the stonemason's toil this condition would exclude I hardly venture to consider, but the condition is absolute'.[49]

At this stage however Ruskin confined his observations to one aspect – the difference between work done by hand and work done by machine. Two years later, however, in discussing the treatment of ornament in volume I of *The Stones of Venice*, he returned to the question, and this time pursued somewhat further its implications regarding the division of labour. Again the starting-point was the thesis from *Modern Painters* I that the role of architecture (that is, architectural sculpture) was to convey the lower orders of power. Now in *The Stones of Venice* I Ruskin developed this notion in the light of the doctrine of Christian art. The rightful expenditure of the lower orders of power, he said, was permitted in Christian (that is, Gothic) architecture, but denied in pagan (that is, classical and Renaissance) architecture. (Both here and in 'The

Nature of Gothic' Ruskin actually made a threefold classification, into 'Servile', 'Medieval' and 'Renaissance'; but he never explained how the 'Renaissance' system differed from the 'Servile', and in practice he treated the two as one.) Furthermore, he said, the nature of this contrast between Christian and pagan was not accidental, but was founded on a theological basis: on the Christian doctrine that every soul, however lowly or ignorant, was of value in itself. The ancient Egyptians, he said, could compel two thousand men to carry out exactly the architect's wishes. But 'those times cannot return':

> We have, with Christianity, recognised the individual value of every soul; and there is no intelligence so feeble but that its single ray may in some sort contribute to the general light. This is the glory of Gothic architecture, that every jot and tittle, every point and niche of it, affords room, fuel and focus for individual fire.[50]

It followed that the only Christian approach was for the architect to work out the general scheme, but for the details to be left to the 'simple act and effort' of the workman, so that the spectator could 'rejoice in its simplicity if not in its power, and in its vitality if not in its science'.[51] The choice was between 'Christian ornament' on the one hand and 'servile ornament' on the other.

GOTHIC AND THE LIBERTY OF THE WORKMAN

According to E. T. Cook, the chapter on 'The Nature of Gothic' in volume II of *The Stones of Venice* was drafted out in Ruskin's 1851–52 diary, and he began writing the chapter properly in Venice in February 1852. Writing to his father on 22 February 1852 Ruskin reported that he was having 'great difficulty in defining Gothic':

> I shall show that the greatest distinctive character of Gothic is in the workman's heart and mind; but its outward test is the trefoiled arch, *not* the mere point.[52]

In fact, in the chapter, as the letter to his father foretold, Ruskin presented two quite different ways of defining Gothic, one in terms of the character of the people who had made it (sections 6–78) and

1.4 John Ruskin: Gothic windows of the Fourth Order (from *The Stones of Venice* II 1853)

the other in terms of the language of its forms (sections 80–105).[53] These two ways of defining Gothic stemmed from the two sides of the Romantic concept of art already noted: on the one hand, the view of the work of art as the material embodiment of the creative powers of the person who made it; on the other, the notion of art as a form of communication or language, with its own rules or 'grammar'. In 'The Nature of Gothic' the two parts sat uneasily with each other. Ruskin was aware of this and tried to justify the two different systems of definition by making an analogy with mineralogy. A mineral, he said, was defined both by its internal nature or elements and by its external forms, and he would follow the same principle by defining Gothic in terms both of inner nature ('the mental tendencies of the builders') and of external forms (pointed arches, trefoils and so on). Even so he had to admit that the analogy did not really work: the absence of any one internal element completely changed the composition of a mineral, whereas it did not remove but only reduced the 'Gothicness' of Gothic.

Of the elements or mental tendencies, he said, the most important was savageness or rudeness. In terms reminiscent of Goethe or Friedrich von Schlegel, Ruskin depicted the savageness of Gothic as the expression of the climate and character of Northern Europe:

> this wildness of thought, and roughness of work; this look of mountain brotherhood between the cathedral and the Alp; this magnificence of sturdy power . . . this out-speaking of the strong spirit of men who . . . show, even in what they did for their delight, some of the hard habits of the arm and heart that grew on them as they swung the axe or pressed the plough.[54]

Following Schlegel, Ruskin said that more important even than this geographical basis was the religious basis of Gothic. He referred here to the distinction made in the first volume of *The Stones of Venice* between 'Christian' and 'servile' ornament. In the 'servile' (that is, classical) system, perfection was achieved only because the workman was 'entirely subjected to the intellect' of another, thereby making the workman a slave; whereas the 'Christian' (that is, Gothic) system, in confessing the imperfection of the human soul and bestowing 'dignity upon the acknowledgement of unworthiness', gave scope for the workman to do as best he could, following the dictates of his soul. This recapitulated the contents of chapter 21 of volume I, but then Ruskin suddenly expanded the argument. He continued:

> But the modern English mind has this much in common with that of the Greek, that it intensely desires, in all things, the utmost completion or perfection compatible with their nature.[55]

In the course of the next two paragraphs it emerged that Ruskin was thinking not so much of the English taste for classical architecture as of the division of labour in production and its ultimate expression, the factory system. According to Ruskin, the industrial system was un-Christian in that it reduced the labour process to the mindless repetition of mechanical tasks, and thereby turned the worker from a human being to a slave. The contrast was no longer between Gothic architecture and classical architecture: it was between the creative labour that had produced Gothic architecture and the sub-human labour of contemporary industrial production.

> Now, in the make and nature of every man . . . there are some powers for better things; some tardy imagination, torpid capacity of emotion, tottering steps of thought, there are, even at the worst; and in most cases it is all our own fault that they *are* tardy or torpid. But they cannot be strengthened, unless we are content to take them in their feebleness, and unless we prize and honour them in their imperfection above the best and most perfect manual skill . . . .
>
> Understand this clearly: You can teach a man to draw a straight line, and to cut one; to strike a curved line, and to carve it; and to copy and carve any number of given lines or forms, with admirable speed and perfect precision; and you find his work perfect of its kind: but if you ask him to think about any of those forms, to consider if he cannot find any better in his own head, he stops; his execution becomes hesitating; he thinks, and ten to one he thinks wrong; ten to one he makes a mistake in the first touch he gives to his work as a thinking being. But you have made a man of him for all that. He was only a machine before, an animated tool.[56]

The rhetoric continued, to the effect that divided labour was sub-human and contrary to Christianity.

> And observe, you are put to stern choice in this matter. You must either make a tool of the creature, or a man of him. You cannot make both. Men were not intended to work with the accuracy of tools, to be precise and perfect in all their actions. If you will have that precision out of them, and make their fingers measure degrees like cog-wheels, and their arms strike curves like compasses, you must unhumanize them. . . .
> On the other hand, if you will make a man of the working creature, you cannot make a tool. Let him but begin to imagine, to think, to try to do anything worth doing; and the engine-turned precision is lost at once. Out come all his roughness, all his dullness, all his incapability; shame upon shame, failure upon failure, pause after pause: but out comes the whole majesty of him also; and we know the height of it only, when we see the clouds settling upon him.[57]

All this was close in tone and style to Carlyle, as was the cadenced contrast made in the next paragraph between the notional slavery of the middle ages and the real slavery of the division of labour.

> Men may be beaten, chained, tormented, yoked like cattle, slaughtered like summer flies, and yet remain in one sense, and the best sense, free. But to smother their souls with[in] them, to blight and hew into rotting pollards the suckling branches of their human intelligence, to make the flesh and skin which, after the worm's work on it, is to see God, into leathern thongs to yoke machinery with, – this it is to be slave-masters indeed; and there might be more freedom in England, though her feudal lords' lightest words were worth men's lives, and though the blood of the vexed husbandman dropped in the furrows of her fields, than there is while the animation of her multitudes is sent like fuel to feed the factory smoke, and the strength of them is given daily to be wasted into the fineness of a web, or racked into the exactness of a line.[58]

But where Ruskin took the critique beyond Carlyle was in the attention he paid to the nature of industrial labour. Carlyle was strong on the horrors of contemporary society, but the target of his criticism was not the factory system but the spirit of commercial-ism and the 'cash-nexus'. Thus Carlyle had interpreted social unrest not as a protest against industrialism, but as

> a voice from the dumb bosom of Nature, saying to us: 'Behold! Supply-and-demand is not the one law of Nature; Cash-payment is not the sole nexus of man with man . . . .'[59]

In the end Carlyle's belief in the redeeming power of work of any kind (his 'gospel of work') always steered him away from criticising industrial labour *per se*: as he wrote in *Past and Present*, 'All work, even cotton-spinning, its noble'.[60]

But with Ruskin this was not the case, despite his general enthusiasm for work. On the contrary: the Romantic notion of art as the outcome of human productive powers at their fullest and most creative made Ruskin acutely aware of the extent to which the divided labour of industrial production fell short of this ideal. Ruskin was therefore in a position to deliver the culmination of his analysis: the contrast between the image of human labour presented by Gothic architecture, and the reality of human labour under the industrial system. In the climax to the chapter he stated:

> go forth again to gaze upon the old cathedral front, where you have smiled so often at the fantastic ignorance of the old sculptors: examine once more those ugly goblins, and formless monsters, and stern statues, anatomiless and rigid; but do not mock at them, for they are signs of the life and liberty of every workman who struck the stone; a freedom of thought, and rank in scale of being, such as no laws, no charters, no charities can secure; but which it must be the first aim of all Europe at this day to regain for her children.[61]

The object of this attack, it should be noted, was not (as with the critique being developed by Marx at about the same time) the social relations of capitalism as a whole, but simply the effect on the individual worker of the division of labour involved in factory production.

> We have much studied and much perfected, of late, the great civilised invention of the division of labour; only we give it a false name. It is not, truly speaking, the labour that is divided;

1.5 John Ruskin: West porch, Rouen cathedral

but the men: – Divided into mere segments of men – broken into small fragments and crumbs of life . . . . And the great cry that rises from all our manufacturing cities, louder than their furnace blast, is all in very deed for this, – that we manufacture everything there except men; we blanch cotton, and strengthen steel, and refine sugar, and shape pottery; but to brighten, to strengthen, to refine, or to form a single living spirit, never enters into our estimate of advantages.[62]

To help overcome the division of labour Ruskin offered a number of suggestions. As consumers, he said, we should choose only 'the products and results of healthy and ennobling labour'[63]; these would be goods marked by rough or imperfect finish, showing that the workman had been allowed a share of invention. As producers, we should abandon the customary division into the thinker and the worker: 'the workman ought often to be thinking, and the thinker often to be working'.[64] While social divisions *per se* should be retained, they should not be based on differences in the kind of work performed by each class:

> It would be well if all of us were good handicraftsmen in some kind . . . . The painter should grind his own colours; the architect work in the mason's yard with his men . . . .[65]

– a significant phrase for subsequent architectural theory.

Of the remainder of the chapter not a great deal needs to be said. Having established the moral obligation of 'allowing independent operation to the inferior workman, simply as a duty to him',[66] Ruskin turned to the rewards gained by the performance of this duty: variety and vitality in the carving, and truth and love in the representation of nature. Three further characteristics (grotesque, rigidity, redundance) completed the enumeration of the moral elements of Gothic.

Ruskin then dealt with the 'outward forms' of Gothic. Here he argued that the pointed arch alone did not define Gothic; rather that it was the combination of the pointed arch with the steeply pitched gable – an idea found previously both in England (Saunders 1811) and Germany (Costenoble 1812); and furthermore that the arch had to be not merely pointed, but cusped, like a leaf – a notion with clear German ancestry, in Schelling and Friedrich von Schlegel. The cusp, Ruskin stated, derived less from structural considerations than from the builders' love and respect for God's work (in this case, foliation) – in other words, the naturalism of the Gothic builders. This was one of the few points at which the two systems of definition overlapped.

At the end of the chapter Ruskin confronted directly the incompatibility of his two methods for defining Gothic. Here he revealed that the second (definition by outward form) would establish whether a building was pure Gothic; but the first (definition by character of the builders) would show whether a building was good architecture. For, he said, 'it may be very impure Gothic, and yet very noble architecture; or it may be very pure Gothic, and yet . . . very bad architecture'.[67] Having thereby thrown some doubt over the whole enterprise – by asserting that the subject was not the nature of Gothic, but the nature of good architecture – Ruskin brought the chapter to an end.

Ruskin had a high regard for the chapter on 'The Nature of Gothic'. As soon as it had been published, in volume II of *The Stones of Venice*, he proposed to his father that the chapter should be reprinted separately as a pamphlet.[68] Nothing came of this – presumably because his father chose not to follow it up. The next year, in the *Lectures on Architecture and Painting* published in April 1854, Ruskin described 'The Nature of Gothic' as the most important chapter in *The Stones of Venice*, and stated wherein its importance lay. It was, he complained, singular

> and far more than singular, that among all the writers who have attempted to examine the principles stated in the *Stones of Venice*, not one has as yet made a single comment on what was precisely and accurately the most important chapter in the whole book; namely, the description of the nature of Gothic architecture, as involving the liberty of the workman.[69]

In October 1854, Ruskin's father notwithstanding, the chapter was reprinted as a pamphlet, when it was used by the Christian Socialists as the foundation manifesto of the Working Men's College. F. J. Furnivall, who was a devotee of Ruskin and one of the founders of the college, later described how this came about.

Through my sending him a prospectus of our Working Men's
College, Ruskin kindly offered to help us, and take the art
classes . . . . I felt that we wanted some printed thing to
introduce us to the working men of London, as we knew only
the few we had come across in our co-operative
movement . . . . F. D. Maurice had written nothing good
enough for this purpose, but Ruskin had. So I got leave from
him and his publisher, Mr George Smith, to reprint this grand
chapter, 'On the Nature of Gothic'; and I had to add to it the
sub-title, 'And Herein of the True Functions of the Workman
in Art', to show working men how it touches them. I had
'Price Fourpence' put on the title; but we gave a copy to
everybody who came to our first meeting – over 400 – and the
tract well served its purpose. Afterwards an orange wrapper
and a folding woodcut from the *Stones* were added to the
reprint, and it was sold at 6d for the benefit of the College.[70]

Although in this way the chapter gained a certain reputation (with,
among others, the undergraduate circle of Morris and his friends
at Oxford), it was events of twenty-five years later that really
established the celebrity of 'The Nature of Gothic'. In the late 1870s
and 1880s, with the onset of the second great crisis of the industrial
economy, the ideas that Ruskin had set out in 'The Nature of
Gothic' were revived by Morris, Webb and their friends, and
formed part of the ideology of the socialist movement in which
they became involved and which developed so dramatically in that
period. In a series of lectures from 1877 onwards Morris proclaimed
the message of 'The Nature of Gothic' as the answer to the problems
of work and art facing society. Morris's espousal gave 'The Nature
of Gothic' a new fame: in 1892 he chose 'The Nature of Gothic' as
one of the early productions of his Kelmscott Press, adding a
preface in which he described the chapter as one of the most
important writings of the nineteenth century, and this was followed
in 1899 by a conventional George Allen edition (including the
Morris preface), which was reprinted many times. It is to this
revival of 'The Nature of Gothic' later in the century that
we must now turn.

2

Philip Webb: Architecture and Socialism in the 1880s

Any enquiry into the relationship between architecture and socialism in nineteenth-century Britain would have to take cognisance of Philip Webb, for with Webb we see an architect of indisputable historical importance who was heavily involved, during the peak years of his career, in the socialist movement.

Philip Webb (1831–1915) came into contact with William Morris and his friends at Oxford in the 1850s and after leaving the office of G. E. Street designed the Red House for Morris in 1858. After a few fairly lean years, Webb's practice took off in the late 1860s and he became one of the most sought-after architects of his day, which he remained until his retirement in 1900. According to Mark Girouard:

> Discriminating people of the time might have agreed that Norman Shaw and Philip Webb were the leading domestic architects of their day. The inner ring of the discriminating would have put Webb above Shaw.[1]

It was in this position as a celebrated architect that Webb became actively involved in the socialist movement, specifically in the Socialist League that Morris and others set up in 1884–85. Webb was a member of the League's Bloomsbury branch, other members of which included Eleanor Marx and her husband Edward Aveling, who was at that time working with Engels on the translation of volume one of Marx's *Capital*. Webb was also active in the national organisation of the League, of which he was treasurer for most of the period of its existence, from the beginning of 1886 to the end of 1890.

This chapter will look at the relationship between Webb's architecture and his socialism, and at the relationship between both and the body of ideas examined in the previous chapter. To what extent did Webb's architecture and his thinking about architecture draw on his experiences in the socialist movement, particularly his encounter with the London marxists? To what extent on the other hand did it draw on the ideas that Ruskin had set out in 'The Nature of Gothic'?

Despite his importance, there has been a dearth of historical studies of Webb, and Lethaby's biography, written shortly after the First World War, still remains the standard work. Before dealing with these questions therefore it is necessary first to say something about Webb more generally, in particular about the very unusual nature of his practice, as the exclusive architect of the exclusive art set.

THE ARCHITECT OF THE PRE-RAPHAELITE GROUP

In Lethaby's telling phrase, Webb was 'the architect of the Pre-Raphaelite group'.[2] To this extent Webb's career rested on the contacts he made early in life, in Oxford in the 1850s, with Morris and the art set centred around Rossetti, G. F. Watts and (at a suitable distance) Ruskin. Throughout Webb's period of practice, from 1858 to 1900, it was for members of this group – both the artists themselves and even more their patrons and friends – that Webb worked.[3]

In the first years of practice it was from the painters and their friends that Webb received commissions: the Red House in Kent (1858) for the aspiring painter William Morris; the Fairmile house in Surrey (1860) for the painter Spencer Stanhope, a protégé of Watts and Rossetti; the workshops in Worship Street, London (1861) for Col. Gillum, an amateur painter and pupil of Ford Madox Brown; Arisaig House, Inverness (1863) for the collector F. D. P. Astley; and the Holland Park studio house for the painter Val Prinsep, who along with Rossetti, Morris *et al.* had been one of the Oxford Union decorators in 1857. Together with Webb himself, all these early clients were members of the Hogarth Club (1858–61), the exclusive club for Pre-Raphaelite artists and their patrons: Morris, Stanhope, Prinsep and Webb as artists, Gillum and Astley as collectors.[4]

When Webb's practice took off in the later 1860s, it was on the basis of this artistic connection. In 1867 Webb received the ultimate accolade of a recommendation from Ruskin: in a letter to Hale White, Ruskin commended Webb as an architect who would give

2.1 Philip Webb, portrait by C. F. Murray (1873)

'perfectly sound and noble work for absolutely just price'.[5] In 1868
Webb received a string of commissions: from George Howard,
amateur painter and future Earl of Carlisle, for a London mansion
on Palace Green, Kensington; from Col. Gillum (whose Euston
Boys Home figured in Ford Madox Brown's painting *Work*) for a
house at East Barnet; from Rossetti's patron the solicitor L. R.
Valpy for an office building in Lincoln's Inn Fields; from G. P.
Boyce the watercolourist, a close friend of Rossetti and disciple of
Ruskin, for a house in Glebe Place, Chelsea (Fig. 2.2); from the
wealthy art collector C. A. Ionides for additions to the Ionides
house in Holland Villas Road, London; and from Hugh Bell, son
of the industrialist and art collector Lowthian Bell, for a house at
Redcar. In all cases these were commissions emanating from the
London art world.

Webb's practice in the 1870s and 1880s continued on these lines,
with work coming especially from the patrons and friends of the
artists. There was a series of major commissions from the Bell
family in the north-east: Rounton Grange (1872) for Lowthian Bell;
Smeaton Manor (1876) for Lowthian's daughter Ada and her
husband Major Godman; and the new Bell Brothers office in
Middlesbrough, first proposed in 1881 but not built until 1889–91.
Equally important was the work commissioned in the same period
by George Howard in the north-west: alterations to Naworth Castle
(1874) and a new house for the agent in the nearby town of
Brampton (Four Gables, 1876); a new church for Brampton (1877)
and also a new vicarage. At the end of 1876 Webb gained another
wealthy client from the world of art patronage when Percy
Wyndham, a friend of Burne-Jones, approached Webb about the
design of a new country house (Clouds) at East Knoyle, Wiltshire –
a project that was to last on and off for the next fifteen years.
Through Howard, Webb was introduced to Gen. Pitt-Rivers (Rush-
more, 1881) and through Wyndham to Ramsden (Lapscombe, 1886)
and Yorke (Forthampton Manor, 1889). Other clients of the 1870s
and 1880s included Sir William Bowman, the eye specialist, who
had treated Rossetti and was a friend and patron of Watts
(Joldwynds, Dorking, 1872); Watts himself (Myddleton Priory, Isle
of Wight, 1873); Mary Anne Ewart, a friend of Ruskin's protégé
Gertrude Jekyll (Coneyhurst, Ewhurst, 1883); and Wickham Flower,
a friend and Chelsea neighbour of Webb's close friend and client
G. P. Boyce (Great Tangley, 1885).

In the last decade of Webb's practice (1890–1900) the pattern was

2.2 Philip Webb: house for G. F. Boyce, Glebe Place, Chelsea (1868), street front

unchanged, with a lot of work for the old clients. For Constantine Ionides there was the Hove house additions (1890); for the Morris family, the Much Hadham cottage (1891), the Clapham Common Institute (1896) and the Morris Memorial cottages at Kelmscott (1899). Additions to their respective houses were made for Bowman and Lowthian Bell, and the tower of East Knoyle church restored for the Wyndhams (1891–93). New clients in this period included the Beales, who moved in the Holland Park set of the Ionides

2.3 Philip Webb: house for G. F. Boyce, Chelsea (1868), dining-room

(Standen, East Grinstead, 1891) and Capt. Baird, who was introduced to Webb by Yorke of Forthampton (Exning House, Newmarket, 1894).

Throughout his period of practice, then, Webb drew his clients from the artistic world in which he himself moved. Many of them knew one another: in writing to one, whether as friend or client, he would often convey greetings from another. What defined this group in their own eyes was that they were if not artists at least artistic. Confirmation of their superiority could be found in Ruskin, with his scornful disdain of the commercial practices and tastes of the ordinary (non-artistic) world. Only a few of the artistic set (notably Madox Brown and Gillum) shared Ruskin's social concerns, but Ruskin's belief in the utter superiority of artistic over ordinary conventional values was accepted as their *credo*, and defiance of ordinary bourgeois conventions by the artists was, if not actually demanded by the patrons, at least treated with indulgence. As Rossetti noted of Morris, his 'very eccentricities and independent attitude seem to have drawn patrons around him': when Morris visited the Howards in 1870, Rosalind Howard (later Lady Carlisle) noted with self-abasing gratitude, 'He is agreeable also – and does not snub me'.[6]

This group was by nature exclusive, with access only by personal contact and introduction. On one occasion, in the early part of his career, Webb did take on a commission from a 'stranger', that is, someone from outside the set, but he drew the lesson of his mistake. In 1871 he wrote to Boyce

> some stranger to me wrote some time back, for a design of mine for some buildings; after considerable care of thought, I send them. I hear this morning that he is much obliged, but that some of the design he does not like, and the rest is unsuitable . . . .[7]

Thereafter new clients in effect needed a personal introduction if they were to be taken on; Howard was careful to supply one for Pitt-Rivers in 1881 and Yorke for Baird in 1894. It was only a slight exaggeration when Webb remarked late in his career that as regards clients, 'I will not take another without a written character'.[8]

Far from seeking out clients in the normal way, Webb made it as hard as possible for anyone outside this set to become his client. From 1864, when he moved his office to what he termed the 'lawful neighbourhood' of Gray's Inn,[9] Webb neither mixed in the architectural circles of London nor sought publicity through exhibiting designs at the Royal Academy and publishing his work in architectural journals. The Worship Street design was published in the *Builder* in 1863 but thereafter Webb avoided publicity. When the critic and historian C. L. Eastlake requested information on Webb's buildings for his book *The Gothic Revival in England*, Webb declined, referring to the 'rule which I've had some satisfaction in keeping up to the present time – viz – not myself to make unnecessarily public any work which I've designed or completed'.[10] This was a rule that he maintained until his retirement.

Webb was equally fastidious in avoiding public appearances at the professional architectural institutions. This applied not only to the Royal Institute of British Architects and the Royal Academy but also to the Architectural Association, where many of his admirers were based. Even when some of the latter formed a more exclusive organisation, the Art Workers' Guild, and conferred on Webb the honour of membership, he remained aloof; although the Guild included some of Webb's disciples, such as Lethaby, it also numbered others, such as the Gothic Revival restorers or 'scrapers' of ancient buildings, towards whom Webb felt nothing but anti-pathy.[11]

There were only two institutions related to architecture that Webb joined. One was the Sanitary Institute, to which Webb was attracted by his rationalist interest in the scientific aspect of architecture. The other was 'Anti-Scrape', the Society for the Protection of Ancient Buildings, which was founded by Morris, Webb and their friends in 1877 and was a mirror of the art world that made up Webb's clients. Membership in the first year included Webb's main clients: Morris, Howard, Bell, Wyndham, Boyce, Flower, Ionides, Ewart, Watts. Other members from the art world included Burne-Jones, De Morgan, Millais and, inevitably, Ruskin. The SPAB was the closest approximation there was to an institu-tional basis for Webb's artistic circle. But even here Webb avoided any role that would cast him, by name or in person, into the public eye. While Webb and Morris worked jointly to create the society, Webb took no office in it; and when the society despatched letters to the press, they might have been written by Webb but they were signed by one of the Honorary Secretaries – an office that Webb would never undertake. Consequently none of the SPAB's public statements appeared over his name.

The result of all this was that, for someone outside the charmed circle, it was almost as difficult to meet Webb as it was to become his client. A Webb disciple of later years, C. C. Winmill, recalled that, having identified Webb as his architectural hero, it nonetheless took him several years to obtain an introduction.

> I had seen 'Joldwynds' and was so impressed that I felt my only chance of knowing anything about building was to know P. W. – it took me three years to get an introduction – you must remember he was not know[n] except to a very limited number.[12]

Such fanatical avoidance of architectural company, to say nothing of architectual publicity, was scarcely the normal route to architectural success. But Webb seems to have decided early on in his career that his goal was neither public fame nor wordly fortune. As Lethaby put it, Webb 'embraced holy poverty. He thought that the worst rot of the age was greed':[13]

In a talk of which the impression remains while the words are gone, he expressed the view that it was impossible to distribute superabundance wisely: the only course was not to have it. Poverty was really his ideal.[14]

This conviction, it seems, dated from the early days at Oxford when the young men in 'the set' – Morris, Burne-Jones, Webb, Cormell Price, Charles Faulkner – declared their 'Crusade and Holy Warfare against the Age'.[15] Webb had no private wealth and was determined not to accumulate any by his work, whether for 'the Firm' (Morris, Marshall, Faulkner & Co) or in his architectural practice. Warrington Taylor, the manager of the firm in the late 1860s, described to Rossetti the decorative work done by Webb on one of the firm's major commissions, the Armoury and Tapestry Room at St James's Palace (1866–67):

> Have you been to see Webb's *chef d'oeuvre*, the decoration of the Palace? . . . The whole of that work was done by Webb; if Webb had been busy with architecture it could not have been done. You could never depend on such work again. Moreover Webb was miserably paid for his designs. This is no fault of the firm for Webb would not have more. He never will charge above a third of what he ought to charge.[16]

This remained the case even when, from 1868 onwards, Webb was indeed 'busy with architecture'. Clients such as Boyce and Lowthian Bell were embarrassed by the modesty of Webb's charges.[17] The Inland Revenue could not believe his tax statements in the 1880s, when he was working on 'Clouds', one of the most expensive houses of the day: in 1882 a net income of £3.13.4 and in 1885 receipts of £5.0.0. Admittedly these were years of exceptionally low income; in 1886 receipts came to £1459.0.0. Nonetheless in the twelve years 1876 to 1887 Webb's net income, according to his own figures, averaged £394.13.4, equivalent to under £8 per week. For one of the most sought-after architects of the day this was a low figure: in contrast, the chief architect of the School Board of London, E. R. Robson, had a salary of £1000 under terms which allowed him in addition to undertake private work.[18]

Having decided that commercial success was not his goal Webb was able to withstand normal commercial pressures, in particular the pressure to staff the office with pupils and assistants capable of producing the vast output of drawings and design work required of a large commercial practice. In this he showed himself a true pupil of his master G. E. Street, who drove himself to an early grave by his obsessive insistence on designing every detail himself, no matter how large the building.[19] Webb had no desire to turn his office into a design-factory, in which design by an 'eminent architect' meant simply that some drawings had gone 'through the mill of his many-handed office'.[20] Webb's staff, housed in the living-room of his chambers in Raymond Buildings, Gray's Inn, consisted of one or at most two assistants and a draughtsman. Before 1882 Basset and Yates were in turn his assistants. In 1882, under the pressure of the 'Clouds' work (which eventually required over 700 sheets of working drawings), he recruited as assistant George Jack, who remained in the office until Webb's retirement. William Weir joined the office in 1888; Detmar Blow, a young protégé of Ruskin, worked for Webb on the restoration of East Knoyle tower in the early 1890s and, according to a note in Webb's address book, was apprenticed to Webb in 1894.

With this system Webb was able to design everything himself. Jack recalled, 'In his office-work every detail was designed by himself, to the smallest moulding'.[21] Working drawings despatched to the builders gave full-scale drawings of every detail from the panel moulding of a door to the chimney-pot of a stable. Nor was anything left to the builder in the interpretation of the drawings, which were covered with Webb's handwriting giving minute instructions for every aspect of construction. Even with 'Clouds', for which Webb's office had great difficulty in producing the working drawings at the rate demanded by the builder, there was no lessening of Webb's control over construction, as the surviving letters show.[22]

ARTISTIC BUILDINGS

Whether artists or art-patrons, Webb's clients saw themselves as artistic, and what they wanted from Webb was a building that would display this fact. In part this meant simply a building that would house their collection of art objects. It was on this aspect of the Val Prinsep studio house – the porcelain collection, the Italian tapestry, the Japanese leather paper – that the *Building News* concentrated in its 1880 review (although it did also applaud the 'singularly original' design of the building itself).[23] Similarly Webb himself, in reporting to Boyce on Rounton, dealt as much with the way the house displayed the Bells' art collection (including pictures by Boyce) as with the architecture.[24] Nonetheless, as well as housing the art collection of the client, a Webb building was also regarded as an art object in its own right. Throughout his period of practice (1858–1900), the buildings designed by Webb were esteemed and appreciated by the members of the art set who commissioned them, not as mere buildings, but as works of art.

The pattern was established at the outset with the Red House. Rossetti, the lynch-pin of the art set, wrote to Ruskin's American friend Charles Eliot Norton in January 1862:

> I wish you could see the house which Morris (who has money) has built for himself in Kent. It is a most noble work in every way, and more a poem than a house . . . but an admirable place to live in too.[25]

The design of the Red House was essentially a piece of 1850s Gothic Revival domestic architecture, and in that sense belonged firmly to the period of Webb's training with Street rather than to his mature work. Designed in the 'modern Gothic' brick style that at the time Webb so much admired in William Butterfield, it was laid out on a simple L-shaped plan, and subscribed to the rule laid down by Pugin in *True Principles* that the appearance of a building should be illustrative of its plan and function. Morris himself was delighted with what he saw as the medieval spirit of the house.[26] No sooner was it completed than Morris, Webb, Burne-Jones *et al.* set about decorating and furnishing it in suitably artistic manner; and from this arose the idea of establishing the decorating and furnishing business – the firm – which was to carry out the *décor* for most of Webb's houses. In 1864 it was proposed that the Burne-Jones family should move down to the Red House and, as Burne-Jones put it, a 'lovely plan was made':

> It was that Morris should add to his house, making it a full quadrangle, and Webb made a design for it so beautiful that life seemed to have no more in it to desire . . . .[27]

It was on the basis of appreciation of this sort that Webb received the commissions of the late 1860s. As Boyce's house in Chelsea was nearing completion in 1869, Webb joked to Boyce about both his own artistic status and the language of art criticism:

> If you want my opinion as to the looks of the building – all I can say is, beautiful!! or in the language of art critics: 'It is wonderful that so simple an effort of a true artist should produce such a result. Form, colour, atmosphere all here – the astonishing gyration of genius, pirouetting, as it were, to a point of painful delights.[28]

In the Glebe Place house and other buildings designed in the late 1860s, Webb left behind him the 'Gothic days' of the Street office and the Red House (Fig. 2.2).[29] In the buildings of the late 1860s we can see for the first time Webb's mature architecture: an idiosyncratic combination of what Webb termed 'rational arrangement' and 'imagination',[30] eschewing 'prettiness' in favour of 'simplicity', albeit of a highly personal sort.[31] In buildings like the Boyce house, or Hugh Bell's house 'Red Barns', the architecture was not based on an imitation or adoption of the architectural style of a particular period of the past; rather it made use of elements of building traditional in the locality, but composed them in a way that defied any easy stylistic classification. At Red Barns Webb used elements of the local vernacular (including red bricks, pantiles and cut brick stringcourses), but not in a way that reproduced any actual vernacular building (Fig. 2.4). Similarly at Boyce's house in Chelsea he used elements from the architecture of the predominantly eighteenth-century locality, but in a way that neither imitated the old buildings nor (as Shaw and others were to do shortly afterwards with 'Queen Anne') repackaged them into a new style. Instead, in Webb's architecture materials and construction were made to 'speak' for themselves, relying to a large extent on the quality of the details for the overall architectural effect.

This remained the character of Webb's architecture for the rest of his career. For many of the small or less expensive houses, such as Smeaton, Coneyhurst, Standen and the Kelmscott cottages, he followed the practice established at Red Barns and the Boyce house of drawing the architectural vocabulary from the local vernacular. But this was not the only source for his architecture: elsewhere, his rule of drawing on the local and the appropriate could lead in rather different directions. For the Howards' agent's house, Four Gables, in the border town of Brampton in Cumbria, Webb drew

2.4 Philip Webb: 'Red Barns', Redcar (1868), street front

on the martial tradition of the border pele-tower (Fig. 2.5). For country houses of the grand sort, such as Rounton and even more Clouds, Webb took as his starting-point the tradition of high architecture, notably English classicism, as exemplified in the works of Vanbrugh. He also looked to the classical tradition for examples of what he considered sensible, regular planning: the main block of Rounton was designed on a plan of bi-axial symmetry. Often, too, houses which in their exterior appearance used an architecture drawn from the vernacular, in their plans and *parti* showed a tight formal conception. Thus, for all its apparent informality, the elevations of the Bowman house 'Joldwynds' were in fact symmetrical; and what appears at first sight as one of Webb's loosest and most rambling designs, Coneyhurst, is actually based on a tight cruciform *parti*.

Since all these commissions were private houses for private individuals, the only opinions that Webb had to satisfy were those of the clients. That those outside the charmed circle of the artistic set did not necessarily appreciate the 'artistry' of Webb's work is evident from the controversy surrounding his one executed church, St Martin's, Brampton (1874). This was one of several commissions

2.5 Philip Webb: 'Four Gables', Brampton (1876), garden front

in Brampton that came to Webb in the 1870s from George Howard who, as son of the Earl of Carlisle, was the *de facto* patron of the church. But in this case the client was not Howard himself but the church Building Committee, and there were many in the town who objected to the way in which, as they saw it, Howard imposed on the parish a fashionable London architect for whose expensive 'art' they were expected to pay. The design of the church was, in itself, remarkable: the plan incorporated the Broad Church views of the new vicar, Henry Whitehead, by placing the chancel virtually within the nave; and the architectural treatment referred less to Gothic than to a notional village church of the border region that had survived centuries of fighting. The composition (a term explicitly used by Webb in this context) and massing of the building derived from the existing cottages which linked the church to the rest of the town: and the two aisles of the church were treated quite differently from each other, both externally and internally. With its broad interior illuminated by the Burne-Jones windows, the church was, as Howard later put it, 'a unique monument which will become more and more striking as years go on'.[32] But to members of the parish at the time the new church was little more than an ossified tax-burden. One of the guarantors, when called upon to make payment, wished 'it had been for a better cause than that precious warehouse of a place'.[33] Webb himself recalled after retirement that he had designed the church for the

> somewhat unliftable citizens, of a really mean north country town. I can assure you when I handed over the work to them some 25 (or so?) years ago they were by no means anxious to express any pleasure in the result of my work.[34]

Among the artistic élite, however, Webb's reputation was secure. In 1883 as Clouds, the mansion commissioned by Burne-Jones' friends the Wyndhams, finally took shape Wyndham told Webb that he was 'very much pleased indeed with the house'.[35] Webb's first design had been planned around an open courtyard, but when that proved too expensive he settled for a top-lit double-height hall. Architecturally the exterior referred clearly to the tradition of high architecture – the architecture of palaces and cathedrals: the details were inspired by Byzantine and Gothic as well as classical design, and only the large gables of the top floor modified the austere and seigneurial character of the main elevations, although the large service wing was much more informal and domestic in character (Fig. 2.6). When the house was eventually unveiled to the members of high society who, along with the artists, comprised the Wyndham's social world, the reception was enthusiastic. 'We have had a good many people here, all of whom are loud in their praise of the house', Wyndham wrote to Webb in January 1886.[36] By the middle of the year Wyndham was warning Webb that his self-imposed isolation was about to be ended by a charge of the aristocracy:

> The Duke of Westminster was here, more delighted with the house than ever. Your capabilities of keeping people at arm's length will be taxed to the uttermost during the next 2 or 3 years as the streets leading to Raymond Buildings will be blocked with would-be clients. Influential people (or donkeys as you would call them) are putting it about that this is the house of the age. I believe they are right.[37]

2.6 Philip Webb: 'Clouds', East Knoyle (1876), south front

A few years later the building's renown had spread to the other side of the Atlantic. In 1893 Wyndham reported to Webb that 'we had an American architect here the other day to see "the masterpiece of modern English Domestic Architecture". . .'. Webb's reply to this undisguised flattery was characteristic: 'It served you right, you brought this stuff on your own head'.[38]

It was at this level of critical approbation that Webb retired from practice in 1900. In 1897 the newly established *Architectural Review* carried an article on Webb's London buildings of the 1860s, a lyrical panegyric which paid tribute to Webb's 'originality' and 'unique position', hailing him as the Walt Whitman of architecture.[39] In 1900 the *Magazine of Art* carried an appreciation by Halsey Ricardo of Standen, the Sussex house designed by Webb for the Beales (1891). The design of such a house, said Ricardo, could spring only from 'that wide human sympathy that we call art': 'the human quality of the building lingers on . . . like a portrait by a fine painter'.[40]

WEBB AND THE SOCIALIST MOVEMENT

In the early 1880s, when Webb was securely established as the architect of the artistic élite, something new entered his life: socialism. The sudden entry of socialism into Webb's life at this time was a reflection at the personal level of the national pattern: as an opponent put it 'in 1833 a socialist movement seemed to break out spontaneously in England'.[41] In 1883 the Democratic Federation adopted a marxist programme and changed its name to Social Democratic Federation; in 1884 the Fabian Society was formed; in 1885 the Socialist League was formed by Morris and others as a secession from the SDF. The socialist movement in these early years was fired with all the confidence of religion. 'It is the ignorance of the workers that alone postpones the day of the social revolution', said the newspaper of the Socialist League, the *Commonweal*: the task was to 'make socialists' by 'convincing people that socialism is good for them and is possible'.[42]

Long before the advent of the socialist movement Webb had been known to his friends for his 'advanced' political views.[43] Politically Webb was at this stage a Radical, that is, an anti-Tory from an advanced Liberal position. In the late 1870s the main Radical platform was the Eastern Question Association, set up at the end of 1876 following Gladstone's attack on the 'Bulgarian Atrocities' (the alleged murder of Bulgarian Christians by the Turks). Both Morris and, to a much lesser extent, Webb were involved in the EQA. When the two of them set up the SPAB a few months later, Webb saw the new venture in similar anti-Tory terms, noting that 'our vandals, like our parliamentary foes, are in a brutal majority'.[44] After the first meeting Webb wrote to Boyce:

> It occurred to me at the meeting on Thursday that you must be unwell or you wd. certainly not have neglected the meeting.
> I knew you had no duchesses who were importunate and thought that the Society was very important. Apart from your reasonable excuse we had many not so reasonable. Duchesses were with them all important no doubt. Our meeting was small, and tho' some business was done it seemed to me that the Turkey case was rather analogous to ours – or ours to theirs, for the suffering of old buildings as well as Christians were as nothing in comparison with a good dinner, or flattery in high places.[45]

The early stages of Webb's involvement in the socialist movement, before his Italian trip of 1884–85, are unclear. Lethaby stated that he heard Webb lecturing to the Hoxton socialists 'about 1883': 'The only point that I remember was an image of the unwinding of the great written scroll of history, unceasingly, unrestingly'.[46] The letters to Morris written from Italy in 1884–85 make it clear that Webb was not just a supporter of 'the Cause' but was also well-informed about the problems and personnel of the socialist movement.[47] To Kate Faulkner (who kept Webb in touch by sending copies of the *Commonweal*) Webb wrote that he was looking forward to 'claiming my place' in the League, 'though in myself of so little strength for helping'.[48] At this stage Webb (who was himself wintering in Italy on medical instruction after severe illness) was mainly concerned about the possible effects of the new development on the health of his friends – with good reason, as it turned out.[49]

After his return from Italy in April 1885 Webb became involved in the Socialist League at both branch and national level. *In absentio* he had been entered for the local branch in Bloomsbury. This was one of the largest branches of the League, with a membership that included Eleanor Marx and her husband Edward Aveling. As one of the three officers of the branch (treasurer, according to Emery Walker) Webb played an active part in arranging meetings and conducting the business of the branch.[50] In October 1885 he wrote to Faulkner:

> I missed you last evening at the Old Compton Street branch as Aveling must keep away without notice and so I *had* to make a meeting go, pretty well on my own lifting and I am not very handy in making people understand what is not quite clear to myself . . . .[51]

Webb was also active in the central direction of the League. Morris, as principal benefactor, had taken the post of Treasurer on the formation of the League at the beginning of 1885, with disastrous consequences for financial organisation. The Auditor's Report of December 1885 indicted Morris for 'the unsatisfactory manner in which the accounts . . . have been kept', 'the troublesome wasteful way in which sums have been paid over', and urged 'the necessity of at once commencing a proper business-like method of book-keeping instead of the chaotic fragmentary mass of scraps and memoranda which your auditors have had to get through'.[52] Webb, punctilious in financial matters, took on the job of sorting out the mess. At the League Council on 1 February 1886 Morris resigned and was replaced by Webb as Treasurer, a post that carried *ex officio* membership of the Ways and Means Committee. At the same time Webb joined the League Council.[53]

From February 1886 onwards virtually all Webb's leisure time was given over to the League, as his life assumed the pattern of the political activist. Monday evenings were spent at the League Council, Thursday evenings at the Ways and Means Committee, and Saturdays at the League offices working on the books with the secretary.[54] In addition there were the weekly meetings of the branch and monthly meetings of London members, which Webb took his turn in chairing,[55] and lectures to other branches: in June 1886 he lectured to the Clerkenwell and Hoxton branches on 'The Necessity for Socialism' and in September to the Bloomsbury branch on 'Foreigners and English Socialism'.[56] In November he attended a meeting of the Oxford branch (run by Charles Faulkner), which prompted some reflections on present and future society, published in *Commonweal* the following month.[57]

By this time Webb's involvement with the League had crowded

out all his other interests and activities, apart from work and the SPAB. The symphony concerts that he and Boyce attended in the 1870s disappeared from his life. As he told Boyce, the only news was 'that *the* Revolution moves slowly but surely':[58] 'my ease-and-dignity evenings are almost all fled and I am the sport of merciless virtue'.[59] The consequence of this frenetic activity was a collapse in health. In September 1887 Webb went down with what he called a 'sharp chill with sore throat'.[60] In the middle of October he was back at League meetings: 'I had a bad throat that is all. If socialists must have throats they should be of cast iron'.[61] In November however he collapsed with what was diagnosed as rheumatic fever, which at one stage threatened to prove fatal and which kept him out of action until September 1888.[62]

After the illness of 1887–88 Webb did not resume his former pace. He carried out his duties as League treasurer, and attended the Monday and Thursday meetings: but there is no record of lecturing, writing or branch activity. Instead he made large financial contributions; as Morris noted, 'most of the money' for the League was provided by Morris, Faulkner and Webb.[63] From July to November 1888 Webb sent a weekly cheque of £4, equivalent to half his average income; he said that the money was from himself and Faulkner, but since Faulkner's stroke at the beginning of October had no perceptible effect, it seems that the contribution must really have been Webb's.[64]

The year of Webb's illness had been a crucial one for the League. A basic division within the League between parliamentarians and anarchists led in May 1888 to the secession of the parliamentarians, including the Marx-Avelings and the Bloomsbury branch. After this the League came increasingly under anarchist control, to the extent that in November 1890 Morris and the Hammersmith branch seceded from the League. From the start Webb had been Morris's adjunct in the League and in November 1890, three days after the secession of the Hammersmith branch, he resigned as Treasurer and severed his connection with the League.[65]

This however was not the end of Webb's socialist activities. In January 1891 he joined the Hammersmith Socialist Society (as Morris's Hammersmith branch was now called), which he attended regularly until 1893.[66] In the winter of 1893–94, however, Webb suffered another serious illness, after which his attendance lapsed, although he still remained a member. It seems that Webb, like many of the activists of the 1880s, could not adjust to the reformist guise that socialism was taking in the 1890s: in January 1895 he wrote to Morris that 'I'm not in tune for cutting a socialistic dash in these waiting days'.[67]

Webb nonetheless retained his faith in socialism. When Mackail was working on the biography of Morris in 1898, Webb tried to get him to include a letter written by Faulkner in 1888, which, Webb said, would throw useful light on 'the time when Morris and his friends were so strenuously engaged in the social movement'.[68] Mackail, who was not sympathetic to Morris's socialism, did not publish the letter in his biography. Lethaby recorded Webb's typically understated comment:

> May 5 1899. Discussing Mackail's Life of Morris which Webb said was very well done he went on to say 'Morris's socialist work was really the making of him . . . . It was his biggest gift to England after all.'[69]

And Lethaby also records Webb's statement from about the same period that notwithstanding all the disappointments 'I am more of a socialist than ever'.[70]

WEBB'S ARCHITECTURAL AND SOCIALIST THOUGHT

Webb was not a great theorist or writer, on either architecture or socialism.[71] His written statements were neither numerous nor particularly cogent. They are nonetheless of considerable interest, in that they reveal the extent to which his thought was derived from Ruskin.

Webb acquired his set of *The Stones of Venice* in December 1855 (shortly before he met Morris) at the substantial price, for a young assistant architect, of £3.10.0.[72] Webb could not accept Ruskin's claim that painting and sculpture constituted the only artistic elements of a building; as he told Lethaby much later, 'J. R. once held ('Seven Lamps'?) that a building wasn't architecture without sculpture and painting – to me a fallacy'.[73] What Webb took from Ruskin was not the notion of architecture as ornament, but the fundamental Ruskinian dichotomy between the middle ages and the nineteenth century. From this conception of the difference between the past and the present, Webb's architectural and social thinking proceeded.

The fullest statement of Webb's architectural thought was made, characteristically, in an unsigned Annual Report he wrote for the SPAB in 1890. The manuscript, initialled 'PW' and dated June 1890, survives at the Society's headquarters in London. In this text Webb reaffirmed the Ruskinian contrast between on the one hand the artistic work of the middle ages and on the other the 'bitter, hopeless work' of an 'age when money alone is the sign of worth'.[74] The contrast was to be seen in every stroke of the workman's chisel. Compare, said Webb, medieval work like the Bronze Bull of Orvieto (on which he had just received a report from his Venetian friend Giacomo Boni) with modern work such as the lions in Trafalgar Square or the new carving in Westminster Abbey.

> Look at the texture of the bull's coat, at the expression of the face; look at his progressive but decoratively restrained movement. Consider the patient work bestowed on the surfaces, smooth and rough, all alive with intelligent direction of hand, as if the worker could not tire in doing well.[75]

As for Ruskin in 'The Lamp of Life' and 'The Nature of Gothic', for Webb it was the hand guided by heart and mind that gave the medieval work its value and that was missing from modern work.

> If the artist had not tired over the surfaces of the Trafalgar Square lions, there would now be something to look at, and wish to touch each time one passed them.[76]

In the case of the new carving in the north transept of Westminster Abbey, Webb conceded that the work had been 'carefully and laboriously done'; but

> there is no sign of inspiration in it, no reward for the labour, which is always visible in a real work of art . . . it is clearly worthless, as such unreasonable work, such bitter, hopeless work, must always be . . . .[77]

Any notion that under such conditions modern workmen could reproduce the art of the past was a cruel delusion:

> It is at such times as ours when the course of human progress, or decay, has turned the art-workman into more of a mere

mechanic than he ever was before; that we set him to match the works of simple and direct ages, the times when the daily life of the craftsman was a positive incentive to imaginative creation.[78]

The entire predicament of architecture in the nineteenth century, said Webb, derived from this contrast.

Our architects are constantly trying to find workmen who can use materials with the simplicity and directness of those of earlier times, so that the workmen themselves should be able to ease the *designer* of the unbearable burden of directing the manipulation of all trades from his office.[79]

As the skill and creativity of craftsmen declined under the impact of commercialism, architects had been forced to attempt the impossible by trying to fill the gap with 'styles' copied from the past. Architecture became a self-conscious process in which architects selected from the copybooks of past styles, leading to the 'parrot cry, that in the nineteenth century we have no "style" of our own'.[80] Trained only to copy form, 'the school of architects bred under this reign of superficial imitation of ancient detail is ill-fitted to deal with buildings where scientific and practical knowledge is required';[81] they lacked entirely the 'scientific skill' to deal with structures and were too jealous to consult those, such as 'an Engineer or other expert accustomed to deal with great weights' who otherwise 'might well be their allies'.[82] Furthermore the commercial pressures that had led to the loss of the craftsman's skill also led the architects to skimp on the work. In the case of ancient buildings the effect was disastrous:

How many unsafe buildings, which have been destroyed in this way, might have remained to us if the business pressure and the want of insight of the architect would have allowed him to spend weeks in his examination of the causes of failure, and their remedy, instead only of hours?[83]

To clothe their ignorance architects clubbed together in professional associations, and protected each other through professional institutions and the professional press.

Like Ruskin, Webb believed that 'restoration' was a fallacy, since 'it is impossible to restore the lost art of one generation of people by the merely imitative art of another'.[84] Patiently, in letter after letter written on SPAB paper, Webb spelt out this 'fact' to the owners of ancient buildings and monuments. In 1887 he wrote concerning the condition of some village crosses in Dorset, which, he said

> only show how different the work of those days was to that of our own time. The masons and carvers themselves were doing their work with full knowledge of the feeling underlying the symbol, and their art was proportionately real. At this time I, as a working architect, know only too well that such feeling is – and must be – wholly wanting in the 19th century.[85]

For the same reasons, as regards new buildings, any idea of a 'Gothic Revival' was an impossibility. The SPAB, Webb declared in his 1890 report,

> will raise no protest against any attempts by our architects to build whole streets, or even towns, in imitative medieval architecture, though failure must stare them in the face.[86]

For himself, from the mid-1860s Webb had no truck with the mock-medievalism of the Gothic Revival; in 1870, in refusing Eastlake's request for information to go into his history of the Gothic Revival, Webb stated that his work did not 'properly come under the category of the "Gothic Revival in England"'.[87]

Like Ruskin Webb believed that the prospects for art in the nineteenth century were bleak; as he informed the errant American architect Mr Ellicott in 1893, in his view 'modern architecture was not worth running about for to see'.[88] Real art was impossible; imitation was futile. All that the architect could do, Webb believed, was to attempt to capture something of the *quality* of the art of the past, accepting that the *means* by which it would be made could never be those of the past.

That quality, Webb believed, was the direct and simple expression found in old work. In real art, he believed, the builders had expressed themselves in a direct and unselfconscious way; all that nineteenth-century architects could do was attempt a similar simplicity and directness of expression in their work. In this case, what was being expressed was the humanity of the person

who made the work of art. Like Goethe and Ruskin, Webb saw
Gothic primarily not as a style or period of architecture, but as
a quality of architecture: what he variously termed the
simple/direct/unselfconscious/barbaric/savage expression in architectural form of the human spirit. In a letter to Lethaby of 1903
Webb stated:

> For years back my brain has worked at the 'essentials' of
> 'Gothic', and in rummaging amongst architectural history
> books of building [I] have more or less concluded that all
> architectures had in some stage of them the 'Gothic' element –
> that is, the barbaric; which led the builders to express
> themselves – and probably when at their best – in direct
> effectiveness, before consciousness of attractive detail.[89]

This quality, of the expression in the work of art of the character
of the art worker, was in Webb's view the only residue of real art
that the nineteenth-century architect could recapture. The division
of labour (in this case between architect and builder) meant that
the insertion of the human spirit into the work of art was coming
at one remove: in the office of the architect, not, as in real art, in
the hand of the craftsman. Only when craftsmen were again free
to express themselves in their work, as in the middle ages, would
real art be produced:

> Till our born craftsmen are stirred to the depths to make *their
> own* designs in the different crafts, there will be none done of
> lasting value.[90]

In the meantime, all that could be done was for the architect to try
to express his or her humanity and personality in the work of art.
For Webb the great exemplar of the expression of the human
spirit in art was Michelangelo. On his visit to Italy in 1884–85 it
was the strangeness and bareness of Byzantine work that most
caught Webb's attention, as his letters show. Nonetheless, as an
artist, Michelangelo remained his great idol: what Tintoretto or
Turner represented for Ruskin, Michelangelo represented for
Webb. From Rome he wrote to Morris in February 1885: 'M. Angelo
is still gold to my mind'; the Sistine Chapel 'always holds its own,
because of the great spirit of the workman who did it'.[91] The
idealist conception of art that Ruskin had inherited from the

German Romantics was in this way retained by Webb in his idea of Michelangelo.

When we turn from Webb's architectural to his socialist thought, we find again that Ruskin was his major source. Webb came to socialism through Ruskin (by no means an unusual pedigree for socialists in the 1880s) and took his main political conceptions from Ruskin. Like Ruskin he saw the commercial system, with its obsession with money, as the principal adversary; and he saw socialism primarily as the obverse of commercialism and the successor to what he termed this 'money-value age'.[92] In the 1870s, in *Fors Clavigera*, Ruskin diagnosed usury (that is, the lending of money at interest) as the cardinal sin on which the commercial system was based, and this Webb accepted as his own creed. In an undated note Webb wrote

> Ruskin is not likely to be popular; Ruskin has called in question 'the spirit of the age', i.e. the spirit of usury. 20 per cent is the nimbus of the modern representative of the 'Ancient of Days'.[93]

In similar vein Webb told Lethaby that his friend Charles Faulkner 'had accepted Socialism wholly and followed Ruskin on usury'.[94]

This Ruskinian thinking was apparent in the 'Jubilee Monument' project of November 1886 (Fig. 2.7). This private architectural satire, dating from the time of Webb's most active involvement in the Socialist League, shows both the nature and the limits of his political consciousness. The scheme was a caricature of the preparations then under way for the celebration of Victoria's Jubilee in 1887: Webb envisaged a fantastic monument that would fill the whole of Trafalgar Square (which had recently been the scene of rioting by the unemployed) and use the latest technology to proclaim the values of royalty and empire. His description of the scheme ends in characteristically Ruskinian terms:

> For the 'Jubilee' Monument to Vic^a in Trafalgar Square.
>   The pyramid to fill the whole square. To receive all the statues now in London and many more. To be filled with Halls, galleries, pavilions, terraces, loggias, orchestras, dancing saloons, restaurants, lifts &c. and have a bronze statue of Vic. in pagoda on the back of a bronze elephant 50 feet long. The bronze work to be perforated and illuminated by electricity; to have horological & astronomical works in it and

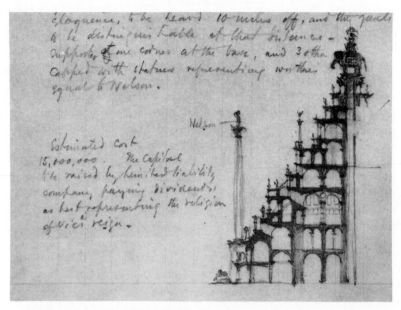

2.7 Philip Webb: the 'Jubilee Monument' (1886)

with a system of steam elocution to trumpet the 'Queens Speech' or other eloquence, to be heard 10 miles off, and the quality of the eloquence to be distinguishable at that distance. To have the Nelson column as supporter at one corner at the base, and 3 other columns at the other corners capped with statues representing worthies considered at this time as equal to Nelson.

Estimated cost 15,000,000. The capital to be raised by limited liability company, paying dividends, as best representing the religion of Vic[a]'s reign.[95]

In this description we can see how little Webb's thinking was affected by his contact with the English marxists at the Bloomsbury branch of the League: for Webb (as for Ruskin) the main characteristic of the existing economic order was the payment of interest on borrowed money, not (as for Marx) the extraction of surplus value from the workforce by means of the wage contract.

The events of the 1880s indeed led Webb not towards Marx and historical materialism, but rather towards anarchism – a trajectory not uncommon within the Socialist League. Webb was on friendly terms with the leading anarchist members of the League, including Joseph Lane, Samuel Mainwaring, Charles Mowbray and Victor Dave, and committed to paper this clear statement of the anarchist position:

> Supposing that the various forms of authority had succeeded in giving a fairly satisfactory life to the masses, there might be some excuse for endeavouring to continue them; but as they have evidently and miserably failed, the masses are bound as honest men to displace authority which has proved itself incapable.[96]

It was in keeping with this view that in 1889, when the League was considering abandoning the publication of *Commonweal* for financial reasons, Webb suggested that in its place they might lend support to the anarchist paper, *Freedom*.[97]

Neither Ruskin's moral fundamentalism nor Lane's anarchism permitted any involvement with the state and its associated institutions, such as parliamentary or municipal elections, all of which were seen as inherently corrupt and corrupting. Nonetheless it was towards the election hoardings that socialism turned in the 1890s. In these conditions socialists – including Webb – who were unsympathetic to the new 'practical socialism' found a new hero: Tolstoy. As the ethical socialist paper *Seed Time* put it in October 1890, 'the name of Tolstoy has become of late a household word in England, and especially among those who are interested in the Social Revolution'.[98] Tolstoy's teaching emphasised inner spiritual regeneration and the need for physical labour and contact with nature. While Webb did not go so far as to join any of the English Tolstoyan model communities, in the period after Morris' death in 1896 it was Tolstoyan socialism that attracted him. In 1898 Webb was 'reading Tolstoy with great interest and approval'[99] and in 1904 he wrote to the architect Alfred Powell:

> Since Ruskin and W. M. have left us to our selves there is but little preaching worth even a tub-pulpit, save – I think – the banned Tolstoi . . . .[100]

In similar vein he wrote to Constance Astley in 1905: 'I am quite at one with the great Tolstoy who raises human love to the highest pedestal of life'.[101] In this new allegiance however Webb was not moving far from his earlier beliefs for, as Pierson noted of Tolstoy, 'in the writings of this foreign prophet, significant features of Ruskin's message reappeared'.[102]

3

The Architectural Theory of William Morris

The period of William Morris's public career, which lasted from 1877 to his death in 1896, was one of crisis in the British economy. The onset of the 'Great Depression' (c.1875–1895) marked the end of the period of prosperity that the country had enjoyed since mid-century, inaugurating a period of declining profits and rising unemployment which came to a head in the mid-1880s. The sense that the mid-Victorian 'age of equilibrium' had passed was reinforced first by the election in 1874 of a strong Tory government under Disraeli, marking the end of the Whig–Liberal dominance which dated back to 1846, and then by the troubles, both at home and abroad, of the Liberal government under Gladstone which was returned in 1880. Already by 1880 Morris noted that the 'century of commerce' had not been able to 'spread peace and justice throughout the world, as at the end of its first half we fondly hoped it would'.[1]

The economic crisis of the late 1870s brought with it a return of doubts and anxieties about Britain's industrial economy on a scale that had not been seen since the crisis of the 1840s. Critiques of society first formulated in the 1840s – whether by Carlyle, Ruskin or Marx – but largely ignored during the boom years experienced a revival of interest. In this process Morris (1834–1896) played a prominent part. His lectures from 1877 onwards explicitly revived the ideas first published by Ruskin around the mid-century, above all in 'The Nature of Gothic'. In his first public lecture, in December 1877, on 'The Decorative Arts', Morris invoked Ruskin's mid-century teaching:

> if I did not know the value of repeating a truth again and again, I should have to excuse myself to you for saying any more about this, when I remember how a great man now living has spoken of it: I mean my friend Professor John Ruskin: if you read the chapter in the 2nd vol. of his 'Stones

3.1 William Morris, photographed by Frederick Hollyer (1887)

of Venice', entitled 'On the Nature of Gothic, and the Office of the Workman therein', you will read at once the truest and most eloquent words that can possibly be said on the subject. What I have to say upon it can scarcely be more than the echo of his words . . . .[2]

This remained Morris's position throughout. In 1892, when he had set up his Kelmscott Press, he chose 'The Nature of Gothic' as one of its early titles, writing for it a preface in which he declared that Ruskin's chapter

> in future days will be considered one of the very few necessary and inevitable utterances of the century.
>
> To some of us when we first read it, now many years ago, it seemed to point out a new road on which the world should travel. And in spite of all the disappointments of forty years . . . we can still see no other way out of the folly and degradation of Civilization.[3]

What Morris presented in his lectures was, in his own words, 'Socialism seen through the eyes of an artist'.[4] In 1883 this led him into active involvement in the socialist movement: in January 1883 he joined the Democratic Federation, at that time 'the only active socialist organisation in England',[5] and for the next six years devoted himself almost full-time to the socialist cause. One of his first steps was to study the work of Karl Marx, whose *Capital* Morris read in 1883.

This chapter is concerned with Morris's theory of architecture. Is it the case, as Graham Hough put it, that in his theory of architecture Morris did little more than regurgitate 'the orthodox Ruskinian view' without significant alteration? Or is it rather, as Paul Meier stated in his encyclopaedic study of Morris's utopian thinking, that although Morris started with the Ruskinian idealist approach, he went on to develop in its place an historical materialist approach to art and architecture based on Marx?[6]

To answer this we must examine Morris's major theoretical statements on architecture, which are to be found in the public lectures on architecture, the arts and society that Morris delivered between 1877 and 1896. Useful evidence is also provided by Morris's correspondence, in which architecture constituted the major theme, and in the recollections of Morris's intellectual development recorded both by himself and his friends.

At the start one point should be made about Morris's personal circumstances as they affected his concept of work. When Morris launched himself on the public platform he was in business as a high-class decorator and designer, with showrooms in Oxford Street, catering to the West End demand for specialist luxury goods. As he put it in 1882, his was a 'peculiar trade', in that originality was 'necessary for our business merely as a commercial affair' and most of his employees were not mere 'hands' but rather 'specialists like myself'.[7] We should note that, although by this stage Morris ran his business on regular commercial lines, he had not been led into this choice of career by the need to earn his living. His father on his death had left a fortune valued at £200,000 (made through the acquisition of shares in mining), which meant that the young Morris was able to choose his career with a view to ends other than mere income. He later recalled the chain of events that led to the formation of the firm:

> At this time the revival of Gothic architecture was making great progress in England and naturally touched the Pre-Raphaelite movement also; I threw myself into these movements with all my heart: got a friend to build me a house very medieval in spirit in which I lived for five years, and set myself to decorating it; we found, I and my friend the architect especially, that all the minor arts were in a state of complete degradation especially in England, and accordingly in 1861 with the conceited courage of a young man I set myself to reforming all that: and started a sort of firm for producing decorative articles. D. G. Rossetti, Ford Madox Brown, Burne-Jones and P. Webb the architect of my house were the chief members of it as far as the designing went.[8]

Morris had thus established his firm not so much as a business proposition as a labour of love. Earlier, in 1855, when justifying to his mother his desire to pursue architecture as a career, he gave as one of his reasons his belief that thereby he might 'reasonably hope to be happy in my work'.[9] This notion that work should be a pleasure – almost a hobby – remained with him, all the more so from the late 1860s when the problems of his marriage led him even more to seek emotional satisfaction in his work. He wrote in 1883

> I could never forget that in spite of all drawbacks my work is little else than pleasure to me; that under no conceivable circumstances would I give it up even if I could.

The almost physical pleasure that Morris took in his own craftwork coloured the way that he thought about work as a whole. In the same letter he continued

> Over and over again have I asked myself why should not my lot be the common lot . . . . Indeed I have been ashamed when I have thought of the contrast between my happy working hours and the unpraised, unrewarded, monotonous drudgery which most men are condemned to. Nothing shall convince me that such labour as this is good or necessary to civilization.[10]

It was in these terms, in which work was equated with pleasurable craft production, that he was to formulate his theory of architecture.

OXFORD ORIGINS OF MORRIS'S THOUGHT

Morris's mature thought on architecture drew largely on the ideas that he first encountered while an undergraduate at Oxford in the early 1850s. Three principal strands can be identified. First and most important was Ruskin, particularly 'The Nature of Gothic', and, in the wake of Ruskin, Rossetti and the Pre-Raphaelites; second was the Oxford history school; and third the design rationalism of Pugin, Viollet-le-Duc and the circle of Henry Cole.

The works of Ruskin constituted the formative influence on Morris's intellectual development. Canon Dixon, a member of the Morris/Burne-Jones 'set', recalled of Morris's undergraduate days (1853–55) that

> Morris would often read Ruskin aloud. He had a mighty singing voice, and chanted rather than read those weltering oceans of eloquence . . . . The description of the Slave Ship, or of Turner's skies, with the burden, 'Has Claude given this?'

were declaimed by him in a manner that made them seem as
if they had been written for no end but that he should hurl
them in thunder on the head of the base criminal who had
never seen what Turner saw in the sky.[11]

It was not *Modern Painters* alone however that affected Morris. In
1892 Morris told Cockerell of his time at Oxford:

> I went up to College in 1852. Ruskin's Stones of Venice (vols
> 2 and 3) came out the following year, and made a deep
> impression . . . .[12]

In 1854 and again the following summer Morris went to France to
see the Northern Gothic praised by Ruskin, and after his return
in September 1855 'had much talk' with Cormell Price 'about
architecture and division of labour'.[13] It was no wonder therefore
that the *Oxford and Cambridge Magazine* which Morris and his friends
were planning at the time and which appeared monthly throughout
1856 should have included the passage from 'The Nature of Gothic'
in which Ruskin denounced the spiritual consequences of the
division of labour.[14]

Through Ruskin, Morris was introduced at Oxford to the work
of Rossetti and the Pre-Raphaelites. Burne-Jones recalled that 1854
saw the publication of Ruskin's *Lectures on Architecture and Painting*:

> I was working in my room when Morris ran in one morning
> bringing the newly published book with him: so everything
> was put aside until he read it all through to me. And there
> we first saw about the Pre-Raphaelites, and there I first saw
> the name of Rossetti.[15]

Two years later, when he had graduated from Oxford and was
working in the office of G. E. Street, Morris came under the
personal influence of Rossetti to the extent that he abandoned his
architectural training to become a painter, and soon afterwards
Rossetti, Morris, Burne-Jones, Val Prinsep, Spencer Stanhope *et
al.* set about the decoration of the Oxford Union. Morris recalled
in 1892:

> We fell under the influence of Rossetti, perhaps I even more
> than Burne-Jones . . . . I left Street after being with him *nine*

months in order to try painting . . . . I was greatly taken up with Mallory, Froissart and anything medieval that I could lay my hands on, my interest in history being essentially with medieval or artistic times . . . .[16]

This equation of 'medieval' with 'artistic' times was to remain with Morris throughout his life. It leads us directly to the second of the strands of Morris's undergraduate thought that we should notice: his fascination with what in 1877 he termed 'the newly invented study of living history',[17] stemming from his romantic love of the middle ages. As an undergraduate, Morris recalled, he 'took very ill' to his formal studies but 'fell-to very vigorously on history and especially medieval history'.[18] He devoured the works of Carlyle, particularly *Past and Present* which was regarded by the Morris 'set' as a quasi-biblical authority; their *Oxford and Cambridge Magazine* ran a five-part series on Carlyle, 'written by one who "believes" in Carlyle'.[19] After he left college Morris kept up with the great advances being made in the subject, reading both the newly-published medieval texts and the work of the Oxford historians, such as Rogers (*History of Agriculture and Prices in England*, 1866), Freeman (*History of the Norman Conquest*, 1867–79), and Green (*Short History of the English People*, 1874). Morris told Cockerell in 1891 that 'whatever study he undertook was interesting only or mainly for the light it threw on history'.[20] As a result Morris developed what Burne-Jones called a remarkable 'bird's eye view' of the centuries.[21]

The discovery of the sense of history and the consequent development of history as a scholarly discipline was, Morris believed, one of the few tangible advances made by the nineteenth century. In an address to the SPAB in 1879, he emphasised 'how different that modern historical research is to the chronicling, the story-telling of times past'. The new sense of history, he said, made it possible to grasp the differences between various historical epochs, and thereby to enter into and understand the lives of people in the past. Whereas in earlier times

neither the chroniclers nor their audience could conceive of their forefathers being different from them in any way . . . we of the present time can understand them just as they are; that is *our* birthright, *our* heritage . . . .[22]

What made the 'new' history particularly appealing to Morris was the fact that the Oxford historians generally took a favourable view of medieval society (stressing both its democratic nature and its high standard of material life), and thus confirming rather than undermining Morris's preferences: Morris later told Lethaby that the 'more we knew about the guilds etc, the more it proved to be like what we supposed'.[23]

Morris's absorption of the advances made by the Oxford history school had two important consequences for his mature thought. First it meant that he had a much more concrete and detailed understanding of the social life of past ages than had been available to Ruskin in the 1840s. Second, when in the 1880s Morris came to read Marx – whose thought was otherwise so unfamiliar – his task was eased by his familiarity with the historical approach, which Marx also employed.

The third strand of Morris's undergraduate thought that was to be of lasting significance was the rationalist approach to architecture and design. Pre-eminently French in origin, the rationalist view of architecture was represented in England by Pugin (*True Principles of Pointed or Christian Architecture*, 1841); by Viollet-le-Duc, whose magisterial *Dictionnaire raisonné de l'architecture française* (1854–68), though untranslated, was well known; and by the circle of design reformers around Henry Cole, including Owen Jones, Richard Redgrave, and Matthew Digby Wyatt, who were best known for their work on the Great Exhibition of 1851 and the subsequent foundation of the South Kensington Museum. Pugin and Viollet both saw Gothic as primarily a rational approach to structure, a working out in construction of the potential of materials and the dictates of logic. The Cole group were concerned with the decorative arts rather than architecture, and put their emphasis on the discipline of utility rather than that of structure, making 'fitness' to use and to material their great theme.

Morris's education in the arts came at a time when these rationalist ideas enjoyed a wide following. At Oxford he subscribed to the *Builder*, whose dynamic and influential editor, George Godwin, shared both Pugin's rationalism and his strong sympathy for Gothic. Under Godwin, the *Builder* promoted the view that truth to materials and the avoidance of non-functional elements or 'redundancies' were the major criteria of good design. Canon Dixon recalled of Morris's undergraduate days at Oxford:

his observations of art began with architecture. He was constantly drawing windows, arches, gables in his books. One of the first things he ever said to me was to ask me to go with him to look at Merton tower. He used to take the *Builder*, and read it, and sometimes talk of the plans and designs in it. Few undergraduates would have done that.[24]

Morris also absorbed the ideas of Cole and his associates. In the *Journal of Design and Manufactures* they demanded 'fitness in the ornament to the thing ornamented', which meant that a flat object like a carpet or wallpaper 'should be treated as a flat surface and have none of those imitations of raised forms' popular at the time.[25] Dixon recollected of Morris:

I believe that his mind was first turned toward decorative art, not actually but in germ, by reading in Faulkner's room an article in *Household Words* which described some of the odd and stupid designs that were then common in furniture, asking, e.g. why we walked over lions and tigers in carpets. I remember his delight at that. (This article was not a remarkable one except in drawing attention to absurdities.)[26]

3.2 Morris & Company showroom, 449 Oxford Street

Here we see the first signs of Morris's life-long enthusiasm for the ideas of 'fitness' in design. When Morris set up as an 'art' decorator and designer in 1861, the ideas of Cole and Owen Jones (whose *Grammar of Ornament* Morris possessed) formed the basic culture of 'enlightened' taste within which he practised. Thus giving 'Some Hints on Pattern Designing' in 1881, Morris spoke of 'this working in materials, which is the raison d'être of all pattern work' and said that, as for 'a carpet-design, it seems quite clear that it should be quite flat'.[27] The rationalist view of Gothic promoted by Pugin and Viollet, once imbibed by Morris, also remained with him: this meant that for Morris Gothic was not just beautiful but also rational, 'an architecture pure in its principles, reasonable in its practice, and beautiful to the eyes of all men'.[28]

MORRIS'S ARCHITECTURAL THOUGHT BEFORE 1883

Morris gave his first public lecture, 'The Decorative Arts', in December 1877 as the first of a series promised for the Trade Guild of Learning, an institution set up with the positivist goal of educating the workmen and moralising the capitalist. Before the lecture Morris admitted to feeling 'nervous at having to face my fellow beings in public',[29] but he was encouraged by its success not just to issue the lecture in published form as a pamphlet, but also to accept lecturing engagements elsewhere: at Birmingham; at the London Institution (where Ruskin, accompanied by Morris, had lectured a few months earlier); and at Burslem, Leek and the Working Men's College.

From these lectures Morris decided to compile a book, *Hopes and Fears for Art*, published in 1882. He wrote to Georgiana Burne-Jones in August 1880:

> By the way, I give my third lecture to the Trade Guild of Learning in October; that will be my autumn work, writing it . . . . Also I have promised to lecture next March at the London Institute – subject, the prospects of Architecture in modern civilization. I will be as serious as I can over them, and when I have these last two done, I think of making a book of the lot, as it will be about what I have to say on the subject, which still seems to me the most serious one that a man can

think of; for 'tis no less than the chances of a calm, dignified, and therefore happy life for the mass of mankind.[30]

In what way did Morris see architecture as involving the happiness of the human race? At the core of Morris's pronouncements was the notion that architecture and art, properly understood, meant pleasure in labour. The 'very kernel and heart of what I have come here to say to you', he told his Birmingham audience in his first lecture there in February 1879 was that

> That thing which I understand by real art is the expression by man of his pleasure in labour.[31]

Lecturing at the London Institution on 'The Prospects of Architecture in Civilization' in 1881 the message was the same:

> Of all that I have to say to you this seems to me the most important – that our daily and necessary work . . . should be human, serious and pleasurable, not machine-like, trivial, or grievous. I call this not only the very foundation of Architecture in all senses of the word, but of happiness also in all conditions of life.[32]

In preaching this, Morris presented himself as nothing more than the messenger of Ruskin. When he and Webb had set up the SPAB earlier in 1877, they based the Society explicitly on the *Seven Lamps*, circulating to all their correspondents a reprint of the passage in 'The Lamp of Memory' on the evils of restoration. Writing to Ruskin in July 1877 Morris said that these words

> are so good, and so completely settle the whole matter, that I feel ashamed at having to say anything else about it, as if the idea was an original one of mine, or of anybody else's but yours: but I suppose it is of service, or may be, for different people to say the same thing.[33]

In the public lectures which began in December of that year he adopted a similar stance to Ruskin. The acknowledgement to 'The Nature of Gothic' made in the first lecture has already been quoted, and similar genuflections continued to pepper Morris's lectures thereafter. In Birmingham in 1880 Morris said that he had been taught so much by Ruskin 'that I cannot help feeling continually as I speak that I am echoing his words',[34] and told his audience at the London Institution that

> the pith of what I am going to say on this subject was set forth years ago and for the first time by Mr Ruskin in that chapter of the Stones of Venice which is entitled, 'On the Nature of Gothic' . . . .[35]

At Oxford in November 1883 (a famous occasion chaired by Ruskin which ended with Morris appealing for recruits to socialism) Morris similarly presented Ruskin as the source of his message:

> ART IS MAN'S EXPRESSION OF HIS JOY IN LABOUR. If those are not Professor Ruskin's words they embody at least his teaching on this subject.[36]

Was Morris correct in this belief? It was undoubtedly the case that his ideas about art and labour were based in large part on Ruskin's teaching: the notion of art as an expression of social life and architecture as a function of the labour process; the favourable view of the middle ages and the antipathy to the Renaissance; and above all the contrast between the free, and therefore human, labour exhibited by Gothic cathedrals and the servile, sub-human labour of the industrial system: these were all major themes taken by Morris from 'The Nature of Gothic'. Yet the differences must also be noted. 'Joy in labour' was not a form of words that Ruskin had used in 'The Nature of Gothic'. The closest that Ruskin had approached to Morris's formulation was in the *Seven Lamps*, when he stated that the proper question to ask about a piece of sculpture was whether the carver was happy when he did the work – a passage curiously that Morris did not cite. Ruskin's own summary of 'The Nature of Gothic' was that it showed the connection between architecture and the 'liberty of the workman'; and indeed 'The Nature of Gothic' dealt with the artistic value not so much of happy labour, as of free labour – something slightly different. In 'The Nature of Gothic' the element of pleasure was less that of the craftsman doing the work than that of the viewer or critic enjoying the result; and pleasure could be given by Gothic as a record of unhappiness as well as of joy. What in Ruskin had been the art critic's pleasure in viewing the work of art as the record of the efforts of 'poor, clumsy men' became in Morris the pleasure of the craftsman, the 'definite sensuous pleasure . . . always present in the handiwork of the deft workman when he is working successfully'.[37]

As well as this difference in emphasis, there were important parts of Ruskin's mid-century thought omitted by Morris. The moral and Christian framework of Ruskin's ideas (the contrast between the pagan and the Christian in art, and the notion of Gothic as the equivalent of the Christian doctrine of the imperfection of the soul), and the equation of architecture with architectural sculpture, were alike absent from Morris's thought. From Ruskin's complex theory, in which art as the expression of the human spirit was related to the conditions of labour which allowed or obstructed such expression, Morris seized on one element which he presented as the nub of Ruskin's teaching: pleasure in labour. Morris was interested in the work of art not as an expression of the necessary imperfection of the Christian soul, but simply as the outcome of a pleasurable and satisfying process of intellectual and physical exertion.

On the doctrine of 'pleasure in labour' Morris built the remainder of his theory. According to Morris, if labour was a pleasure to the producer, that pleasure would reveal itself in the object produced; and the way that it would do so was through decoration. The decorative arts were nature's gift, the means whereby the necessary labour of the human race was turned from a curse to a blessing: only let them

> beautify our labour . . . and there will be pretty much an end of dull work and its wearing slavery; and no man will any longer have an excuse for talking about the curse of labour, no man will any longer have an excuse for evading the blessing of labour.[38]

Nature constituted not just the source but also the content of decoration:

> For, and this is at the root of the whole matter, everything made by man's hands has a form, which must be either beautiful or ugly; beautiful if it is in accord with Nature, and helps her; ugly if it is discordant with Nature, and thwarts her; it cannot be indifferent . . . .[39]

This belief in nature as the source of beauty in art stood firmly in the tradition established by Ruskin in *Modern Painters*. For the manner in which nature was to be rendered in decoration, however, Morris followed the design rationalism of the Cole group. In the decorative arts, he said, it was neither possible nor desirable to 'imitate nature literally': therefore decorative work should be 'suggestive rather than imitative' of nature.[40] By 'the conventionalizing of nature' into 'beautiful and natural forms', the user would be reminded 'not only of that part of nature which . . . they represent, but also of much that lies beyond that part'.[41] In these sentiments we see Morris reiterating the doctrines of Owen Jones *et al.*

An object decorated in this way, looking 'as natural, nay as lovely, as the green field, the river bank or the mountain flint', Morris stated, could not fail to give pleasure to whoever used it. 'To give people pleasure in the things they must perforce *use*' was thus, after giving pleasure to the maker, the second 'great office of decoration'.[42] It was this whole process, of investing objects of everyday use with pleasurable beauty and thereby making them works of art, that constituted the definition of

> Architecture: the turning of necessary articles of daily use into works of art.[43]

If this constituted architecture, when if ever did it exist? Here Morris followed directly 'The Nature of Gothic': architecture had existed in the middle ages but no longer existed in the nineteenth century. According to Morris, in the middle ages everything made by human beings, from cups to cities, had been beautiful: not because they were made by specially gifted people, but because conditions of labour at that time had meant that work was a pleasure, not a toil. The 'wonderful works' on show at the South Kensington (now the Victoria and Albert) Museum, he claimed, were no more than

> the common household goods of those past days . . . made by 'common fellows', as the phrase goes, in the common course of their daily labour,

but made with enjoyment:

Many a grin of pleasure, I'll be bound . . . went to the carrying through of those mazes of mysterious beauty, to the invention of those strange beasts and birds and flowers that we ourselves have chuckled over at South Kensington.

Similarly with the houses and churches of the middle ages:

who was it that designed and ornamented them? The great architect, carefully kept for the purpose, and guarded from the common troubles of common men? By no means . . . 'a common fellow', whose common everyday labour fashioned works that are to-day the wonder and despair of many a hard-working 'cultivated' architect.[44]

In contrast, the nineteenth century had destroyed the pleasure of work for the mass of the population, subjecting them to 'the greatest of all evils, the heaviest of all slaveries': the division of labour. In a manner descended directly from 'The Nature of Gothic', Morris denounced

that evil of the greater part of the population being engaged for by far the most part of their lives in work, which at the best cannot interest them, or develop their best faculties, and at the worst (and that is the commonest, too) is mere unmitigated slavish toil . . . . And this toil degrades them into less than men . . . .[45]

This was a direct revival of the critique of the de-humanising effects of the division of labour formulated by Ruskin in the 1840s.

While Morris followed Ruskin on the main lessons of history, nonetheless on the specific conditions prevailing in the various periods he provided a somewhat different (and rather more sophisticated) account. While the art of the ancient Greeks had been, in formal terms, perfect, 'its demand for perfection in quality of workmanship' had 'crushed all experiment, all invention and imagination' in the arts.[46] Morris credited the Romans with having effectively 'invented architecture' by adopting the arch, but they had used it only structurally, not realising its potential for architectural expression.[47] This realisation occurred in sixth-century Byzantium, when the workman was liberated from the tyranny of the architect and allowed to 'do something that people would stop to look at no less than the more intellectual work of his better-born fellow'.[48] The outcome of this 'freedom of the many, in the realm of art at least' was Santa Sophia, the first demonstration of a rational, popular and beautiful architecture and hence 'the crown of all the great buildings of the world'.[49]

The rehabilitation of Byzantine architecture – St Mark's above all – had been one of the themes of Ruskin's mid-century architectural writings. But Ruskin, relying as always on direct observation, had not pressed the claims of Santa Sophia (even if it was implicit in his treatment of St Mark's), tending to defer to the unfavourable views of Byzantine architecture held by his contemporaries (although this was something that he later revised, particularly in the 1880 reissue of the *Seven Lamps*).[50] It was the French nineteenth-century theorists – including Lenoir and Vaudoyer (*Études d'architecture en France*, 1841–42) and Viollet-le-Duc (*Entretiens sur l'architecture*, volume one, 1863) – who saw Byzantine architecture and above all Santa Sophia as a turning-point in the history of architecture. No more than Ruskin had Morris been to Constantinople to see Santa Sophia; instead he relied on the photographs specially obtained for him in 1878 by his friend Aglaia Ionides Coronio. On this basis nonetheless Morris was prepared to present Santa Sophia as the turning-point in architectural history, even though (unlike the French) he considered that the most valuable contribution to Byzantine architecture had come from the Romans rather than the Greeks.

According to Morris, the Gothic era, when art was the free and unselfconscious product of a 'multitude of happy workers', lasted from Santa Sophia to the Renaissance.[51] Once 'the brightness of the so-called Renaissance faded', it emerged that the attempt to imitate the perfection of classical exemplars had destroyed popular art, leaving only a stale academicism in its place.[52] Under the division of labour imposed by the commercial system, art was separated from artifacts and artists from artisans. Instead of being 'a gift of the people to the people . . . a part of everyday life', by the nineteenth century art had become 'an esoteric mystery shared by a little band of superior beings' and the only buildings of the nineteenth century with any artistic merit at all were those

> few houses built and mostly inhabited by the ringleaders of the rebellion against sordid ugliness, which we are met here to further to-night.[53]

SOCIALISM AND MARXISM

In the lectures given between 1877 and 1883, Morris, drawing on Ruskin's ideas of thirty years before, criticised society on the grounds that it suffocated art. Morris later recalled that

> the study of history and the love and practice of art forced me into a hatred of the civilization which, if things were to stop as they are, would turn history into inconsequent nonsense, and make art a collection of the curiosities of the past which would have no serious relation to the life of the present.[54]

At this stage Morris admitted privately that he sought not a piecemeal improvement in but a transformation of society. In 1878 he wrote of Matthew Arnold's lecture, 'Equality', that while he agreed with Arnold's main point,

> if he has any idea of a remedy, he dursn't mention it: I think myself that no rose-water will cure us: disaster & misfortune of all kinds, I think will be the only things that will breed a remedy: in short nothing can be done till all rich men are made poor by common consent . . . .[55]

Similarly at the start of 1881 he wrote to Georgiana Burne-Jones that his mind was 'very full of the great change which I hope is slowly coming over the world . . . the abasement of the rich and the raising up of the poor . . . till people can at last rub out from their dictionaries altogether these dreadful words rich and poor . . . '.[56]

The problem however was to see how this fundamental change might be brought about; as Morris later recalled, in this 'period of political radicalism . . . I saw my ideal clear enough, but had no hope of any realization of it'.[57] During these years (1877–83) Morris was politically a Radical: following his work for the Eastern Question Association in 1876–78, he became Treasurer of another Radical pressure group, the National Liberal League, and at the 1880 general election campaigned enthusiastically for the return of Gladstone. But the new government was unable to live up to the hopes of the Radicals, particularly over Ireland and imperial issues; 'if I say I don't trust the present government, I mean to say that I don't trust it to show as radical', Morris wrote to his wife in

February 1881, 'Whig it is and will remain'.[58] By the end of the
year his disenchantment with the Radicals had reached the point
where he resigned his post in the National Liberal League.

At this stage Ruskin was Morris's acknowledged 'master'.[59] But
according to Morris's own account it was not Ruskin but J. S. Mill,
the most 'advanced' of the orthodox liberal political economists,
who put 'the finishing touch to my conversion to Socialism'. In
1879 Mill published in the *Fortnightly Review* a series of articles on
socialism which

> put the arguments, as far as they go, clearly and honestly,
> and the result, so far as I was concerned, was to convince me
> that Socialism was a necessary change, and that it was possible
> to bring it about in our own days.[60]

In January 1883 Morris joined the Democratic Federation. This
body had been founded two years previously as an alliance of
Radical clubs, but under the leadership of H. M. Hyndman soon
took on a socialist hue, a change that it signalled in 1883 by adding
the prefix 'Social' to its name. From then on, for the next six years,
Morris was to lead the life of a socialist activist – 'the pernicious
practice of what may be called professional agitation, professional
though unpaid'[61] – first in the Social Democratic Federation and
subsequently in the Socialist League, which was formed as a
secession by Morris and others, with Engels' support, at the end
of 1884.

Marxism constituted the main intellectual platform of the British
socialist movement of the 1880s, if for no other reason than that,
as Morris put it in 1885, Marx 'is the only completely scientific
Economist on our side'.[62] In 1890 Morris told an interviewer that

> It was Carl Marx, you know, who originated the present
> Socialist movement; at least, it is pretty certain that that
> movement would not have gathered the force it has done if
> there had been no Carl Marx to start it on scientific lines.[63]

When he joined the Democratic Federation Morris was quite
ignorant of political economy and had no knowledge of Marx: 'I
had never so much as opened Adam Smith, or heard of Ricardo,
or of Karl Marx'.[64] Accordingly he set down to remedy the

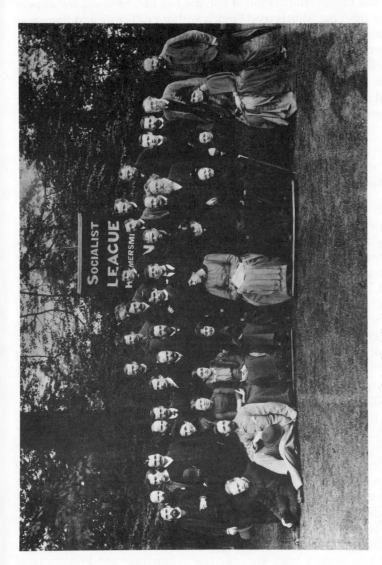

3.3 The Hammersmith Branch of the Socialist League: a photograph by Frederick Hollyer (1885). Morris is the prominent bearded figure standing to the right of the banner

deficiency by studying Marx's *Capital*. Morris read no German and the full English translation of volume one of *Capital* did not appear until 1887; but Morris read French without difficulty and there was a French edition available, which had been published with Marx's approval in 1872–75. This French edition of the first volume of *Capital* Morris acquired and started to study: in February 1883 he 'was bubbling over with Karl Marx, whom he had just begun to read in French'.[65] Further reading revealed the difficulty of coming to terms with political economy as a novice: Morris later recalled

> I must confess that, whereas I thoroughly enjoyed the historical part of 'Capital', I suffered agonies of confusion of the brain over reading the pure economics of that great work.[66]

Nonetheless he persevered, recognising that the subject of socialism was 'a difficult and intricate one, and to understand really requires a great deal of reading'.[67] By 1884 his copy of *Capital* had become so frail, 'worn to loose sections by his own constant study of it', that he had it rebound by his young artist friend, T. J. Cobden-Sanderson.[68]

Morris's reading of marxist texts other than *Capital* was confined to what was available in English and French. After *Capital*, the work from which he drew the most was Engels' *Socialism: Utopian and Scientific*, a succinct history of both socialist thought and the emergence of capitalism, which Engels had published in French in 1880. These two formed major sources for the series of articles on the history and theory of socialism, 'Socialism from the Root Up', which Morris wrote with E. B. Bax for *Commonweal* in 1886–87 (reissued in book form in 1893 as *Socialism: its Growth and Outcome*).[69] Other texts available to Morris included the *Communist Manifesto* (in a scarce English edition of 1850 and a readily available French edition of 1885), *The Civil War in France* (written and published in English in 1871), and the early short piece *Wage Labour and Capital*. While the key economic and political texts of marxism were thus available to Morris, it is important to note that the early writings of Marx dealing with ideology (the 'Economic and Philosophical Manuscripts', and *The German Ideology*) were not.

Morris's education in marxism was aided by the personal contacts that he made in the socialist movement. His contact with the pre-eminent marxist, Friedrich Engels, was limited to a few meetings held at the time of the formation of the Socialist League and the first year or so thereafter; and, although they were his allies in the formation of the League, Morris did not acknowledge any particular debt to Eleanor Marx or her husband Edward Aveling. Bax, Hyndman and Scheu were named by Morris as the three friends from whom he had learned about socialist theory. Scheu was an Austrian socialist refugee with strong anarchist leanings; he and Morris were close friends from the time of meeting in 1883, and there is evidence to suggest that Scheu may have helped Morris with his knowledge of some of the German socialist texts. Hyndman, the founder of the SDF, had been friendly with Marx until the latter discovered the plagiarism of his doctrines in *England for All* (1881); from Marx's theories Hyndman emphasised the theory of surplus value and the doctrine of the class struggle, thereby, as Pierson put it, reducing marxism from dialectical materialism to a form of economic utilitarianism.[70] When Morris was undergoing his education in marxism in 1883–84 he was in continuous and close contact with Hyndman, whom he described as the person 'allowed by Socialists to be capable of giving a definite exposition of the whole doctrine'.[71] A very different view of marxism was represented by E. B. Bax, who approached the subject from the side of German idealist philosophy: while going along with Marx in his materialist view of society, Bax believed that Marx had been one-sided in omitting metaphysics from his dialectic, and called for a socialist ethics or metaphysics to stand alongside Marx's socialist economics. Bax was Morris's ally in the break with Hyndman and the establishment of the Socialist League, and the two collaborated on the series of articles 'Socialism from the Root Up'.

How then did Morris understand Marx's teaching? Firstly, as a theory of history. Asked in 1890 by a non-socialist interviewer to give Marx's teaching in a nutshell, Morris replied that

The general purpose of his great work is to show that Socialism is the natural outcome of the past. From the entire history of the past, he shows that it is a mere matter of evolution, and that, whether you like it or whether you don't, you will have to have it; that just as chattel slavery gave way to medieval feudalism and feudalism to free competition, so the age of competition must inevitably give place to organism. It is the natural order of development.[72]

Morris thus grasped Marx's notion of the stages of historical development, of which capitalism was merely the most recent. For most people, Morris wrote in July 1883,

> it seems a part of the necessary and eternal order of things that the present supply and demand Capitalist system should last for ever: though the system of citizen and chattel slave under which the ancient civilisations lived, which no doubt once seemed also necessary and eternal, had to give place, after a long period of violence and anarchy, to the feudal system of seigneur and serf: which in its turn, though once thought necessary and eternal, has been swept away in favour of our present contract system between rich and poor.[73]

Morris followed Marx not just on the three main stages of development (ancient, feudal, and capitalist), but also on the stages of the development of capitalism, citing 'the admirable account of the different epochs of production given in Karl Marx's great work entitled "Capital"'.[74] From Marx Morris also took the point that history had a direction that could not be reversed:

> We cannot turn our people back into Catholic English peasants and Guild craftsmen, or into heathen Norse banders, much as may be said for such conditions of life: we have no choice but to accept the task which the centuries have laid on us . . . .[75]

Under Marx's influence Morris reluctantly modified his strong personal antipathy to machinery ('Why infernal machines? All machines are infernal!', he told Lethaby), accepting the view that it was the exploitative relations of capitalism rather than machines *per se* that were at fault and that machinery and factories would have a necessary place in the socialist future.[76]

Morris also followed Marx in the materialist conception of society. He wrote in 1888:

> Socialism is a theory of life, taking for its starting point the evolution of society; or, let us say, man as a social being.
>
> Since man has certain material *necessities* as an animal, Society is founded on man's attempts to satisfy those necessities . . . .[77]

In the process of satisfying these material needs, classes arose opposed to each other. The main feature of capitalist society was this class struggle, resulting from the monopolistic ownership by the capitalist class of the means of production necessary for the sustenance of life. Morris wrote in 1888 that

> as long as there is individual ownership of capital (to put it short) there must be a superior and an inferior class; and between these classes there must be antagonism, each can only thrive at the other's expense.[78]

But the antagonism of classes which was necessary to the capitalist system was also 'the natural and necessary instrument of its destruction'.[79] In October 1883 he wrote to his Manchester friend C. Horsfall:

> you think that *individuals* of good will belonging to all classes of men can, if they be numerous and strenuous enough, bring about the change. I on the contrary think that the basis of all change must be, as it has always been, the antagonism of classes . . . . Commercialism, competition, has sown the wind recklessly, and must reap the whirlwind: it has created a proletariat for its own interest, and its creation will and must destroy it: there is no other force that can do so.[80]

Socialists aimed at 'the abolition of the monopoly in the means of production' and the establishment of a society in which 'the possession and control of all the means of production and exchange' rested with the whole people.[81] Thereafter, with 'the class struggle, now thousands of years old, having come to an end', the real history of humanity would begin: nations as political units would cease to exist; politics and the political system, as 'the reflection of our class society', would be transformed; and government would change from a 'government of *persons*' into an 'administration of *things*'.[82]

Although to this extent Morris's political thought as a socialist followed Marx, we must note that in one major respect Morris was not an orthodox marxist by the standards of the day. As Bernard Shaw noted, while Morris accepted Marx as the socialist authority on economics and 'was on the side of Karl Marx *contra mundum*', he hardly ever referred to what was held to be the central tenet of

Marx's economics, the theory of surplus value, and in his socialist propaganda he tended to focus on aspects other than the economic.[83] Morris's silence on this central point of socialist doctrine was due in part to his low opinion of himself as an economist. In February 1887, when his series with Bax on 'Socialism from the Root Up' had reached Marx's *Capital*, Morris noted in his diary:

> Tuesday to Bax at Croydon where we did our first article on Marx: or rather he did it: I don't think I should ever make an economist even of the most elementary kind: but I am glad of the opportunity this gives me of hammering some Marx into myself.[84]

The following month he wrote *à propos* a forthcoming lecture that 'I am not very likely, I fear, to overload it with economics'.[85]

But there was another factor involved as well. Morris stood in the English ethical tradition which held that, as the future society was to be morally superior to that of the present, so socialists, as the apostles of that new society, should demonstrate a morality superior to that normally accepted. In this view, not only was the appeal of socialism primarily ethical, but that appeal stood to be undermined by any reference to 'sordid' material interests – a belief fundamentally at odds with Marx's materialist conception of the roots of human action. Hence Morris emphasised the 'higher' or ethical aspects of socialism; as he told C. J. Faulkner, he was positively 'afraid of such successes that come of appealing to people on the side of their immediate interests'.[86]

This ideal of socialists as a higher species of being, untainted by the corruption and materialism of the everyday world, also lay behind Morris's political strategy, the policy of 'abstention' from parliamentary involvement, which in 1888 drove out the English marxists (including Eleanor Marx and Edward Aveling) and split the Socialist League. For Morris, the commitment to revolution meant precisely a commitment to overthrow the kind of unprincipled behaviour that politics and commercial life alike necessitated. He expressed his attitude in a letter to Bruce Glasier at the end of 1886:

> I really feel sickened at the idea of all the intrigue and degradation of Concession which would be necessary to us as a parliamentary party: nor do I see any necessity for a

revolutionary party doing any 'dirty work' at all, or soiling ourselves with anything which would unfit us for being due citizens of the new order of things.[87]

As E. P. Thompson has shown, this left Morris in the 1880s in the anomalous position of trying to bring about the advent of Socialism while refusing to take part in the engagements of that class struggle which, according to marxist theory, offered the only route to success.[88]

'LOOK BACK! LOOK BACK!'

How did Morris's entry into the socialist movement and his discovery of Marx affect his attitude to Ruskin? Did Morris after reading Marx in 1883 follow the marxist orthodoxy and reject Ruskin as pre-scientific and non-socialist? A letter written in September 1882 to a correspondent who had congratulated Morris on one of his writings shows clearly Morris's view of Ruskin immediately before his entry into the socialist movement:

> I thank you for your kind and sensible letter . . . . I have little I think to add to what you have read of mine: I do not like however to be praised at the expense of Ruskin, who you must remember is the first comer, the inventor; and I believe we all of us owe a hope that still clings to us, and a chance of expressing that hope, to his insight: of course to say one does not always agree with him is to say that he and I are of mankind.[89]

On becoming an active socialist, Morris accepted that, so far as immediate socialist politics were concerned, Ruskin and the idiosyncratic ideas he been expounding, particularly in *Fors Clavigera*, had to be set aside. He wrote in July 1884 that

> though I have a great respect for Ruskin, and his works (beside personal friendship), he is not a Socialist, that is not a *practical* one. He does not expect to see any general scheme even begun: he mingles with certain sound ideas which he seems to have acquired instinctively, a great deal of mere whims . . .

anyhow his idea of national workshops is one which could only be realised in a State (that is a society) already socialised: nor could it take effect in the way he thinks.[90]

But while rejecting Ruskin's particular nostrums, Morris remained committed to Ruskin's critique of society. Not only would he not allow Ruskin to be maligned by his fellow socialists, but he even defended Ruskin as an economist. In May 1886 an article in *Commonweal* by Bax ended with a vigorous polemical attack on Ruskin and on Ruskin's notion of reforming society through art. Morris in an editorial footnote sprang to Ruskin's defence.

> I think that whatever damage Ruskin may have done to his influence by his strange bursts of fantastic perversity, he has shown much insight even into economical matters, and I am sure he has made many Socialists; his feeling against Commercialism is absolutely genuine, and his expression of it most valuable.[91]

To press home the point, the following month Morris started a four-part series, 'Ruskin as a Revolutionary Preacher', to make available to the socialist movement the many passages from Ruskin that were 'helpful to our side',[92] and subsequently through the office of the Socialist League published a penny pamphlet, *The Rights of Labour according to John Ruskin*.

Nor did the genuflections to Ruskin in Morris's public lectures come to an end. After the famous sentence in the Oxford lecture of November 1883 in which Morris presented as the core of Ruskin's teaching the doctrine that 'ART IS MAN'S EXPRESSION OF HIS JOY IN LABOUR', he commented:

> Nor has any truth more important ever been stated . . . .[93]

The following year Morris spoke of 'Professor Ruskin's unrivalled eloquence and wonderful ethical instinct', and in 1888 referred to the 'marvellous inspiration of genius' shown by Ruskin in 'The Nature of Gothic', to which he paid full tribute in his preface to the Kelmscott edition four years later.[94]

How was it that Morris's old allegiance to Ruskin was able to co-exist with his new enthusiasm for Marx? A curious incident from the end of 1885, when Morris was fully involved in his agitation for the Socialist League, provides a clue. A list of the

'Hundred Best Books', drawn up Sir John Lubbock, was published by the *Pall Mall Gazette* and sent to various public figures, including Morris, who were asked for their emendations. Rather than work from Lubbock's list, Morris produced his own list of those books, fifty-four in all, 'which have profoundly impressed myself'. The list included the classics (Homer, Boccaccio, Scott *et al.*) and the works of Ruskin and Carlyle – but not Marx. Morris explained his choice:

> My list seems a short one, but it includes a huge mass of reading. Also there is a kind of book which I think might be excluded in such lists, or at least put in a quite separate one. Such books are rather tools than books; one reads them for a definite purpose, for extracting information from them of some special kind. Among such books I should include works on philosophy, economics, and modern or critical history. I by no means intend to undervalue such books, but they are not, to my mind, works of art; their manner may be good, or even excellent, but it is not essential to them; their matter is a question of fact, not of taste. My list comprises only what I consider works of art.[95]

For Morris, evidently, Marx belonged with the philosophers, economists and historians in the category of 'rather tools than books'. Marx essentially provided Morris with technical aid, explaining both the history of the various epochs of production and the character of capitalist society; but the overall conception, of human life and the place of art and architecture within it, remained the one that Morris had taken from Ruskin.

This can be seen directly in the paper Morris gave to the 1884 meeting of the SPAB, entitled 'Architecture and History', where Morris used the analysis of the capitalist mode of production that he had just read in *Capital* to account for the contrast between the middle ages and the nineteenth century given in 'The Nature of Gothic'. Morris set out to show that the impossibility of 'restoration' (the impossibility of reproducing medieval work under nineteenth-century conditions) was

> not accidental, but is essential to the conditions of life at the present day; that it is caused by the results of all past history, and not by a passing taste or fashion of the time . . . .[96]

To do this Morris presented a summary history of the 'conditions under which handiwork has been produced from classical times onward', drawing directly on the analysis given by Marx, particularly as regards periodisation. Morris stated that he had

> read the full explanation of the change and its tendencies in the writings of a man, I will say a great man, whom, I suppose, I ought not to name in this company, but who cleared my mind on several points (also unmentionable here) relating to this subject of labour and its products.[97]

Whereas in the classical period manufacture had been the work of slaves, Morris stated, in the feudal system craft guilds grew up in which handwork was carried out by freemen in an undivided labour process. The guild craftsman enjoyed a good standard of life and

> being master of his time, his tools, and his material, was not bound to turn out his work shabbily, but could afford to amuse himself by giving it artistic finish.[98]

But then in the early sixteenth century came the 'great change': men were driven from the land and forced into towns to sell their labour, where as journeymen they were collected in larger units under a single master. This, the first stage in Marx's periodisation of capitalism, in turn gave rise to the second stage, based on the division of labour, in which instead of carrying through the entire process of production himself each craftsman was 'condemned for the whole of his life to make the insignificant portion of an insignificant article'.[99] This was followed by the third stage, the factory system, in which the worker did nothing more than tend a machine:

> what thoughts he has must be given to something other than his work . . . 'tis as much as he can do to know what thing the machine (not he) is making.[100]

We can see here Morris making use of Marx's analysis of history, seeing the past in terms of the stages of development of the mode of production and periodising it accordingly. But the phenomenon that this analysis is used to explain – the existence of art in the middle ages and the non-existence of art in the nineteenth century – is derived from Ruskin. While Morris now followed Marx in his concept of history, his concept of art remained unchanged: art was still seen as 'pleasure in labour', a suprahistorical and rigid definition against which the different epochs were to be weighed and judged. Unaware of Marx's earlier work on ideology, which might have enabled him to see the Ruskinian concept of art as itself historically produced, Morris simply incorporated some elements of marxism into his pre-existing theory, with Marx's analysis of the growth of capitalism replacing Ruskin's notion of the decline in moral value as the explanation of the contrast established by Ruskin between the middle ages and the nineteenth century.

By the end of the 1880s Morris realised from the fissures in the socialist movement that the advent of socialism was unlikely to occur 'for a while' and gradually abandoned his role as a 'professional' socialist agitator and returned to his artistic interests.[101] He resumed regular attendance at the meetings of the SPAB and inspected threatened buildings on their behalf. He began his work on printing, setting up the Kelmscott Press in 1890. He lent support to the activities of the Arts and Crafts Exhibition Society and the Art Workers' Guild by attending their meetings and giving lectures for them.

The result was a further corpus of lectures and articles on the history of architecture and the arts. In these writings, dating from the last years of his life (1889–1896), Morris reiterated without substantial alteration the theory of architecture that he had set out in the lectures of the period before his entry into the socialist movement. Indeed, far from modifying his architectural thought in the light of his socialist experience and encounter with marxism, we find Morris restating with renewed emphasis some of those ideas about architecture which he had first imbibed in Oxford in the 1850s.

The first of these was the Pre-Raphaelite notion of beauty. Unlike Webb, Morris never abandoned the Pre-Raphaelite belief that any search for beauty should be derived directly from the art of the middle ages. Reviewing the Royal Academy exhibition for the socialist paper *To-Day* in 1884, Morris had asked:

What . . . is to feed the imagination, the love of beauty of the artists of to-day while all life around them is ugly; sordid

3.4 E. Burne-Jones: frontispiece drawing for William Morris's *A Dream of John Ball* (1888)

poverty on the one hand, insolent or fatuous riches on the other? . . . those only among our painters do work worth considering, whose minds have managed to leap back across the intervening years, across the waste of gathering commercialism, into the later Middle Ages . . . .

This, Morris said, applied not only to painting but to all the arts.

Anyone who wants beauty to be produced at the present day in any branch of the fine arts, I care not what, must be always crying out 'Look back! Look back!'[102]

Lecturing to the Arts and Crafts Exhibition Society on 'Gothic Architecture' in 1889 Morris made it clear that he included architecture within this prescription. Architecture, he said, had 'reached its fullest development in the Middle Ages':

remote as those times are from ours, if we are ever to have architecture at all, we must take up the thread of tradition there and nowhere else . . . . In the future, therefore, our style of architecture must be Gothic Architecture.[103]

In the same lecture Morris also showed that he still held to the rationalist concept of Gothic that he had imbibed in the 1850s. Gothic, he said, 'was the first style since the invention of the arch that did due honour to it, and instead of concealing it decorated it in a logical manner'.[104] This was close both in concept and language to Pugin's *True Principles* of 1841. A similarly Puginian note was sounded in the paper that Morris gave to the Art Workers' Guild in 1891, 'The Influence of Building Materials upon Architecture': like Pugin in *True Principles* Morris treated architecture in terms of the different building materials (stone, brick, wood), defining architecture as 'the art of building suitably with suitable material'.[105]

The 'Gothic Architecture' lecture however did reveal one new element in Morris's thought: the discussion of architecture in terms of the expression of mind or spirit. Discussing the architecture of ancient Greece, Morris asked

What is to be said about the spirit of it which ruled that form? This I think: that the narrow superstition of the form of the Greek temple was not a matter of accident, but was the due expression of the exclusiveness and aristocratic nature of the ancient Greek mind . . . .[106]

Other lectures of this period also spoke of buildings in terms of their 'spirit' or 'soul'.[107] This might be considered as insignificant were it not for an incident recorded by Lethaby. In February 1893 a social evening was held by the Hammersmith Socialist Society at Kelmscott House, attended by Lethaby, Cockerell, Gronlund and others, at which Morris entertained the company with recitations and readings. In his notebook Lethaby recorded Morris mouthing Hegel:

> Beauty is a revelation of Reality, as Hegel said, 'The idea revealed in the finite'. A vindication of God . . . . A call to the spirit.[108]

Lethaby's notebook records other comments of Morris from this period along similar lines.

Where had Morris got his Hegelian aphorism from? As undergraduates at Oxford, Morris and his friends had been introduced to German philosophy by Carlyle, but the focus had been on Goethe, not Hegel. German philosophy was not an interest that they pursued thereafter; in part perhaps because of Ruskin's outburst in the third volume of *Modern Painters* (1856), leading to a lack of interest in German thought on their part, and in part because of their simple inability to read German. Morris's late reference to Hegel must therefore be attributed to influences from elsewhere.

One possible source was Morris's friend and collaborator E. B. Bax, who had included a brief summary of Hegel's theory of art in the section on Hegel in his *Handbook of the History of Philosophy for the Use of Students* (1886). But Hegel's view of art was not a major theme for Bax and this seems an unlikely source for Morris's aphorism. More plausible as a source is Bernard Bosanquet, the Oxford neo-Hegelian philosopher. In 1886 Bosanquet published the first English translation of *The Introduction to Hegel's Philosophy of Fine Art*, the text in which Hegel set out his notion of art as the point at which the absolute and infinite was revealed to the mind through the finite and sensuous. In 1892 Bosanquet followed this with *A History of Aesthetic*, a monumental work of scholarship that not only gave great prominence to Ruskin and Morris, but explicitly presented them as the culmination of German aesthetic thought from Goethe to Hegel. Bosanquet wrote of Morris's thought that 'the true correlative to these conceptions is Kant's doctrine of genius, and, I may add, Schiller's doctrine of play and Hegel's of the ideal'.[109] Bosanquet was a close friend and colleague (at University College, Oxford) of Morris's friend Charles Faulkner, and he was on the council of the Home Arts and Industries Association, in which capacity, he wrote, he had 'learned to appreciate the writings of Mr Ruskin and Mr Morris'.[110] Altogether it is hard to believe that no-one in Morris's circle would have drawn to his attention so powerful a tribute to his importance as a theorist.

The reference to Hegel constituted the one significant new element in Morris's thought of the 1890s; for the rest his architectural thinking remained as it had been in the 1880s and thus largely as formed in the 1850s. How are we to account for this continuing attachment to the ideas that Morris had imbibed in his youth? His famous essay on 'The Revival of Architecture' of 1888 tells us how he himself saw the matter. In this largely (albeit never explicitly) autobiographical account, Morris set out his view not just of nineteenth-century architecture, but also of the relationship between the artistic and socialist sides of his own life. In so doing he showed the extent to which his understanding of architectural history, far from having been transformed under the impact of historical materialism, remained that of the Romantics, telling a story not of classes, material change and ideology, but of ugliness and revolt.

In 'The Revival of Architecture' Morris presented the nineteenth-century revival of architecture as a single all-embracing movement, a revolt against the ugliness of industrialism, that had started early in the century and continued up to the time of writing. Originating with the literary Romantics, the movement had taken shape first with the discovery (clearly by Pugin) that Gothic was 'a logical and organic style',[111] and then with the hope that art might again become, as it had been in the middle ages, living and popular. But although it produced some 'interesting' buildings and works of art, this hope was ill-founded, 'for though we had learned something of the art and history of the Middle Ages, we had not learned enough'.

At last one man, who had done more than anyone else to make this hopeful time possible, drew a line sternly through these hopes founded on imperfect knowledge. This man was John Ruskin. By a marvellous inspiration of genius (I can call it nothing else) he attained at one leap to a true conception of medieval art which years of minute study had not gained for others. In his chapter in 'The Stones of Venice', entitled 'On the Nature of Gothic, and the Function of the Workman therein', he showed us the gulf which lay between us and the Middle Ages.[112]

This marked the turning-point: from then it was evident that the revival would have to turn from an architectural to a social movement. For the purely architectural side of the revival, the story thenceforth was one of decline, as the architects were forced, by the recognition of the gap separating the fourteenth from the nineteenth century, to progressively lower their sights: first from Gothic to the fifteenth century, and then to the 'brick style in vogue in the time of William the Third and Queen Anne'.[113] With the Queen Anne style the revival had 'come down, a long weary way from Pugin's "Contrasts"'; although a few buildings of value followed, the overall result was 'too limited in its scope, too much confined to an educated group, to be a vital growth'.[114]

But while the architectural side of the revival floundered, the social side took new life. Once Ruskin had demonstrated that 'the social life of the Middle Ages allowed the workman freedom of individual expression, which on the other hand our social life forbids him',[115] it became evident that the hopes of the revival could be met only by a change in society. The socialist movement of the 1880s, in Morris's presentation, was the result.

> The enthusiasm of the Gothic revivalists died out when they were confronted by the fact that they form part of a society which will not and cannot have a living style, because it is an economical necessity for its existence that the ordinary everyday work of its population shall be mechanical drudgery . . . . The hope of our ignorance has passed away, but it has given place to the hope born of fresh knowledge. History taught us the evolution of architecture, it is now teaching us the evolution of society . . . .

In the 'society developing out of ours', work would no longer be a drudgery and architecture would again be possible:

> we are waiting for that new development of society, some of us in cowardly inaction, some of us amidst hopeful work towards the change . . . .[116]

In this way Morris explicitly presented his socialist agitation of the 1880s as the logical outcome of the education in architectural thinking that he had undergone thirty years before. Implicitly, he also recognised what this investigation has shown: that while Morris's architectural thought may have led him to socialism, his encounter with socialism (and particularly with historical materialism) had no substantial effect on his architectural thought, which to the end of his life remained substantially as formed in the 1850s.

4

W. R. Lethaby and the Fabians

Of all the disciples of Ruskin, W. R. Lethaby (1857–1931) is generally considered the most important in terms of architectural theory. Trained as an architect and in his early years the chief assistant to Norman Shaw, Lethaby in his forties abandoned architectural practice to concentrate on writing and teaching. For these he rapidly acquired a European reputation, above all for the Central School of Arts and Crafts which, under the aegis of the London County Council, he set up in 1896. Here, as also at the LCC School of Building founded in 1904, Lethaby established a scheme of instruction directed to the Ruskinian goal of overcoming the division of labour and thereby reinvesting production with art.

The curiosity in this was the regime under which this Ruskinian programme was instituted. The educational work of the LCC was the responsibility of a semi-autonomous agency, the LCC Technical Education Board, where Lethaby was employed from 1894 to 1904. The Board had been set up by, and was under the control of, the Fabian Sidney Webb, whose interests were not spiritual or artistic, but economic and political. Dedicated to the cause of 'national efficiency', Webb sought to improve the competitive standing of London's economy in relation to its international rivals, and set up the Central School and the School of Building as a part of a comprehensive scheme to provide training in the skills required by London's manufacturing trades.

Sidney Webb and the Fabians were pioneers of a new version of socialism – social democracy – that from the 1890s onwards was to become increasingly important, particularly in Britain and Germany. Lethaby's work at the Technical Education Board, centering on the foundation of the Central School of Arts and Crafts and the School of Building, raises directly the question of the relationship between Ruskinian ideals and the modernising goals of social democracy. How was it that, in Lethaby's work for the TEB, the Ruskinian critique of the division of labour married so well with the Fabian drive to increase efficiency? How did an ideology that was antagonistic both to the state and to commercialism become the adjunct of a political programme aiming to improve commercial competitiveness by an extension of state activity?

LETHABY'S INTELLECTUAL DEVELOPMENT UP TO 1894

In the decade before his appointment to the Technical Education Board in 1894, Lethaby underwent a major process of intellectual development. Unlike Ruskin or Morris, Lethaby did not have a private income; but his work, as chief assistant in Norman Shaw's office (1879–89) and thereafter in practice on his own account, did not occupy all of his time and he was able to spend time studying at the British Museum.[1] The main strands in Lethaby's thought in this period consisted first of the Romantic art theory of Ruskin, to whom Lethaby was 'converted' in 1884–85, and second of the rationalist doctrine of Viollet-le-Duc, whose writings on medieval architecture provided a major source for Lethaby's own researches. In attempting to resolve these two very different ways of thinking about architecture, Lethaby sought guidance from William Morris and Philip Webb, whose thought, as we have seen, similarly mixed the idealist with the rationalist and who, from 1890 onwards, became Lethaby's personal and intellectual mentors.

The intellectual distance that Lethaby was to travel in the decade up to 1894 we can see from an article on the 'English and French Renaissance' that he published in 1883. Here he dismissed Ruskin's 'moral' criticism of Renaissance architecture out of hand, on the grounds that it 'can surely have little weight when he admires so profoundly the painting and sculpture of the same age'.[2] Pugin and other rationalist or 'utility' doctrines were also discounted, on the grounds that Gothic could not be explained any better than classical architecture on a utility basis. The main aesthetic issue facing the architect was the selection of a style (Lethaby recommended English Renaissance). All these were views that he would later disown. The only point made in the article to which he remained committed was the belief that all periods of art were valid and valuable.

The conversion to Ruskin was the major intellectual event of Lethaby's life. Early in 1884 Lethaby and Gerald Horsley, a

4.1 Portrait plaque of W. R. Lethaby as Master of the Art Workers' Guild (1911)

colleague from the Shaw office, attended Ruskin's lectures on *The Storm-Cloud of the Nineteenth Century* at the London Institution – the only time that Lethaby saw Ruskin in person. Robert Schultz Weir, who joined the Shaw office about this time, later recalled with a touch of hyperbole that 'by the time I got to know him he had read everything that Ruskin had ever written and absorbed his teaching'.[3] In 1885 Lethaby was studying the major Ruskin texts: *The Stones of Venice, St Mark's Rest, Val d'Arno*.[4] The results of this were apparent by the end of the decade. In 1889 Lethaby spoke approvingly of Ruskin in a lecture at the Architectural Association, and in a lecture on cast iron given to the Royal Society of Arts in February 1890 presented himself as a Ruskinian.[5] This lecture opened with quotations from 'The Lamp of Truth' and *The Stones of Venice* and interpreted cast iron in Ruskinian terms as a once worthy art that had been degraded into a mere commodity.

The cast iron lecture ended with an epigrammatic summary of the Ruskinian view of the relationship of art and society: ' "There's always good iron to be had; if there's cinder in the iron, 'tis because there was cinder in the pay"'.[6] The source of the epigram was the American transcendentalist Ralph Waldo Emerson, whom, along with Whitman and Hawthorne, Lethaby was reading and annotating in the mid-1880s. In this respect it is significant that Lethaby in 1895 included Thoreau along with Ruskin and Morris in his intellectual ancestry.[7] In his reading of the mid-1880s, in other words, Lethaby was reading Ruskin as part of a tradition that included the American transcendentalists who, even more than Ruskin, emphasised personal and spiritual fulfilment as against political action.

Lethaby's interest in mythology, evident in his sketchbooks throughout the 1880s, led eventually to the publication of *Architecture, Mysticism and Myth* at the end of 1891. Mythology was one of the major intellectual preoccupations of the day, both in Ruskin (*The Queen of the Air*, 1869, and *St Mark's Rest*, 1877–84) and in the London art circles in which Lethaby moved – not least with Morris, Burne-Jones and the Pre-Raphaelite set. In his 1883 Oxford lectures Ruskin treated Burne-Jones and G. F. Watts as the 'Mythic Schools of Painting'.[8] Particularly important for Lethaby in this regard were Alma-Tadema, whose house he visited early in 1884, and the example of William Burges (1827–1881), who had combined architectural practice and art scholarship in a way that appealed strongly to Lethaby. Lethaby made numerous references to Burges in his sketchbooks, and in *Architecture, Mysticism and Myth* commented on the egg symbolism in Burges' house, which he had seen in the early 1880s.

Lethaby's attraction towards Ruskin in the 1880s was part of the more general movement by young London architects, particularly those in the Shaw office, in the direction of what became the 'arts and crafts'. The story of the formation of the Art Workers' Guild in 1884 and the Arts and Crafts Exhibition Society in 1887, and of Lethaby's involvement in both, is well known. The 'elder statesman' in the formation of the arts and crafts was J. D. Sedding (1837–1891), who, of all the London architects of the day, had the closest personal devotion to Ruskin. Sedding had been an ardent Ruskinian since the age of fifteen, when he had discovered the *Seven Lamps* and copied its plates line by line; he had taken personal instruction from Ruskin in the 1870s in the art of drawing; and he shared entirely Ruskin's conviction that art meant communication between human spirits through the agency of material animated by the artist's hand.[9]

Lethaby and Sedding met in 1883 in the discussions that were to lead to the formation of the Art Workers' Guild. In 1885, when he was making notes from Ruskin in his sketchbook, Lethaby began with a statement from Ruskin that had been published by Sedding.[10] Two years later, in 1887, Sedding proposed to Lethaby that they should collaborate on a book on Saxon and Norman architecture (Sedding doing the text, Lethaby the illustrations), and over the next two years they spent a good deal of time together, going on architectural expeditions for sometimes as long as a week or more. Although in the end the book was not produced, intellectually the relationship was important: in reading Ruskin in the 1880s, Lethaby had Sedding, with his fine-art approach to Ruskin, as guide.

At the same time Lethaby was involved in another area of study which was to expose him to a view of Gothic rather different from that of Ruskin. He later recalled:

> It happens that my days of studentship were in the time when there was a special enthusiasm for French cathedrals, and I must have been one of the last of those who concentrated on the 'professional' study of these masterpieces of structural art. I have worked, measuring and drawing, at all the great monuments of Northern Gothic art, at some of them again

and again, and I may set down three dozen as they occur to me . . . .[11]

Study trips in the 1880s included Normandy (1880), the Loire (1882) and Burgundy (1885 and 1887), in each case taking in the cathedral district of the Ile-de-France. Through these studies Lethaby was led not just to an admiration for the French as masters of architecture (an admiration strong enough to overcome his dislike of their *beaux arts* system), but even more importantly to an appreciation of the French rationalist interpreters of medieval architecture, particularly Viollet-le-Duc (1814–1879). From the 1840s onwards Viollet had developed his view of Gothic as above all a rational structural system (in Gothic, he believed, the builders 'simply followed their reason'),[12] and this view he set out in the magisterial ten volumes of the *Dictionnaire raisonné* of 1854–68. In the famous entry on 'Construction' (itself virtually a book), Viollet wrote that 'the beauty of a structure' lay 'in the judicious employment of the materials and the means placed at the disposal of the constructor'.[13]

Viollet's dictionary was well known and highly esteemed in Britain. For Lethaby, researching medieval architecture and building, it was an essential source; he used the article on construction both in its original form and later in its 1895 English (New York) translation, and cited Viollet in his own writings from 1890 onwards. For the 1893 book on leadwork he drew on Viollet not only for information but also for the epigraph:

> That which gives to the leadwork of the Middle Ages a particular charm is that the means they employed and the forms they adopted are exactly appropriate to the material.[14]

Viollet followed the Saint-Simonians in seeing Gothic and Byzantine architecture as the product of a system of free, guild-based labour. The fact that Viollet shared Ruskin's belief in the 'free craftsmen' of the middle ages made it easier for Lethaby to regard the two authorities as compatible, even though in fact their theories – the one positing art as spiritual communication, the other as the application of reason – were profoundly at odds. In attempting to combine the two, Lethaby was following the example of Morris and Webb, whose circle he entered after 1890 and of both of whom he became a devoted admirer.

Lethaby first came across Webb and Morris in the 1880s, at the time of their active involvement in the socialist movement. As already noted, his later recollection was of hearing Webb lecture to the Hoxton socialists 'about 1883'.[15] In October 1885 he attended Morris's lecture on 'Socialism' at the Working Men's College and in May 1886 on 'Art and Labour' at the Socialist League, and his sketchbooks for 1885 and 1886 include various and lengthy quotations from Morris.[16]

From Morris in the mid-1880s Lethaby imbibed socialist enthusiasm. Schultz Weir, who was in the Shaw office with Lethaby at the time, later recalled:

These were the days of active socialistic propaganda. Morris was much involved in it, Lethaby also in his quiet way took part. Several societies were formed such as 'the Social Democratic Federation' and 'the Socialist League'. There was a good deal of discussion in the office and Lethaby propounded the ethics of socialism to us all and roped some of us into the fold. What particular fold it was I don't remember, but I remember our going to meetings in some small hall in Bloomsbury [probably the Old Compton St hall used by the Bloomsbury branch of the League].

Norman Shaw was much amused at all that went on, rumours of which reached his ears. He was never surprised at anything Lethaby said or did. Not so however the father of one of his pupils. Lethaby had arranged to go on a sketching tour with this pupil and when his father got to know of it he rushed up to see Shaw in a great state. 'I hear my boy is going sketching with a socialist', to which Shaw replied, 'he's perfectly harmless, I assure you, perfectly harmless'.[17]

In the event Shaw's confidence was well-founded, for Lethaby's active involvement with the socialist movement did not develop beyond what was recounted by Weir. It is possible that the violence of 'Bloody Sunday' (13 November 1887) had an effect: 1887 always remained for Lethaby the year of 'Riot Sunday in Trafalgar Square',[18] and certainly the injuries and deaths that occurred that day presented a picture of socialism very different from the vision of Whitman or Ruskin. There is no evidence that Lethaby joined Morris's Socialist League, nor in the later period, unlike many other Morrisites, did he join the Fabian Society; and in lecturing on Morris in 1901 Lethaby contrived to avoid making any reference at all to politics or socialism.[19]

Lethaby came under the close personal influence of Morris and Webb only after the demise of the Socialist League. The introduction came through Ernest Gimson (1864–1919). Lethaby and Gimson met in the summer of 1889 and became close friends; the following year they made several trips together, including in November an outing to see Webb's 'Joldwynds'. Webb they regarded as their 'particular prophet': to be near Webb, at the end of 1890 Gimson and his partner Sidney Barnsley moved to rooms in Raymond Buildings, two stairs along from Webb, and in the spring of 1891 Lethaby followed, moving to Gray's Inn Square 'just opposite Raymond Buildings'.[20]

Thereafter Lethaby was fully admitted to the inner Webb-Morris circle. At Gray's Inn he was in close contact with Webb. His notebook records visits in 1893 to Hammersmith and Merton with Morris and to Epping Forest with Webb. Above all there were the Thursday evening meetings of the committee of the Society for the Protection of Ancient Buildings, followed by supper at Gatti's tearooms. Lethaby joined the SPAB in the autumn of 1891 (proposed by Morris, seconded by Gimson); Rubens states that he was soon attending committee meetings, although he was not formally elected to the committee until 1893.[21] The meetings and Gatti suppers, attended by Morris, Webb, Lethaby, Blow, Cockerell and Walker, became legendary.

In the wake of Morris and Webb, Lethaby sought to combine the two major discoveries of his intellectual journey of the 1880s, Ruskin's view of art as personal expression and the French structural view of Viollet. This is not to say that Lethaby simply reproduced Morris and Webb: his direct contact with Viollet meant that he was stronger than either Morris or Webb on structural experiment as the basis of true architecture, and the fact that his reading of Ruskin came in the 1880s rather than the 1850s meant that he was more explicit than they were about both mysticism and the role of personal expression or, as he termed it, 'expressionism' in art.[22]

Lethaby's conflation of Ruskin and Viollet, foreshadowed in his 1890 lecture on cast iron, was clear in his 1892 essay 'The Builder's Art and the Craftsman'. Architecture, Lethaby wrote, 'is the easy and expressive handling of materials in masterly experimental building'.[23] The essay went on in Ruskinian fashion to diagnose the division of labour as the basic problem in architecture, and to propose as the answer the creation of architects who worked on the building site and craftsmen who had an opportunity to think as well as to make. What made the art of the past so powerful, said Lethaby, was that it met direct needs in a direct way: 'the construction of buildings done with such fine feeling for fitness . . . that the work was transformed into delight and necessarily delighted others'. Only where the building artist (whether the builder who 'thought' or the architect who 'built') still had direct control over the materials could design again become, as it should be, 'insight as to the capabilities of material for expression when submitted to certain forms of handiwork'.[24]

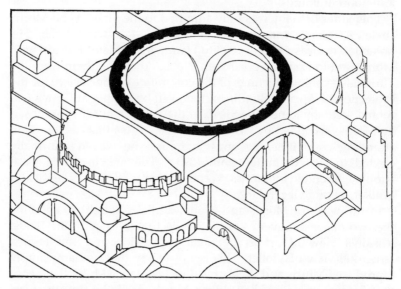

4.2 W. R. Lethaby and H. Swainson: the vaulting system of Santa Sophia (from *The Church of Sancta Sophia*, 1894). Lethaby's drawing was adapted from Choisy

It was in his book on Santa Sophia, published in 1894, that Lethaby's architectural thinking was given its most forceful expression (Fig. 4.2). Lethaby was led to Byzantine art by Ruskin. In his 1884–85 sketchbook Lethaby transcribed two key passages from Ruskin on the subject: the passage from 'The Nature of Gothic' stating of Byzantine architecture that its 'highest glory is, that it has no corruption. It perishes in giving birth to another architecture as noble as itself';[25] and the passage from *St Mark's Rest* (1877–84) on the 'one Greek school':

> Let us leave, to-day, the narrow and degrading word 'Byzantine'. There is but one Greek school, from Homer's day down to the Doge Selvo's . . . .[26]

Although there was keen interest in Byzantine architecture in London art circles (not least with Morris and Webb), nonetheless in the study of Byzantine architecture the English lagged behind the French. Encouraged by Viollet-le-Duc, Auguste Choisy undertook a major study, *L'Art de Batir chez les Byzantins* (1883), which presented Byzantine architecture as a rational structural system created by the Greek system of guild labour. Lethaby and his co-author Harold Swainson, a Cambridge classics graduate working in the Shaw office, freely acknowledged their debt to Choisy's work, for which they professed 'great admiration'.[27]

'Sancta Sophia is the most interesting building on the world's surface', Lethaby declared in the opening sentence of the book. For Lethaby Santa Sophia (which he and Swainson visited in 1893) was the ideal both of the rational building espoused by Viollet and the artistic expression demanded by Ruskin. Lethaby followed Choisy in depicting Santa Sophia as the product of a guild system of labour, in which there was no division of labour and hence neither non-executive architects nor mindless 'hands'. Only by re-adopting this form of organisation, he believed, would the production of a rational and expressive architecture once more become possible:

> In such craft organisations of labour, free of the financial middlemen who now rightly call themselves 'contractors', we see the only hope that building for service, and ornamenting for delight, can again be made possible.[28]

According to Lethaby's depiction, with architects and workmen working together on the building site, building problems at Santa Sophia were faced directly and experimentally, rather than by recourse to scholastic formulae; materials were used 'in the frankest and fullest manner';[29] beautiful and practical forms, such as the capitals, were worked out 'on the mason's banker';[30] and problems of structure were explored in a direct, experimental way.

4.3 W. R. Lethaby, Henry Wilson, R. W. Schultz Weir, Halsey Ricardo, F. W. Troup, Stirling Lee and Christopher Whall: Liverpool Cathedral Competition entry (1902) (montage)

It is evident that the style cannot be copied by our attempting to imitate the Byzantine builders; only by being ourselves and free, can our work be reasonable, and if reasonable, like theirs universal.

L'ART C'EST D'ÊTRE ABSOLUMENT SOI-MÊME.[31]

FABIANISM AND TECHNICAL EDUCATION

In 1894, within months of the publication of the Santa Sophia book, Lethaby was appointed art inspector to the Technical Education Board of the London County Council. The Board, set up in 1893, was more or less the personal creation of Sidney Webb, the Fabian leader, who had been elected to the LCC the previous year.[32] Sidney Webb came from the English Radical tradition (his father had been a vehement supporter of John Stuart Mill), but he also drew on other sources, in particular the French philosopher Auguste Comte. Webb shared Comte's belief that society was moving inevitably towards a far more organised condition, in which social and economic life would be controlled not by individual capitalists but by a new class of administrative experts. During the 1880s Webb, Bernard Shaw and others formed a reading club at Hampstead, which initially (1884–85) concentrated on the first volume of Marx's *Capital* (in the French translation); Shaw recalled that 'Sidney Webb, as a Stuart Millite, fought the Marxian value theory tooth and nail', preferring the far less politically contentious Jevonsian explanation of value.[33]

The Fabian Society, at first a small group of London intellectuals, attained national significance with the publication in 1889 of *Fabian Essays in Socialism*. Here they presented their belief that socialism meant above all an extension of state activity: as a Fabian publication put it, 'The socialism advocated by the Fabian Society is State Socialism exclusively'.[34] In his contribution to the *Fabian Essays*, Sidney Webb presented socialism not as something new and unknown, but simply as a continuation of the trend of the previous fifty years towards an extension of the activities of the state, particularly at municipal level. In Webb's description there was nothing more involved in the advent of socialism, with municipalities taking over more 'museums, parks, art galleries, libraries . . .' and so on, than there was in the purchase of shares on the stock market.[35] The great benefit, Webb argued (echoing Comte), was the greater efficiency that would result from the 'gradual substitution of organised co-operation for the anarchy of the competitive struggle'[36] and the replacement of inefficient individualism by efficiently administered collectivism.

Efficiency was one of the great concerns of the 1890s. In the second half of the nineteenth century Britain lost its global economic hegemony and started to fall behind its rivals, Germany, the United States and Japan. In Britain this generated a belief in the need to increase economic and social efficiency – the 'quest for national efficiency'. One means proposed to this end was technical education, since it was thought that the efficient provision of industrial training in Germany and other countries was one of the factors that had enabled them to make such rapid economic progress. In 1887 a National Association for the Promotion of Technical Education was set up, led by a Liberal MP, Arthur Acland, and in 1889 the Conservative government passed the Technical Education Act, giving county councils powers to provide technical education, and more importantly a further Act in 1890 securing the funds for them to do so.

Before the LCC election of 1892 Webb was involved in discussions with the leaders of the technical education lobby, Arthur Acland and his assistant Llewellyn Smith, over a programme of technical education for the capital; and immediately after the election he secured the establishment of an LCC Special Committee on Technical Education, with himself as chairman and Llewellyn Smith as secretary. The Committee's first step was to commission a report on technical education in London from Llewellyn Smith.

The structure of employment in London at this time was unusual, in that, as Stedman Jones has shown, while London's commerce benefited greatly from the economic changes that accompanied the Industrial Revolution, for London's industries the effects were largely destructive. Manufacturers in London were disadvantaged by the high rents in the capital (itself largely consequent on the transformation of the City into a commercial and financial centre) and could not compete with factory-based competition from the provincial centres of the north and abroad. London's industries did however have the advantage of proximity, both to the centres of luxury consumption in the West End and Westminster, which supported trades such as jewellery, watchmaking and printing, and to the large mass market offered by the London population. Prevented by high rents from converting to factory production,

London manufacturers responded with the expedient of 'sweating', that is, dividing the process of production between a number of unskilled workers, each of whom worked from their own premises where they were paid low wages and bore the overhead costs of space and energy themselves. Clothing was the best-known case of sweating, but it also prevailed in the wood and furniture trade and elsewhere. Building, the other main trade catering for the mass market, in London as elsewhere did not industrialise but instead underwent a process of deskilling which involved a similar subdivision of production.[37]

Llewellyn Smith's report dealt with London's main skilled trades: building (136,000 employees), clerical work (100,000), wood and furniture (60,000), engineering and metal (53,000) and printing (50,000). In none of these, Llewellyn Smith stated, were training facilities adequate. Except in a few cases, apprenticeship 'is practically dead in London', and in many trades 'nothing has taken the place of apprenticeship. There is no systematic method of training'.[38] As a result

> London boys who should be receiving a training in the workshops and technical schools are too often qualifying as 'odd boys' and porters for a subsequent career at the docks.[39]

The lack of adequate training disadvantaged London in regard not just to continental rivals, but also to the major provincial towns; unless the LCC intervened, Llewellyn Smith argued, London's competitive position could only deteriorate further. Accordingly, he proposed a complete overhaul of technical education in the capital, with the LCC introducing a comprehensive system based on scholarships (to ensure that the right trainees got the right training), grants (to enable the existing instruction in the schools and polytechnics to be improved), and inspection (to ensure that the Council's requirements were met). Only by these means, he argued, would London ensure the adequate training of the next generation of skilled workers.

There were a number of reasons, according to Llewellyn Smith, for the collapse of training: but the most important was 'the extreme division of labour in these trades as practised in London'; this 'made it less and less possible for lads to obtain . . . a competent all-round training'.[40] A worker destined to work on only one particular part of the production process learned neither the general skills needed for the trade as a whole (for example, technical drawing in the case of the building trades) nor a general grasp of the trade beyond 'the particular branch at which he usually worked'.[41] What was needed was some means to help 'counteract the evils of excessive division of labour':

> We want all-round men, not one-sided specialists – a boot-maker, not a 'clicker' or a 'finisher' – an engineer, not a 'fitter' or a 'turner' or a 'machine hand'. One important function in fact of a technical class is to give a workman some insight into the general principles of the whole of his trade, not only of the special branch to which he may chiefly be confined.[42]

It should not be thought that Llewellyn Smith arrived at this Ruskinian conclusion purely on the evidence of his enquiry. For Llewellyn Smith had been an undergraduate at Oxford, at Ruskin's adopted college, Corpus Christi, during Ruskin's second tenure of the Slade professorship (1883–85). Along with others from Oxford he had gone on to work at Toynbee Hall in the East End; here he taught crafts to the workmen, at first with Ashbee in the School of Handicraft and then at the rival Whitechapel Craft School which Llewellyn Smith set up in 1891. His attachment to the Ruskinian belief in the need to heal the division of labour thus pre-dated his engagement by the LCC.

In general, Llewellyn Smith proposed that the training in the principles of the trade should be given by the 'doers' (that is, those experienced in the trade) if only because they were the only people to whom the learners would pay any regard. But in the art industries a workman-instructor would be able to teach only the 'vicious customs' of existing practice, whereas the aim had to be to lift 'the industry out of the rut in which it is fixed, on to a new plane'.[43] What was needed here was instruction by those approaching the subject from the artistic rather than the trade side: educated people, like Llewellyn Smith himself, rather than those with the debased notions of the trade. Llewellyn Smith's model was the Municipal Art School of Birmingham, which was not only the largest of its kind in Britain but the only one where the teaching was based explicitly on Ruskin's ideas.[44]

His recommendation was that London's art schools, instead of teaching amateurs and instructors, should be reorganised to provide training specifically directed at the workers in London's art industries. The same steps should be taken for art as for technical education as a whole: grants should be introduced, payable only to schools if they met specified requirements; a scholarship system should be introduced, to feed the schools 'yearly with the best material'; and to inspect the schools and set the standard for art teaching, a 'first-rate' teacher/inspector should be appointed. At some stage in the future, the Council might establish 'a great Municipal Art School of its own' and also, to improve the training of architects, 'a school of architecture and the building trades'.[45]

In February 1893 the LCC accepted the Llewellyn Smith report and set up the Technical Education Board to implement its recommendations. One of the Board's first steps was to appoint a small staff of 'experts' who, in line with Fabian doctrine, were to be of the highest calibre. The first appointment was the secretary to the Board: Prof. William Garnett, from the new science-based universities of Nottingham and Newcastle. Following this, in July 1894, the Board decided to advertise the post of adviser/inspector for art.

THE CENTRAL SCHOOL OF ARTS AND CRAFTS

At this date Lethaby, five years after leaving Shaw's office to set up on his own, was short of both money and architectural employment. At the prompting of Emery Walker and Sydney Cockerell, Lethaby decided to apply for the TEB art inspectorship. In October 1894 he wrote to Cockerell:

> If I do not see Mr Morris I shd be glad if you would tell him that I am not taking it up as a *pis aller*: for a time at least I feel I could do the work with real enthusiasm: for I believe if I could succeed in interesting the pupils I shd at the same time do myself a lot of good in being dragged out of my present cul-de-bag.[46]

Walker was Morris's collaborator on the Kelmscott Press and secretary of Morris's Hammersmith Socialist Society (1890–96), and Cockerell was Morris's secretary and subsequently his executor. Testimonials were secured by Lethaby from Shaw and by Cockerell from Morris and Burne-Jones, with further testimonials from Crane and Walker, and Philip Webb, Haywood Sumner and William Richmond as referees. With this list of names, it was obvious that in applying for the TEB post Lethaby was the candidate of the Morris group.[47]

The TEB wanted someone with experience of the art industries. Of the 166 applicants for the post of art inspector, two 'possessed qualifications of a different order' from the others, 'especially with reference to their connection with art industries and their practical acquaintance with many of the trades which it is our special object to develop'.[48] These were Lethaby and George Frampton, the sculptor and Royal Academician, who like Lethaby was a prominent member of the Art Workers' Guild and the Arts and Crafts Exhibition Society. It was agreed that the two should be appointed jointly, on the basis of each giving three evenings and two half-days to the post. This arrangement worked amicably but did not last long: in 1898, under pressure of professional work, Frampton bowed out of his inspection duties, although he remained as titular co-director of the Central School. Even before then however it is clear that Lethaby provided most of the energy, and that in ventures such as the establishment and direction of the Central School, in which Frampton and Lethaby bore nominal joint responsibility, Lethaby was the driving-force.[49]

A good deal of Lethaby's time as art inspector was taken up with routine work: inspecting the art schools, instituting scholarship exams and organising the collection of casts for use in schools. Our main interest is in the creation of the two new schools, the Central School and the School of Building.

The Central School of Arts and Crafts had a twin function: to train architects on the basis of collaboration with the crafts; and to train workers in London's specialised art industries, such as enamelling and silversmithing. For both of these Llewellyn Smith had envisaged that a municipal school might be needed. Following his appointment in 1894, Lethaby in June 1895 took up the idea of a new school of architecture. In place of the 'merely theoretical' training provided by the architectural offices, Lethaby proposed that the Board establish a school of 'positive architecture' in which the training would be based in the workshop. Lethaby wished

> especially to bring before them the view that we have in (1) good building (2) sympathetic choice and handling of materials (3) sensibility as to expression by means of colour, texture and form; all the factors necessary for building up a *positive architecture* such as is at present nowhere taught . . . .[50]

The workshop-based training for architects could be supplied by the polytechnics (such as Regent Street and Chelsea) in the coming session, if they would open their trade classes to architects and organise additional instruction in 'practical architecture'. But on top of this a 'continuation school' or 'higher Polytechnic' was needed, where selected students could complete their training by working alongside students of the crafts. As a start, Lethaby proposed to give two or three lectures in the autumn 'generally opening up the course of instruction in "Positive" or "Constructive" Architecture"'.[51]

For the benefit of Board members, Webb and Garnett provided a gloss on Lethaby's proposal. The 'distinctive objects' of the proposed higher school of architecture were, they said, twofold.

(a) The partial training of young architects in association with craftsmen in order that they may become practically familiar with the conditions under which work is carried out, and the capabilities and limitations of various materials.

(b) The adaptation of the architectural character of the building to the special purposes for which it is to be used instead of restricting the utility of the building by adherence to traditional styles inconsistent with modern conditions and requirements.[52]

This was a significant revision of Lethaby's programme. While the emphasis on workshop training (the notion that design occurs at the point of production) and the antipathy to scholasticism (the notion that rational design is possible only if the designer is free from adherence to past formulae) was retained, Webb and Garnett omitted what for Lethaby was the purpose of the whole enterprise: the creation of an expressive architecture, that is, an architecture that constituted art in the Ruskinian sense.

Although it received a favourable response from the Board, the implementation of Lethaby's scheme in the 1895 session was limited to the opening of polytechnic trade classes to architects' pupils (at the Borough and South Western Polytechnics), and the delivery by Lethaby of two lectures in the autumn on 'Modern Building Design'. The lectures, given at the TEB's School of Lithography at Bolt Court and introduced by Garnett, were clearly intended as quasi-official statements of the Board's programme.

Lethaby restated the argument of the Santa Sophia book: expression in architecture was the goal, rational design the means; the necessary basis of this was the healing of the division of labour, so that architects built and builders thought about design; and this in turn meant doing away with the contracting system and getting the building unions to take on again the role of guilds, controlling both quality and output. At the least, architectural education had to be based on the workshop, not the office. (Incidentally the *Builder*, which reported the lectures in full, was not impressed either by Lethaby's argument or by his authorities: Morris was 'a pronounced Socialist' and Ruskin was 'entirely passé'.[53])

The impetus for the creation of a new school was resumed in February 1896 when Webb prepared a long paper reviewing the work of the Board and pointing to the urgent need to provide training for art industries. 'No branch of the Board's work is more important, and none is more difficult, than that of improving the teaching of art, especially in its relation to handicraft and design', Webb stated.[54] Despite the Board's efforts in this regard, the art schools were still 'not attended, to any but the smallest extent, by handicraftsmen', which meant that little had been done to bring the teaching into relation with local industries. The only way to do this was to establish a Central Art School, to provide 'specialised art teaching in its application to particular industries in close relation with the employers and workmen in those industries'.[55] This would extend what the Board had already done with the National Society of Lithographic Artists at the Bolt Court school. The new school might eventually grow 'into a central municipal art school of the type at Birmingham', but it should proceed on a step-by-step basis, the immediate task being to find suitable premises so that the school could open quickly.

Lethaby and Frampton responded to Webb's paper with a proposal for a Central School that would teach both the art industries and architecture. At the 'Central School for Artistic Crafts' all teaching would be directed purely at those engaged in the various industries. Architecture would be taught as 'experimental building', including building mechanics, practical building crafts and the design of modern buildings. Teaching in the decorative crafts would include crafts such as stained glass, lettering, illumination, design for cabinet-makers, wood-engraving, silversmithing and enamelling.[56]

On this the TEB agreed and decided in May 1896 to lease

premises in Regent Street and open the School the following October. The directors were Frampton and Lethaby; to carry out the day-to-day administration the Board appointed C. W. Beckett, the former secretary of the Arts and Crafts Exhibition Society and a member of the Fabian Society. Since teaching was directed purely at those engaged in the various artistic trades, all classes were in the evening. The 1896 prospectus showed how the teaching of the School was seen as a corrective to the excessive division of labour in the London trades.

> This School, opened on Monday 2nd November, has been established by the Technical Education Board of the London County Council, to provide instruction in those branches of design and manipulation which directly bear on the more artistic trades. Admission to the school is, within certain limits, only extended to those actually engaged in these trades, and the School makes no provision for the amateur student of drawing and painting.
>
> The special object of the School is to encourage the industrial application of decorative design, and it is intended that every opportunity should be given to the students to study this in relation to their own particular craft.
>
> There is no intention that the School should supplant apprenticeship – it is rather intended that it should supplement it by enabling its students to learn design and those branches of their craft which, owing to the sub-division of processes of production, they are unable to learn in the workshop.
>
> The instruction is adapted to the needs of those engaged in the different departments of Building Work (Architects, Builders, Modellers and Carvers, Decorators, Metal Workers, etc), Designers in Wall Papers, Textiles, Furniture, Workers in Stained Glass, Bronze, Lead, etc, Enamellers, Jewellers and Gold and Silver Workers. Other departments will be opened in response to any reasonable demand.[57]

Between 1896 and 1902 the number of classes increased from 12 to 31 (new subjects included enamelling, woodcuts, writing and illumination, embroidery, carving and gilding, and cabinetwork), and the student roll increased from 177 to 600. The most popular classes were those in the art industries of the West End, especially silversmithing (taught by Augustus Steward) and bookbinding

4.4 Central School of Arts and Crafts, London: the silversmiths' room (1911)

(taught by Douglas Cockerell, the brother of Lethaby's friend Sydney Cockerell), and also the architecture class run by Halsey Ricardo. The School's reputation spread across Britain and Europe, particularly Germany: Muthesius in 1901 called it 'probably the best organised art school of our age'.[58]

Teaching at the School was based on Ruskinian principles: artistic expression through direct contact with materials; nature as the source of ornament; and above all countering the division of labour by reuniting the hand and heart in the act of design. In teaching silversmithing Augustus Steward aimed to counter that 'specialisation' in the trade that 'simply makes the workman a mere unit in the factory, a mechanic who understands the production of one article, and sometimes only a part' (Fig. 4.4).[59] Against this, students were taught to undertake the whole process of design and production, starting with studies from nature and continuing through modelling to the production of the completed item. Cockerell's bookbinding class was run on the same lines: each workman was 'encouraged to carry out the work of binding books from start to finish, irrespective of the particular craft he may be employed upon in the shop in which he works'.[60]

Following Lethaby's proposal of 1895, architecture at the school was taught in three parts: as design, craft and construction. Students were also encouraged to attend the drawing classes, where 'studies from natural forms are made a basis for the consideration of ornament'.[61] Stone-cutting and leadwork for architects (the latter originating in Lethaby's book of 1893) were taught one evening per week; likewise the lectures on the mechanics of construction. Design was taught two evenings per week under Ricardo's supervision, where a determinedly rationalist regime prevailed: in their first year, students were set to design a house,

> as many determining conditions, as to cost, nature of site and materials, etc, being given as practicable, from the point of view that architecture should respond directly to the facts of modern life.

As well as studio instruction, there were lectures on

> past examples of architecture, of Roman and Gothic times, mainly based upon Choisy's analysis of Roman construction and Viollet-le-Duc's of medieval buildings . . . .[62]

Students were also expected to make decorative designs for a given material (such as tooled leather) and see the process through to the finished object.

The architectural instruction at the Central School fulfilled the Ruskinian ideal of approaching architecture as one of the arts. In terms of what Lethaby had written in the Santa Sophia book, however, the instruction provided at the School was one-sided in that it maintained the separation of architects from other members of the building trades: architects were being taught alongside other artists, but not alongside other building craftsmen. The Central School was however seen as a higher school; basic training was to be provided by expanding the instruction in the building trades already provided by the polytechnics. It was to improve training in this latter respect, and root design in the practical building skills, that the School of Building was established.

THE SCHOOL OF BUILDING

The great problem in the London building trades, all parties agreed, was the vacuum in training caused by the breakdown of the apprenticeship system. Llewellyn Smith stated that if London had its full complement of learners in the building trades, there would have been 2000 more learning carpentry, 1400 house-painting, 1200 engineering and 800 bricklaying.[63] With London boys unable to get an adequate training, the London building trades were recruited largely from the country, and employers and men alike called on the TEB to take steps to remedy the situation. Between 1893 and 1897 the Board was pressed to launch or finance new classes by representatives of the painters and decorators, plumbers, building workers, plasterers, master builders, and stonemasons. Trade classes in the various building trades at the nine polytechnics supported by the TEB were expanded and advertised through the local trade unions, with the result that in 1897–98, of the 10,269 students enrolled in the polytechnics, over a third (3548) were in building. The employers welcomed these efforts by the Board and the trade unions to improve training, and even suggested that the trade unions should take over responsibility for apprenticeships, issuing 'certificates to members of their trades who have served proper apprenticeship, and qualified as tradesmen by examination'.[64]

Lethaby was sympathetic both to the idea that unions should be responsible for training and to the idea that the Board should assist them in this endeavour. As we have seen, in his view one of the great lessons of Santa Sophia was that building should be controlled not by contractors but by guilds. A lecture given at Birmingham in 1896 set out his thinking on 'Arts and the Function of Guilds'. Trade unions, Lethaby declared, should set themselves higher goals than merely looking to the material interests of their members:

> The bettering of the conditions of labour, in respect to shortening hours of work and increasing wages as much as may be, is not a very large or philosophic programme for the immense organization of the modern trade unions.[65]

Rather, anticipating the theories of the building guilds, Lethaby gave the unions the task of fulfilling the Ruskinian ambition of reintegrating art and labour. The true role of the unions was to reintroduce art into the production of items of everyday use, 'finding a way in which beautiful craftsmanship will once again become . . . common' and thereby transforming labour from a mindless burden into a creative pleasure. In this view the tuition mounted jointly by the TEB and the trade unions was a step towards the resumption by the unions of the guild functions of controlling both the quality of output and the training of those entering the trade.

In 1897 the TEB set up an enquiry into the educational needs of the building trades. The ensuing report (January 1899) pointed to the need for instruction not just for the trades but also for the 'officers' of the industry – architects, clerks of works, foremen, and builders – who also needed a thoroughly practical training ('the officer does not neglect his drill because he is trained in strategy').[66] Both the employers and the unions wanted the trade classes to be open only to members of the trade, but on Lethaby's advice this was not accepted by the enquiry. To provide an institution where architects and workmen could learn their skills side by side, Lethaby called for the TEB to set up a School of Building.

> I should like a school of building. The inquiries of the Building Trades Committee have shown that there is no institution where architects and engineers (so far as they deal with other

than metal), builders, clerks of works and foremen can get a knowledge of building as a whole. A consequence is that architects have become mere draughtsmen or accountants, according to their bent; 'builders' need know nothing of building, but only of contracting, and clerks of works and foremen can get only a smattering of the circle of building crafts. Supposing this could be done, I would like the school to be open to the ordinary craftsman – mason, plasterer and what not; possibly he would then be ready to allow *bona fide* builders to go into his own classes at the several polytechnics.[67]

By this stage a possible venue for the School had become available, in the form of the land and buildings of the disused swimming bath in Ferndale Road, Brixton; the TEB was told that the 'great hall of Lambeth baths would provide unrivalled accommodation' for those aspects of building tuition that required a large space.[68] There was strong local pressure for the creation of a new polytechnic, but this was outside the powers of the Board, which instead decided on a 'monotechnic' – the School of Building. After long delays the acquisition of the Brixton site was eventually completed in May 1901.

The following month Lethaby gave a paper at the RIBA on 'Education in Building'. In this paper (which included the first detailed presentation of his work on the masons of Westminster Abbey) he spelled out the theory on which the School of Building was based. In the middle ages, said Lethaby, architecture had been carried out as naturally as any other 'work', in an ordinary, unselfconscious way; 'there was no art nonsense when work was *The Work*', and the finished result was 'as natural as a honey-comb or a bird's nest'. The same was true of Ancient Greece, Persia, India, Constantinople and Italy before the Renaissance: 'everywhere the art of building was developed by the continuous experiments of practical masons and builders'.[69] This was the only true style of architecture: 'the art of experiment, the art of reasoning on given data, the art of impressing on work the evidence of thought, care, mastery, nobility of purpose . . .'.[70]

Building today, said Lethaby, must be studied in the same way. Architects should spend time on site, not in the office – like Lethaby's friends Gimson and Blow, acting as resident architects, 'digging fresh earth with the scent of new cut wood in the air . . .'. Echoing Ruskin's Romantic adulation of the 'savage' workman in

'The Nature of Gothic', Lethaby called on architects to learn from and respect, not despise, the building workers:

> These rough, tired men . . . are after all the true artists in building, the representatives of the medieval architects . . . . As it is, I never go on a building which I call my own but I want to beg their pardon for my vulgarity, pretentiousness and ignorance. It is they and only they who sufficiently know what stones are sound . . . .

In turn the workmen's unions should turn from the 'crude war of strikes' and assume 'more and more the functions of the old guilds', taking on responsibility for training in the wake of the collapse of the apprenticeship system. 'By means of schools, and a system of apprenticeship to the guilds, masons will again see to the training of masons . . . .'[71] These schools where builders would work beside architects, and journeymen instruct learners in the building skills, would continue the tradition of the building workshops of the middle ages and develop the art of building through experiment.

It was another three years before the School of Building opened at Brixton. The director was H. W. Richards, a former builder responsible for the highly regarded building course at the Northern Polytechnic, and both the staff and the syllabus for the building and trade subjects were directly imported from the same source. But Lethaby emphasised that in addition to the trade classes the School was also to train the 'officers' of the industry, and that to do so it would have to undertake 'experimental research of an educational type in connection with (a) Builders' materials (b) Composite structures'.

> There are at present a very large number of problems which are only imperfectly understood, and in connection with which it is necessary that complete and systematic investigation should be conducted on purely educational grounds in order to enable the school authorities to be in a position to impart the knowledge required by those who are responsible for architectural design.[72]

For Lethaby this was the prime attraction of the Brixton baths building: its great hall provided a 'unique opportunity' both for a

4.5 School of Building, Brixton: construction of full-scale cottage in the Great Hall (1911)

'testing laboratory' and for the various trades to work together on practical projects of construction (Fig. 4.5). Adjacent to the hall were the workshops and studios for the various building skills: the plasterers' and bricklayers' workshops to one side, the metalwork and plumbers' workshops and the drawing office for building construction on the other. Above, on the first floor, 'approached by a gallery running the whole length of the hall', were the architectural drawing office, the painters' and decorators' loft and the carpenters' and joiners' workshop.[73] In the great hall of the School Lethaby saw a modern equivalent of the medieval ideal, with all the building skills and all the building classes collaborating on a central laboratory of experimental building.

Teaching at the School had a dual emphasis: on the one hand, on the principles (particularly the scientific principles) underlying everyday practice in the building world; and on the other, on the practical application of the various skills in collaborative building work. The prospectus stated that the purpose of the School was to

> enable artisans and others engaged in the building and allied trades to acquire an intimate knowledge of the principles that underlie the processes which they have to carry out in their daily work . . . .
>
> Every facility is given for full size work, and when practicable, the various trades will work in conjunction, for which purpose a portion of the Large Hall will be devoted.[74]

The emphasis was on the 'practical combination of the studies in the several trades and branches' covered by the School, with the students of the trades, building and architecture pursuing their respective studies in the workshops and laboratories and then collaborating in the Great Hall on the construction of temporary and permanent examples of full-scale work.

The School was officially opened in February 1904. All classes took place in the evening. Liaison with the industry was provided by an advisory body which included representatives of the trades (bricklayers, plumbers, plasterers, masons, painters) and of the employers. Teaching began in January 1904 with building and trades subjects and in the first full session, 1904–5, the number of students at the school, at 643, was the highest of any LCC institution.[75] In July 1905 Beresford Pite, Lethaby's colleague from the Royal College of Art, was appointed architectural director and formal tuition in architecture began the following year. The original building proved too small, and plans were soon drawn up for an extension, providing workshops, laboratories, classrooms and lecture theatre (completed in 1909) that doubled the available accommodation.

The opening of the School of Building – the culmination of the programme set out ten years before in the Santa Sophia book – is a good point at which to leave Lethaby. Although Lethaby himself was still art advisor to the TEB and principal of the Central School, and indeed heavily involved with the construction of the Central School's new premises in Southampton Row, the TEB itself was wound up only days after the official opening of the School of Building, and the functions of both the TEB and the School Board of London were taken over directly by the London County Council. The LCC Education Committee was a far less flexible and more bureaucratic body than the TEB; as Schultz Weir recalled, 'difficulties began, and Lethaby suffered much from the education machine of the London County Council'.[76] By this stage Sidney Webb had broken with the ruling Progressive group on the LCC and was kept out of the chair of the new Education Committee. The result was that, while Lethaby remained head of the Central School until 1911 and art advisor to the LCC until 1918, his relationship with the LCC after 1904 was neither particularly happy nor particularly fruitful.

Lethaby's period with the TEB had opened with the Santa Sophia book; it closed, ten years later, with the publication of his book *Medieval Art* – a subject on which he had been working on and off for twenty years. The book was a record of the varied intellectual allegiances that Lethaby had developed over this period. Dedicated to Philip Webb, the book took its epigraph from Ruskin's *Val d'Arno*. The main contention of the book, that medieval art was to be seen as a single entity, stretching 'from the Peace of the Church to the Eve of the Renaissance, 312–1350', followed Morris and retrospectively made sense both of Ruskin's confusion between Byzantine and Gothic in *The Stones of Venice*, and of Webb's indifference to the distinction between the two in his architecture. Lethaby's emphasis on the continuity of the Hellenic tradition, from the fifth century BC to the fifth century AD, also drew on

Ruskin's idea in *St Mark's Rest* of the 'one Greek school'. There was plenty of reference too to Viollet, Choisy and the French structural interpretation of Gothic; the 'most penetrating criticism of Gothic architecture that has been made', said Lethaby, was that of Viollet's mentor Prosper Mérimée, with his suggestion that a cathedral like Amiens 'is more like an engine than a monument'.[77]

The main weight of *Medieval Art* however was given not to structural rationalism nor somewhat surprisingly (given what Lethaby had told the RIBA only three years before) to the guild basis of architecture. Rather Lethaby stressed medieval art as the product of mind or spirit: art was defined as 'man's thought expressed in his handiwork' and medieval art was presented as the product of a single 'consciousness' or 'period of culture' that lasted from the establishment of the Church to the Renaissance.[78] Medieval art was the expression of the 'medieval spirit' and Gothic cathedrals were 'manifestations of the minds of men working under the impulse of a noble idea'.[79]

In this regard Lethaby's *Medieval Art* was the clearest statement yet within the Ruskinian tradition of the idealist concept of architecture that lay at its roots. As such it points both backwards, to the origin of that tradition in German idealist thought of the early nineteenth century, and forwards, to the idealist notion of architecture that was to be inherited by architectural modernism. With Lethaby's *Medieval Art* we are only a stone's throw from the interpretation given by Niklaus Pevsner, in his *Outline of European Architecture*, of Western art as the expression of the spirit of the European civilisation.[80] In both cases architecture is presented as the expression of a mind or spirit that exists independently of material conditions, and the history of architecture is seen as the record of changes in that spirit. In this sense Lethaby's book points to the idealist thinking that lay at the heart of both the Ruskinian tradition and the modernist tradition that succeeded it.

5

Raymond Unwin: The Education of an Urbanist

The notion that Ruskin and Morris provided Raymond Unwin (1863–1940) with much of his intellectual inspiration derived from pronouncements made by Unwin himself in his later years. In his inaugural presidential address to the Royal Institute of British Architects in 1931 Unwin stated that

> my early days were influenced by the musical voice of John Ruskin, vainly striving to stem the flood of a materialism which seemed to be overwhelming the arts, and much else; and later by the more robust and constructive personality of William Morris, and his crusade for the restoration of beauty to daily life.[1]

On other occasions in the 1930s Unwin recalled that as a schoolboy in Oxford in the 1870s he had seen Ruskin leading the road-diggers at Hinksey, and that while working in Manchester the following decade he had been inspired by William Morris to set up a local branch of the Socialist League. On receiving the RIBA Gold Medal in 1937 Unwin again spoke of the formative influence of Ruskin and Morris, although he also mentioned alongside them James Hinton and Edward Carpenter.

> One who was privileged to hear the beautiful voice of John Ruskin declaiming against the disorder and degradation resulting from laissez-faire theories of life; to know William Morris and his work; and to imbibe in his impressionable years the thoughts and writings of men like James Hinton and Edward Carpenter, could hardly fail to follow after the ideals of a more ordered form of society, and a better planned environment for it, than that which he saw around him in the 'seventies and 'eighties of [the] last century.[2]

The notion that Ruskin and Morris were fundamental to Unwin's intellectual development raises two questions that will be addressed in this chapter. The first relates to the socialist strategy informing Unwin's architectural thought. In the 1880s Unwin fully endorsed the argument of Morris and the Socialist League that socialists should avoid any entanglement with the electoral process and the state. Yet his thinking as an architect and town planner as set out from 1901 onwards was predicated on precisely the opposite point of view – on using the state to further socialist reform, particularly in the area of housing and town planning. How did Unwin come to make this change from the 'abstentionism' of the Socialist League to the 'municipal socialism' of the early 1900s?

The second question involves Unwin's relationship to one of the central tenets of the tradition derived from 'The Nature of Gothic', the concern with architecture as the product of free labour. Although Unwin periodically made obeissance to the notion of architecture as the expression of joy in labour, in practice his thinking was concerned with the role of architecture in giving satisfaction, not to its producers, but to its users. Unwin's interest was in the role that architects and architecture could play in the process of transition to a socialist way of living, whether at the level of the individual, the community or the city. How did Unwin come to differ from the rest of the English Ruskinian tradition in this respect and think about architecture from the point of view not of the builders but of the occupants?

The answer to both these questions is to be found in Unwin's position as an intellectual active in the socialist movement in the north of England in the 1880s and 1890s. Here the decisive intellectual influence on Unwin was not Ruskin or Morris, but Edward Carpenter (1844–1929), the socialist, poet, erstwhile clergyman, advocate of sexual (particularly homosexual) liberation and propagandist of 'the simple life'. But even more than any particular intellectual influences, Unwin's development was moulded by the dynamics of the socialist movement in the industrial north in these decades. From this position in the northern socialist movement Unwin was led away from both the concern with joy in labour and the abstentionist politics that appealed so strongly to the socialist intelligentsia in London and the south, towards the application of his architectural skills to the attempts being made to produce 'practical socialism', particularly on the basis of the municipality.

In the autumn of 1901 Unwin was transformed from an obscure

5.1 Raymond Unwin, from a family photograph (1898)

provincial architect into a figure with a national reputation. Within the space of a few weeks his book *The Art of Building a Home* (written with his partner Barry Parker) was published, gaining wide attention, and Unwin gave widely reported lectures to three national bodies, the Garden City Association, the Workmen's National Housing Council, and the Fabian Society, the last being published under the title *Cottage Plans and Common Sense*. The ideas on housing and town planning that Unwin set out here and in other publications over the next few years have come to be seen as a turning-point in the relationship between architecture and the city, with major effects not only in Britain but throughout the world.[3] In this chapter we will trace the development of Unwin's thought and see how he came to formulate these ideas.

THE IMPACT OF EDWARD CARPENTER

In later life Unwin recalled that he 'had grown up among liberal ideas in religion and politics'.[4] In particular he took from his family a marked antipathy to the ethics of commerce. When Unwin was 'ten or eleven years old', his father sold the family business in Rotherham, West Yorkshire, in uncertain circumstances and moved with his family to Oxford, to become a student at Balliol College, matriculating in 1875.[5] Unwin's father alerted his son to the social questions of the day (together they attended the first meeting of the Land Nationalisation Society in 1881) and inspired him with a hatred of business. Several years later Unwin quoted his father's comment that a limited liability company was 'a company with unlimited ability to lie'.[6] In his first published article, written for Morris's *Commonweal* in June 1886, Unwin asked:

> What is likely to be the result on the character of a race of men if they are set to compete with one another, each to get the better of his neighbour? Surely they must become selfish and heartless. The most selfish will get on best . . . . Where would the modern business man be who, when selling out shares which he believes will go down, should stop to think of the ruin he may bring to some poor family? Again, has it not become a bye-word that a certain amount of dishonesty is necessary in all trades?[7]

5.2 The Simple Life: Edward Carpenter (right) and friends outside the cottage at Millthorpe in the 1890s

This picture of the inherently corrupting effects of the competitive system sprang from family lore as much as from political analysis.

On leaving Magdalen College School, Oxford, in 1880, Unwin's initial intention was to enter the Church. But he was not sufficiently sure of his vocation to proceed with the expense of a university education, and instead he went back to the north, to Chesterfield, where he served a training as an apprentice engineering draughtsman/fitter and continued to debate his future. At Chesterfield he lived for a time with his wealthy cousins, the Parkers; Robert Parker was a banker, who disapproved of Unwin both for his penury and his socialism, all the more so when Unwin and his daughter Ethel Parker fell in love.

In Chesterfield Unwin encountered Edward Carpenter. Carpenter's conviction that in 'the simple life' he had found the way to reconcile his belief in socialism with his economic position as a *rentier* was to be of profound importance to Unwin's entire thought. At this stage Carpenter was in the process of abandoning lecturing to pursue 'the simple life' in the country – a pursuit that took him in 1880 via the Totley farm of Ruskin's Guild of St George to life in a cottage nearby with his friend Albert Fearnehough and his wife. Unwin, who attended Carpenter's lectures in Chesterfield in 1880–81, recalled in a tribute to Carpenter:

> From about the year 1881 Edward Carpenter became a great influence in my life. He was then giving one of the last of his courses of University Extension Lectures on Science . . . . A year or two later, when intercourse with working people and close contact with their lives brought home to me the contrast with all that I had been used to in my Oxford home I turned again to Edward Carpenter for help, as the overwhelming complexity and urgency of the social problem came upon me.[8]

In 1883 Carpenter acquired some land in the country outside Sheffield, at Millthorpe, and built a cottage where with the Fearnehoughs he set up as a market gardener (Fig. 5.2). In a letter to Ethel Parker in May 1884 Unwin described his first visit to Millthorpe, in terms that uncannily forecast his future conception of the ideal physical setting of the home:

> I had a little note from Mr Carpenter saying he is now at Millthorpe & asking me to go and see him yesterday. So I

walked over and found that he has built a little house just beyond that old tannery . . . . He has the next three fields on the same side . . . . Oh it was so beautiful! . . . .

The house he has built is a long one only one room deep, as all the rooms face South, and look over to a beautiful ford. One field is laid out in oats for the horse and wheat for fowl use, the other is in grass with a few young apple trees in it, the centre one in front of the house is planted with fruit, vegetables and flowers – lots of young rose trees – there is a stream running at the bottom where primroses grow.

He is living with a man who was a scyth maker in Sheffield, his wife and daughter, they all share alike the living room where cooking is done and there is a piano in the same room, they seem a very happy family.[9]

From then on Carpenter was the major influence on Unwin's intellectual development. He and Unwin were in close personal contact from 1884, when Unwin 'spent helpful and happy weekends with him and his companions' at Millthorpe, with 'long days and nights of talk'.[10] Unwin lived within walking distance of Millthorpe until October 1884 and again from May 1887 until 1896. Even Unwin's time in Manchester (early 1885 to the end of 1886) did not interrupt the relationship, for Carpenter came several times to Manchester to lecture for Unwin's Socialist League branch and Unwin continued to go over to Millthorpe for weekends. For Carpenter doubtless the attraction of the relationship was in part sexual; Unwin seems to have managed to remain unaware of this, even though they slept together. Carpenter figured prominently in Unwin's letters to Ethel Parker, and when in 1891 Unwin was urging her to deepen her knowledge of socialism Carpenter was the first author he recommended.[11] When the Unwins' first child was born in 1894, he was named Edward and Carpenter was godfather.

In October 1884, when Unwin was leaving Chesterfield, Carpenter gave him a copy of *Towards Democracy*, the long poem recounting Carpenter's search for spiritual and emotional freedom that had been published the year before. Despite the personal contact he had had with Carpenter, the effect of the book on Unwin was overwhelming: it was a 'bewildering revelation'[12] that 'opened [the] door to [a] new world'.[13] In 1931 Unwin recalled that

The feelings compounded of mystification, escape and joy with which I read it through on the journey to Oxford, are still a vivid memory . . . the sense of escape from an intolerable sheath of unreality and social superstition which the first reading of *Towards Democracy* brought to me is still fresh . . . .

The message that Unwin took from Carpenter's poem centred on the need for inner spiritual reform as the basis for new relations both between people and between people and nature. Unwin wrote:

It is difficult to convey any intelligible idea of such a poem, ranging as it does over all things in heaven and earth – and hell; and depending as it does for its main influence on the artistry of expression, the turn of a phrase, the intimacy of a touch. There are, however, two or three main conceptions towards the expression of which all tends, and every touch is made to contribute. They begin with a new understanding, relation and unity to be realized between the spirit of man and his body, the animal man no longer a beast to be ridden, but an equal friend to be loved, cherished, and inspired.

Growing out of this, made possible by it, there then emerges a new sense of equality and freedom in all human intercourse and relationships.

Content, in happy unity with its body, the soul of man, thus accepting equality of spiritual status, and enjoying free communion with its fellows, discovers a new relation to the universe, to nature, and to the Great Spirit which pervades it; a new faith, not of belief in this or that, but of trust.[14]

On another occasion Unwin described *Towards Democracy* as the story of 'a soul's slow disentanglement from [the] sheath of custom & convention'.[15] The great theme towards which Carpenter was working was the 'Simplification of Life', which he set out in a paper of that name in 1886. The fundamental antithesis posed by Carpenter was between 'convention' (artificial, unnatural, unhealthy and unnecessary) and the 'real needs' of life (simple, natural, open, and non-exploitative). Accepting both Marx's theory of surplus value (which for Carpenter rendered dividends morally soiled) and Ruskin's proscription of usury, Carpenter argued that the only course for right-thinking people of wealth such as himself was to abandon the extravagant life style to which they were accustomed in favour of 'the simple life'; by reducing their requirements to, for example, a single dish for each meal, they could minimise the expenditure of labour and wealth required to support their daily lives, using the now superfluous income from their dividends for socially progressive causes, such as promoting socialism.

These ideas became basic to Unwin's thought, both about socialism and later about architecture. In 1887 he wrote to Ethel Parker:

> sometimes there comes across me a sort of misty idea of some society in which there shall be a 'better way' . . . a better land altogether where life would be freer & happier, more natural, everything made pure & clean, clean food, clean lives, clean bodies, & all open & above board. Of course it is the idea of *Towards Democracy*. Only dear Ettie don't you know how at times it comes over one with more power & seems for ever new . . . .[16]

Carpenter, according to his own account, took the 'style and moral bias' of his socialism from Ruskin and the 'economics' from Marx. By the latter, he meant chiefly the theory of surplus value, extracted from Marx and popularised by Hyndman in *England for All*; when Carpenter read this work in 1883 he found in the chapter on surplus value the essential basis he needed to get 'the mass of floating impressions, sentiments, ideals, etc in my mind . . . into shape'.[17] For Unwin there was nothing new in the Ruskinian element in Carpenter; he was familiar with Ruskin's teaching from Oxford and went on to read several of Ruskin's works after meeting Carpenter (including *Modern Painters* and *Unto this Last*), but without any particular expression of enthusiasm.[18]

The Marxian theory, by contrast, was unfamiliar to Unwin. Carpenter introduced Unwin to Hyndman's writings (on that first visit to Millthorpe Unwin went away with a copy of one of Hyndman's books) and in 1885, as part of his programme of self-education in socialist theory, Unwin decided that he needed to gain a 'better understanding of its scientific basis as given by Marx'.[19] The result was a lecture, 'The Dawn of a Happier Day' (January 1886), which set out at some length what Unwin explicitly called 'the theory of surplus value'.[20]

This early grounding in the value theory of Marx sets Unwin apart from the other figures studied in this book. But it is important to note that, with Unwin as with Carpenter, acceptance of the value theory did not imply acceptance or even understanding of historical materialism as a whole. Carpenter incorporated the value theory of Marx within an ethical, transcendental socialism; his view of history showed no debt to Marx, being biological and evolutionary rather than materialist, and his concept of art and architecture, as communication between human souls, was Ruskinian and transcendentalist. Unwin followed Carpenter in the idealist notion of both socialism and art: the change to socialism had to start, he believed, with the spread of 'the spirit of socialism'; and he endorsed the Emersonian definition of art, as the 'manifestation afresh of the universal mind or Soul which is behind all things'.[21]

UNWIN AND THE NORTHERN SOCIALIST MOVEMENT

From 1885 until the early 1890s, the main focus of Unwin's interests and energy was the northern socialist movement, first in Manchester and then across the Pennines in the adjacent towns of Chesterfield, Sheffield and Clay Cross. In the course of this work as a socialist speaker and organiser, Unwin was led away from the abstentionist politics espoused by Morris and the London socialists towards the programme of immediate and pragmatic reform developed by the northern socialists during these years.

Unwin left Chesterfield in October 1884. After a few months at home in Oxford he returned north, early in 1885, to Manchester, close to Ethel Parker at Buxton. In Manchester he had obtained a job as an engineering draughtsman, but he regarded as his real work the voluntary activities he undertook for various social causes. These included the temperance movement, the Ancoats Brotherhood (a social mission with which Morris was connected) and above all the Socialist League. In retrospect Unwin came to regard this period as the heyday of his political activism. He recalled in 1902:

> During the lifetime of the Socialist League I found a sphere of work so congenial that I descended for a time into the arena of actual struggle . . . . Times have changed since the League

days. Many who know our movement now would find it difficult to realise the frame of mind in which we worked in '85 or '86, when the coming Revolution loomed large in our imaginations . . . .[22]

The early stages of Unwin's attachment to the Socialist League are unclear. Carpenter's lead was initially ambiguous: personally he supported Morris in forming the League, but Carpenter also had loyalties to Hyndman and the SDF and it was not until September 1885 that he joined the League. Unwin moved a good deal faster. At the end of January 1885 Unwin wrote to Ethel Parker:

I see there has been a split in the Socialist party. I think I told you Morris and several more have left the Social democratic Federation and have started a 'Socialist League'. I see they are going to issue the first no. of their organ the 'Commonweal' tomorrow, I have ordered a copy to see what it is like. Morris is going to manage it himself so I hope it will be a good paper. May I send you a copy . . . .[23]

A visit to Manchester by Morris in July 1885 won Unwin for the League. The following month Unwin organised the take-over of the local Socialist Union and became secretary of the new Manchester branch of the Socialist League.[24] From then he was indefatigable as organiser and, along with Morris, Carpenter and others, as speaker at the meetings held both indoors and in the open air.

But things did not go well for the League in Manchester: during the winter of 1885–86 membership of the branch fell steadily (from 41 in October to 28 in February) and by March Unwin reported that it was 'not easy for me to say how we stand now that our meetings are so irregular'.[25] Returning in June 1886 from the League's national conference (at which he made friends with May Morris) he found things no better:

I am afraid there is little to report while I have been away, only one open air meeting was held on two Sundays. Last Thursday 3 turned up to hear my report of conference though I sent all P.cards. It is very disheartening.[26]

In an attempt to revive its fortunes the League branch decided to move, to Openshaw in the north-east of the city, where Unwin and another branch officer took a house, but to little effect. At the end of September Morris paid a visit to Manchester in a vain attempt to restore morale. In November *Commonweal* reported that Unwin had resigned as branch secretary on leaving the district, and the branch faded away thereafter.[27]

The failure of his socialist activity in Manchester weighed heavily with Unwin; it was, he felt, his 'want of enthusiasm' that 'made my work in Manchester come to so little'.[28] A more likely cause was the League's policy of 'abstention' from parliamentary elections, for, as Unwin told League headquarters in June 1886, 'most of our old members are not much good, and the two or three that are have gone head first into the election!'.[29] In this regard it is significant that while the League floundered in Manchester the SDF, which was not committed to the anti-parliamentary line, prospered.

At this stage Unwin adhered unequivocally to the League's abstentionist line; 'personally I am strongly in favour of the League keeping non-parliamentary', he wrote in July 1886,[30] a view that he argued with vigour in an article in the *Commonweal* the following month. Reforms aiming to alleviate the condition of the working class within the framework of the existing system were dismissed altogether as a deliberate means of 'postponing any attempt to get at the real cause'. The only answer was to 'revolutionise society':

> I use the word revolutionise, because nothing short of a revolution will do. We have got to a stage where mere reforms are useless, often worse. If you have a good system founded on rightness and harmony, it can be improved by reforms; but where the system is bad . . . . there is no place for reform . . . .[31]

This was much the same view as that taken by Philip Webb and his friend Charles Faulkner about the same time.

After leaving Manchester in November 1886 Unwin returned for a few months to Oxford. In May 1887 he started a new job as a draughtsman for the Staveley Coal and Iron Company at Barrow Hill, near Chesterfield, where his work included the design of machinery for the pits. The head of the firm, Charles Markham, was a socialist sympathiser and poet who had contributed to

Commonweal, but even so Unwin had to be careful not to mix work and politics directly. Instead he involved himself in socialist activity in three nearby towns: Chesterfield, Sheffield and Clay Cross.

In Chesterfield, his friend Joe Cree told him as soon as he arrived in May 1887, the prospects for socialism were not rosy and a reading or discussion group was the most that they could aim at. The group was instituted, meeting on Sundays, and was kept going by Unwin until 1891.[32] Speakers included, as well as Carpenter and Morris, the Christian Socialist John Furniss, from the nearby Moorhays commune, and Unwin himself, on the ethical teaching of James Hinton. Unwin found a strong secularist feeling among the Chesterfield socialists and warned them

> that they must be careful in condemning the ordinary orthodox Xtianity not to imagine they had said anything against what Christ really taught.[33]

The Sheffield Socialist Society was a larger venture. It had originated during the general election of November 1885, when Furniss, Carpenter and others had put up an independent parliamentary candidate against the Liberals. At the end of February 1886 Morris visited the Sheffield socialists with the hope of gaining their adherence to the League, but found them resistant, mainly because of 'our repudiation of a Parliamentary method, the reasons for which I did my best to explain'.[34] Carpenter provided a programme for the Sheffield Socialist Society, as they called themselves, which included among its immediate objectives 'Labour Representation . . . in all forms – Parliamentary, Town Councils, Boards of Guardians, School Boards, etc'.[35]

While living at Manchester Unwin travelled over to lecture to the Sheffield socialists and on his return to Chesterfield in May 1887 he became a regular member of the Sheffield group, lecturing for them frequently. It was as such that Carpenter described Unwin in his autobiography: 'Raymond Unwin, who would come over from Chesterfield to help us, a young man of cultured antecedents, of first-rate ability and good sense, healthy, democratic and vegetarian . . . .'[36] In Sheffield Unwin met socialists from other parts of the country who were making the pilgrimage to Millthorpe, including in September 1887 the ethical socialist Percival Chubb, of the Fellowship of the New Life, whose ideas on ethical education appealed to him.

Unwin remained involved in the Sheffield group until 1890. At this date, after the collapse of the League but before the emergence of the Independent Labour Party, the anarchists in Sheffield and elsewhere were able to gain a hearing for their policy of immediate revolution. In Sheffield the anarchist group included the so-called 'Dr' Creaghe, who, it was stated, would be 'helping us to get the Rev. over speedily';[37] a 'most revolutionary beggar' was Unwin's comment after having brought Creaghe over to lecture at Chesterfield in January 1891. Unwin listened to the anarchist argument in favour of immediate revolution but was not convinced that 'blowing up bridges' was really the way to bring about socialism.[38] This was perhaps fortunate, since two of the Sheffield anarchists were soon afterwards arrested in connection with the 'Walsall Bomb Plot'.

The third of Unwin's socialist *fora*, Clay Cross, brought him into direct contact with the parliamentary strategy in the person of the young socialist agitator J. L. Mahon. Encouraged by Engels, Mahon sought to bring socialism and the labour movement together by 'taking hold of the working-class movement as it exists at present, and gently and gradually moulding it into a Socialist shape'.[39] Basing himself in the northern coalfields (particularly Northumberland, where a bitter strike was in progress) Mahon set up the North of England Socialist Federation, with a clear commitment to parliamentary action.

Unwin acted as behind-the-scenes organiser for Mahon in the Derbyshire coalfield. In June 1887 Mahon asked Unwin to help organise a socialist rally of the Derbyshire miners at Clay Cross, to which Unwin agreed, although worried at the danger 'if it gets known to our boss that I am stirring up the miners!'.[40] *Commonweal* reported that on 12 July 1887

A large meeting of the Derbyshire miners was held. Raymond Unwin [and others] . . . spoke. Mahon explained the lines on which the Socialist organisation of the Northumberland miners had been formed, and sixty names were at once given to form a similar society.[41]

Other meetings followed; on 2 August Unwin 'spoke for some time on the programme of the North of England Socialist Federation which we have adopted'.[42]

The following week Unwin wrote to the Socialist League headquarters on behalf of the Clay Cross socialists to enquire about the conditions under which the League would accept them as an affiliated society, and received the uncompromising reply that if they wished to affiliate to the League they must sign a pledge renouncing parliamentary action. A month later Unwin informed the League that at

> a meeting held at Clay Cross last Tuesday your letter was read & the matter of joining the League was discussed. It was decided not to join the League, the majority not being willing to sign any pledge on the parliamentary question. I must say that we regret that the League has decided to push this question in a more extreme manner than formerly.

It was not that they wanted immediate parliamentary action:

> in fact the majority at Clay Cross are of opinion that Education and organization outside all parliamentary work is the best course to follow at present, & would have been glad to join the League as the best organisation for carrying out that work. But they do not feel free to sign anything which might be construed into a repudiation of parliamentary work in the future . . . .
> Our position shortly is this. We believe parliamentary action for the present & for some time to come to be useless or worse but we think that eventually the changes may be made through the means of Parliament.[43]

Under the immediate impact of these events Unwin's thinking about the merits of the revolutionary and the parliamentary routes to socialism changed. An article written early in September 1887 set out his change of view. Instead of arguing the abstentionist case against the parliamentary, Unwin now sought for 'a third course', which without being a compromise would take account of the strengths and weaknesses of both sides of the argument. The objection to revolutionary action was that it had no popular support; the objection to parliamentary action was that it was 'likely to lead to no good'. Instead, he believed, a third course was offered by education; this was really the old Socialist League line, but now given an even stronger ethical emphasis. The need was to address the people,

> teach them Socialism, and try by any means in our power to
> spread also the true Socialist sentiments of brotherhood,
> freedom, and equality . . . .

because spiritual had to precede social change:

> There must be more of the spirit of Socialism, more regard for
> other's good, before any social changes can be of much use.[44]

This remained Unwin's position until the rise of the Independent
Labour Party transformed the political landscape in the 1890s:
revolution was futile; parliamentary action was unlikely to yield
any result; the 'great work' was to educate the people in socialism.[45]

Unwin thus deferred to some indefinite point in the future the
likely date of the advent of socialism. In August 1887 he noted that
his youthful belief in the imminence of socialism was passing:

> somehow each time I come to seriously think of it I seem to
> see that there will be longer and longer to wait. I used to think
> of 3 or 4 years, now I think of 7 to 10 or even 20 years![46]

The problem, as Unwin had found when addressing the Derbyshire
miners, was that it was hard to get them 'to work for anything
distant, they want something at once'.[47]

In the meantime there was one form of immediate action that
Unwin felt was legitimate: the founding of socialist colonies or
communes. In the area around Sheffield and Chesterfield this was
a strong tradition, with the St George's Guild farm at Totley,
Carpenter's Millthorpe (which acted as a sort of training ground
for other would-be colonists), and the Christian Communist settlement at Moorhays led by John Furniss. On his first visit to
Millthorpe Unwin had wondered 'whether a place something like
Mr C.'s would not be a good thing', 'a little centre of socialism and
refinement for some country place';[48] and even while in Manchester
he had written an article for *Commonweal* commending these 'social
experiments'. His return to Chesterfield in 1887 strengthened this
interest:

> I have been thinking that Edward is right in trying to do
> something in a small way even now as well as agitating for a
> large change . . . I wish I could do more in that sort of work.[49]

Unwin visited and was strongly impressed by John Furniss's commune at Moorhays, some four miles from Millthorpe, where 120 acres had been taken over by a group of twenty settlers:

> The communists seem to be doing pretty well . . . . We dined off a regular communist apple dumplin, the finest I ever saw! There is something very interesting in these fellows, uneducated simple fellows as we should call them, living together a life so much more noble than most of us are able to do.[50]

Furniss impressed Unwin, not only by his socialist work in Sheffield and by his commune, but also by his primitive Christianity. At this stage Unwin was almost as much concerned with questions of ethics and religion as with politics. His diary entry for 22 May 1887 is characteristic:

> Joe [Cree] & I get on very well, we talked of social matters and religious, Sunday keeping and worshipping God by serving man.
>   I can't quite make up my mind about morality, whether we are to start with the good of others as the basis & take moral laws as merely the expression of what wise men have thought to be for the good of others, or are we to take them as moral laws given from heaven to be obeyed in spite of all appearances because they are from God . . . .[51]

Unwin's major intellectual interest at this time was in the ethical writings of James Hinton (1822–1875), an interest that he shared with Carpenter. In Hinton, with his belief in the service of humanity and his insistence on the primacy of the moral or spiritual faculty over the intellectual, Unwin found a confirmation of his own beliefs. Unwin even felt that it might be his vocation to proselytise for Hinton. Hence his delight in finding in the uneducated Furniss a philosophy similar to that of Hinton:

> You know I said I wanted to translate Hinton to the people, well there's Furniss, he's hardly read anything but the bible and he has grasped all the vital parts of Hinton . . . . He thinks nothing can be done unless we have that real religion, we must all be 'saved', that is, from selfishness.[52]

It was not surprising, given this, that Unwin was repelled by the positivist philosophy of Auguste Comte, which he studied at this time but found both anti-spiritual and anti-democratic.[53] Unwin preferred spiritual fare: Emerson, Tolstoy or the *Bhagavad Gita*.

Although none of the three socialist groups with which Unwin was involved between 1887 and 1890 were branches of the Socialist League, Unwin's loyalties remained with Morris and the League. After leaving Manchester Unwin became an individual member of the League and he continued to write regularly for the *Commonweal*. But with the collapse of the League at the end of 1890 – a part of the general disarray of the socialist movement – Unwin found his socialist commitment being put to the test. Like many others he found it hard to maintain socialist enthusiasm when the only prospect was an indefinite period of the rather thankless work of 'education'. At the beginning of 1891, after a 'rather poor' lecture and meeting at Chesterfield (his only remaining arena of socialist activity), he reaffirmed his belief in socialism:

> The ideal of Socialism is to some of us a religion, & it does Ettie not only tell us what is right but help us to do it

but admitted that he was finding the work of organising socialist meetings increasingly tedious.[54] A few months later, while still affirming that 'the Socialists hold the ideas which seem to me right'[55] he admitted that socialism no longer filled the role of a religion in his life.

> You see Ettie at one time I was sort of given up to Socialism, it was my religion and I feel the loss of it as such. But I think it quite possible for some other side of the work besides the agitating to take the same place.[56]

As a result, as he later put it, in the early 1890s he largely 'yielded to . . . idle and cowardly impulses, and retired to my peak'.[57] In these years Unwin was largely preoccupied with personal matters, in particular with advancing his career prospects sufficiently for Robert Parker to drop his objection to Unwin and Ethel Parker becoming engaged. In 1891 agreement of a sort to an engagement was obtained, but then retracted; marriage eventually followed in 1893, whereupon the Unwins set up home in Chesterfield.

THE ARCHITECTURE OF SOCIAL EXPERIMENTS

A new period in Unwin's life began in 1896, when he went into partnership with his brother-in-law Barry Parker in architectural practice at Buxton, on the west side of the Peaks. At the same time the Unwins moved from Chesterfield to Chapel-en-le-Frith (close to the moors but also on the main route from Manchester to Sheffield), where they occupied a lodgehouse that remained their home until they moved to Letchworth Garden City in 1904.

Setting up in practice meant for Unwin not just a new kind of employment but also release from the constraints so long imposed on his political activities by his employment in industry. This freedom became apparent in January 1897 when for the first time Unwin's name appeared in the list of lecturers published by the *Labour Annual*.[58] More importantly it gave Unwin for the first time the opportunity to combine his skills as a building designer with his interest in socialist ventures.

Throughout this period Unwin retained his belief in the ethical mission of socialism. His activities in this regard centred on the Labour Church, of which he was an active member in the late 1890s, lecturing regularly at Labour Churches in the midlands and the north.[59] In an article for the *Labour Prophet and Labour Church Record* in March 1898 Unwin stated that the name 'Labour Church'

> directs attention at once to the two great ideas which have caused the movement to spring into existence. The first of these may be expressed in this way: that the Labour Movement is powerless to move society sufficiently deeply to realise its aims, without the help of religion . . . . The other idea which is somewhat the converse of this may be put thus: A religion which stands aside from any great movement of social regeneration must cease to be vital and shrivel into mere formalism.

Echoing both Carpenter and Hinton, Unwin wrote that the religion of the labour movement was based not on mere doctrine or intellect, but on something deeper, the religious feelings inspired in the 'simple soul' by 'the words of love, and the life of goodness' of Christ. It was the job of the Labour Church to unite the labour movement around

> the broad ethical principles and ideal feelings which are common to us all, putting these forward as the main basis

of our movement. Those merely intellectual beliefs about economic laws, or political tactics, must be subordinated and kept in their due place; they are matters on which all thinking men will tend to differ, at least in details; it is upon these points that we split. There will always be the opportunist group, the uncompromising revolutionary group, and the purely educational groups in the movement. But in the Labour Church all these must meet and be fused, as it were, by the heat of common feeling for common ideals, into one force.[60]

After 1900 the Labour Church declined and as Unwin became increasingly involved in his architectural schemes his ethical work lapsed. His beliefs however remained intact. After the move to the fledgling Letchworth Garden City in 1904, where no church had yet been built, the large living-room in the Unwins' house was the setting for 'Sunday Evening Services' which, like the Labour Church services of the 1890s, were of a non-denominational nature 'such as could be joined in by those of any, or no, creed'.[61] The services were organised by Bruce Wallace, formerly of the Fellowship of the New Life, who had also been active in the Labour Church in the 1890s. Lecture notes survive for an address given to this group by Unwin *c.* 1905; the subject, appropriately, was the ethical ideas of Hinton.[62]

From the time of his first visit to Carpenter's Millthorpe Unwin retained his belief in what he called 'social experiments'. In 1887 in *Commonweal* he affirmed:

> Unlike some Socialists, I hope for great results . . . from individual efforts, from men who try to practise common interests and to do useful work, from small societies for working co-operatively in farming and other branches of industry – in short, from all who, by living, in spite of conditions, as far as possible in accordance with their ideal of life and society, are helping to spread the ideals and sentiments which will make our life in the future happier than it has been in the past.[63]

Between 1896 and 1904, Unwin pursued the architectural implications of this belief. At the level of the individual home, it shaped the Unwins' family life at Chapel-en-le-Frith and the recommendations on house design made in *The Art of Building a*

Home. At the level of the model community, it shaped the ideas presented by Unwin in article form in 1900–1901 and embodied in the design of Letchworth Garden City in 1903–4.

Unwin's thinking about the home centred on 'the simple life'. In part 'the simple life' was a development of the injunction issued by Ruskin in 'The Nature of Gothic' to purchase only such goods as were the product of undivided labour. It was this point that Unwin put in a lecture at Sheffield in 1897:

> As workers our first thought should be of the conditions of work, of its effect on us, of our joy in our work . . . . As consumers we should think of the lives of the men we consume. Everything we buy, every service we accept, is so much human life & it depends on us largely whether we buy & consume the joyous happy hours of labour or the weary hours of drudging toil.[64]

At their cottage at Chapel-en-le-Frith, described by their friend and neighbour Katherine Bruce Glasier, the Unwins carried this out enthusiastically, with curtains, blankets and clothes made from 'Ruskin' flannel, hand-woven in the Isle of Man, and wrought-iron fittings 'that had brought the village blacksmith a new delight in life'.[65]

But more importantly 'the simple life' drew on the radical antithesis between 'convention' and 'real needs' established by Carpenter in the 1880s. In place of the conventional life style of the wealthy, which in this view enslaved both those on whose labour it depended and those who were its supposed beneficiaries, Unwin called for 'a simpler form of life, one which need not cost so much of the labour of others to maintain, or so much of their own to produce'.[66] The application of this notion of 'the simple life' to domestic architecture was the main theme of *The Art of Building a Home*. As one reviewer noted, the authors

> insist on the importance of designing a house with a primary view to the comfort and convenience of those that will occupy it, and of making it as far as possible a truthful expression of the life that is to be lived there, instead of a mere echo of conventions.[67]

In *The Art of Building a Home* Parker and Unwin took as their target the ordinary house which, 'sacrificed to convention and custom, neither satisfies the real needs of its occupants nor expresses in any way their individuality'.[68] 'Real needs', according to Parker and Unwin, started with nature, and it was from nature, in the form of the site, that the design of the house should proceed:

> The site is the most important factor to be considered, for it usually suggests both the internal arrangement and the external treatment.[69]

Nature's influence operated on the design in three ways: first, aspect (every living-room had to be open to the sun); second, prospect (the best possible view had to be secured from the main rooms); and third, landscape (the house had to adorn rather than deface the landscape in which it stood). In urban or suburban building this meant that merely conventional ideas, such as 'the convention that a cottage should face to the street',[70] would have to be abandoned, and the arrangement of roads and buildings, as much as the internal plan of the house, be suited to these dictates of nature. In language reminiscent of Ruskin's advice in *Modern Painters* to 'go to Nature', Parker and Unwin stated that

> to produce a good plan, one should go to the site without any preconceived conventions, but with a quite open mind, prepared . . . to receive all the suggestions the site can offer.[71]

Beyond that it was a question of attending to the life and 'real needs', as opposed to the 'conventional wants', of those who were to live in the house. In the case of a labourer's cottage, this would produce a radical transformation in the internal plan, eliminating the parlour (demanded only by 'a false convention of respectability') and replacing it with a single large living-room, with the right aspect and a good view, and containing everything needed for daily living from the cooking-range to the piano.[72] A middle-class house too would be closer to this simple cottage than to a conventional villa.

> Those whose main desire is for beauty in their lives are coming to see that to the rational cottage as sketched above, with its ample living-room and the other necessaries of a decently comfortable life, they must add with great caution and reluctance, and only as dictated by really pressing needs.[73]

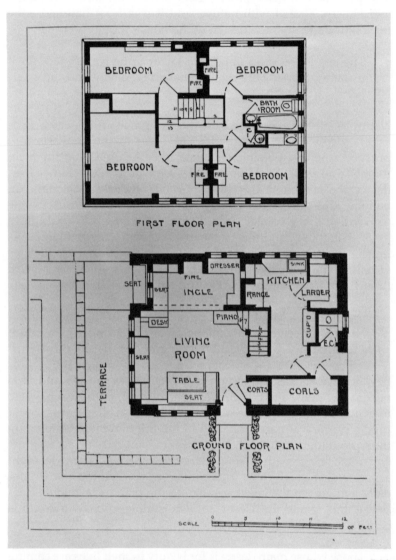

5.3 Parker and Unwin: design for a cottage for the Unwins, Chapel-en-le-Frith (1897), plans (from *The Art of Building a Home*, 1901). The kitchen and living room formed different parts of a single volume

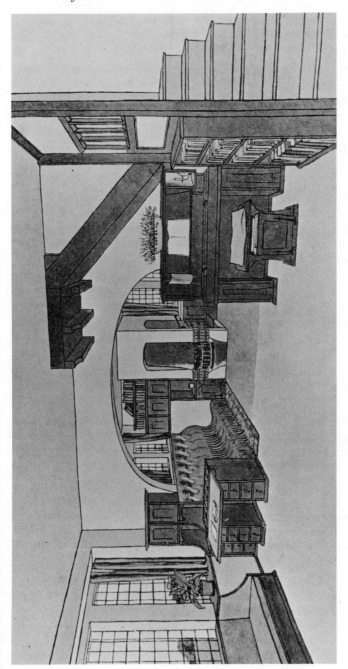

5.4 Parker and Unwin: design for a cottage for the Unwins, Chapel-en-le-Frith (1897), interior perspective: view into inglenook (from *The Art of Building a Home*, 1901)

The result would be something closer to a Japanese interior as described by the orientalist Lafcadio Hearn than to a conventional English home.

The Art of Building a Home included an unexecuted design made about 1897 for a new cottage for the Unwins on a site at Chapel-en-le-Frith (Figs 5.3 and 5.4). As with other Parker and Unwin projects of this period, the design was a good deal less assured than the prose and, for all the talk of simplification, for a small house the form was one of considerable complexity. (When challenged at the Society of Architects on the way in which their planning cut rooms up 'into nooks and crannies', Unwin replied rather ungenerously that the 'sketches were his partner's work, and most of the originality was due to him'.[74]) Nonetheless in Unwin's eyes the plan represented the expression of the simple life, with conventional ideas, such as the upstairs/downstairs distinction between parlour and kitchen, eliminated and everything designed according to need and purpose, 'so that there is no incongruity between the desk and the dresser, the piano and the plate rack'.[75]

Although to this extent Unwin's notion of 'the simple life' as set out in *The Art of Building a Home* followed Carpenter, one important difference should be noted. For Carpenter, a crucial element in 'the simple life' was the break with the convention not just of manners and surroundings, but also of heterosexuality and the family – a notion entirely absent from Unwin. Whereas for Carpenter 'the simple life' meant in part the opportunity to live more or less openly in a homosexual relationship, for Unwin, whose relationship with his wife and children was orthodox, this sense of a transformation of gender and family roles was absent. While proposing a transformation in the physical setting of the home, Unwin's writings unlike Carpenter's tended to reinforce rather than challenge the conventionality of the social relations that were to exist within it.

Whatever might be achieved by individual attempts to lead a higher form of life, more might be expected from social experiments in which not just an individual or family but a whole community was involved. To Unwin socialist colonies such as the Moorhays colony constituted the germ of the the socialist life of the future.[76] In 1889, describing a Sunday outing by the Chesterfield socialists to the early-eighteenth-century Sutton Hall, Unwin wrote:

Small wonder that, as we stood looking at the house and the splendid view it commands, we should fall to talking of the 'days that are going to be', when this Hall and others like it will be the centre of a happy communal life. Plenty of room in that large house for quite a small colony to live, each one having his own den upstairs . . . and downstairs would be large common dining-halls, dancing-halls, smoking rooms – if indeed life shall still need the weed to make it perfect.

And we chatted on, each adding a bit to our picture; how some would till the land around and others tend the cattle, while others perhaps would start some industry, working in the outbuildings or building workshops in the park, and taking care not to spoil our view . . . . Others, again, could work in the mines and bring up coal, of which there is a good supply just now being worked by a neighbouring company . . . .[77]

The 1890s was a great period for communitarian experiments that sought to realise visions of this kind. One of the Unwins' closest friends, the ethical socialist Katherine Bruce Glasier, was involved in the early 1890s in one of the most famous, the Starnthwaite colony near Kendal. The late 1890s saw a new wave of communitarian experiments, largely triggered by the setback received by the ILP in the 1895 election; the English Tolstoyans, led by J. C. Kenworthy and Bruce Wallace of the Fellowship of the New Life, were involved in several colonies (Purleigh, Whiteway and others) where they attempted, as one report put it in 1898, 'to *live* Socialism'. Nor was this a purely insular phenomenon: in Leeds in 1897 an outbreak of 'Cosme fever' was reported, with local socialists being attracted by the lure of the socialist colony in Paraguay.[78] By the turn of the century many of these ventures had collapsed from inadequate organisation, and the rump of the Tolstoyan group transferred their allegiance to what appeared to be the more promising venture of Ebenezer Howard and his Garden City Association, founded in 1899.

Letchworth Garden City, based on Howard's ideas, was a more highly organised version of the simple life colonies of the 1890s. Howard had approached Unwin for a design early in 1903 and (following a competition which Lethaby and Ricardo also entered) Unwin's plan for the new city was formally adopted a year later. Early settlers at the new venture along with the Unwins included veterans from the colonies of the 1890s, including Bruce Wallace and Carpenter's erstwhile companion George Adams, who brought with him the sandal-making business he had started at Millthorpe. According to Charles Lee, who moved to Letchworth in 1907, a 'typical Garden Citizen'

> Wears far-and-near spectacles, knickerbockers and of course sandals . . . . Vegetarian and member of the Theosophical Society . . . . Over his fireplace – which is a hole in the wall lined with brick – is . . . a large photo of Madame Blavatsky. Some charming old furniture, several Persian rugs etc. Books – works of Kipling, Lafcadio Hearn, 'Isis Unveiled', Wm Morris, Edward Carpenter, H. G. Wells, Tolstoi, etc.

To those unfamiliar with the socialist version of colonial life, Letchworth was quite confusing, 'a morris dance of many-coloured movements – Buddhism, Theosophy, Christian Science, Female Suffrage, several brands of Socialism and who knows how many varieties of Vegetarianism?'.[79]

It was in the context of this tradition that Unwin developed the ideas about the design of socialist colonies that he presented in his paper 'Co-operation in Building', published in article form in December 1900 and January 1901[80] and reprinted in *The Art of Building a Home*. In his earliest surviving lecture, 'The Dawn of a Happier Day', written under the influence of Hyndman and Carpenter in 1886, Unwin had derided the notion of a 'Golden Age' in the past, stating that there had been much violence, ignorance and drudgery in the middle ages and that socialists should look for their Golden Age to the future.[81] By 1900 however he had come to share the medieval enthusiasm of Morris and regarded the middle ages as the model for the architecture of communitarian experiments. What made the buildings of the middle ages – the village, the manor house, the college quadrangle – so appealing, according to Unwin, was the orderly social life that they expressed.

> The village was the expression of a small corporate life in which all the different units were personally in touch with each other, conscious of and frankly accepting their relations, and on the whole content with them. This relationship reveals itself in the feeling of order which the view induces . . . .[82]

The socialist colonies would revive the collective life of the middle ages which had been shattered in the period of individualism.

> Association for mutual help in various ways is undoubtedly the growing influence which is destined to bring to communities that crystalline structure which was so marked a feature of feudal society, and the lack of which is so characteristic of our own.[83]

Accordingly for their architecture the colonists should revive the building forms of the middle ages: 'Why should not cottages be grouped into quadrangles, having all the available land in a square in the centre?'[84] Or, if a full quadrangle did not fit the site, houses could be built on just three sides of the quadrangle, an arrangement that Unwin had found in the manor houses of the late middle ages.[85]

In these forms a new life would develop. Relationships between people would change: as well as domestic life in the individual cottages, each quadrangle would provide for communal life by including common rooms for relaxation, baking, laundry and bathing.

> From this to the preparation of meals and the serving of them in the Common Room would be only a matter of time; for the advantage of it is obvious. Instead of thirty or forty housewives preparing thirty or forty little scrap dinners, heating a like number of ovens, boiling thrice the number of pans and cleaning them all up again, two or three of them retained as cooks by the little settlement would do the whole, and could give better and cheaper meals into the bargain.[86]

The relationship to nature would change also: instead of the land being divided up into individual private plots of a diminutive area, it would be grouped into the central space of the quadrangle where it would constitute a large garden for collective use. Thereby

> association in the enjoyment of open spaces or large gardens will replace the exclusiveness of the individual possession of backyards or petty garden-plots . . . .[87]

5.5 Parker and Unwin: design for a quadrangle of cottages (1898–99), perspective of quadrangle (from *The Art of Building a Home,* 1901)

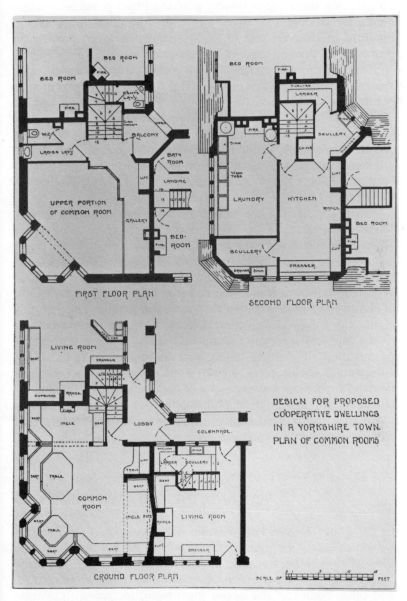

5.6 Parker and Unwin: design for a quadrangle of cottages (1898–99), plans of
communal units (from *The Art of Building a Home*, 1901). The double-height
living-room had a gallery at first floor level; at second floor level were the
kitchen, scullery and laundry

To illustrate these ideas Unwin published two possible arrange-
ments for co-operative dwellings. One (designed for a site in
Bradford in 1898–99) was of the quadrangular form that Unwin
proposed for general use, with individual dwellings on four sides
and common rooms occupying one corner, and the central open
space laid out as a garden or lawn (Figs 5.5 and 5.6). Two versions
of this plan were shown, one with three-bedroom cottages and the
other with five-bedroom houses. The other scheme illustrated by
Unwin was a design for a south-facing slope: a group of houses
arranged informally around three sides of a green. This design
originated in a tentative commission received in 1899 from Isabella
Ford of Adel Grange near Leeds, a friend and disciple of
Carpenter's.

Unwin approached the design of Letchworth Garden City in
1903–4 as essentially an elaborated version of a co-operative
scheme. He discussed the housing for the garden city in the paper
he gave to the Bournville conference of the Garden City Association
in September 1901: the design was to follow the ideas set out in
The Art of Building a Home, that is, being based on the 'real needs'
of nature and social life rather than mere convention. The planning
of the city followed the same notions, paying attention both to
nature (not just aspect and prospect, but also topography and the
preservation of existing trees), and to the 'real needs' of the
occupants (such as access, employment, economy). Ownership of
the land by the community – one of the unchanging fundamental
tenets of Unwin's political philosophy since the 1880s – would
mean that at the garden city the community for the first time
'secured freedom to express its life adequately' in its architecture.[88]

ART AND THE CITY

In his paper to the 1901 Garden City Association conference,
Unwin called for the municipal authority in the garden city to lead
the way in building housing. By this date there was a widespread
demand for municipal provision of housing from trades councils
and other bodies in the labour movement, including the Fabian
Society, the Workmen's National Housing Council (set up
in 1898) and above all the Independent Labour Party. The ILP,
launched in Bradford in 1893, saw in housing a strong argument

for its policy of labour representation on local councils and in parliament. The first issue of the Leeds ILP's *Labour Chronicle* in May 1893 carried an article on 'Unhealthy Dwellings':

> The disgraceful action of the Corporation in regard to back-to-back houses should prove a wholesome lesson to the working classes of Leeds; and we hope it will open their eyes to the blind folly of sending the monied classes to represent them.[89]

This journal also carried a front page article on 'Labour May Day' by Unwin. Unwin was sympathetic to the ILP from the outset but was doubtful how much a socialist political party could really achieve. In 1900 however the ILP received a crucial boost when it gained the adherence of the trade union movement and shortly after Unwin declared for the new party. In January 1902 an article in the *ILP News* (which was edited by his friend Bruce Glasier) set out Unwin's position.

Writing as a former 'member of the old Socialist League', Unwin declared that times had changed since the days of the League. The League's belief in the coming revolution had been proved wrong: 'the change was not destined to come in the way we thought and feared'. Now the idea of socialism was widely accepted and people worked to advance it in many different ways, not least through 'municipal and political life'. Unwin still believed that the political route held 'immense dangers . . . dangers of corruption and compromise': it was essential therefore that 'if we are to enter this life we must follow a policy that has at least some chance of success'. The alliance with the trade unions offered 'the best chance we ever had of getting a Socialist Labour Party in Parliament' and, if the parliamentary route was to be followed at all, this alliance should be pursued determinedly.[90]

Within the arguments of the time Unwin's article was an attack on the Social Democratic Federation and its notion of a 'pure' Socialist political party and a defence of the ILP's attempt to form a Labour Party in which socialists and trade unions would co-operate – the strategy that Mahon had advocated to Unwin's Clay Cross socialists in 1887 and the one on which the Labour Party was to be founded. In an editorial Bruce Glasier commented of Unwin's article:

Although idealist as ever in his conceptions of the goal of Socialist effort, and although by disposition recoiling from the turmoil of electioneering, he frankly conceded the main ILP contention that the municipal and political Labour way is the right road to practical Socialist achievement.[91]

Keir Hardie, one of the main instigators of the alliance with the trade unions, was sufficiently impressed by Unwin's article to poach it for his paper, the *Labour Leader*.[92]

Unwin's ILP article came shortly after he had presented his ideas on municipal housing at three major gatherings: in a speech to the Garden City Association conference (20 September 1901); in a lecture to the Workmen's National Housing Council (4 November 1901); and in a lecture to the Fabian Society (22 November 1901). This last, entitled 'Light and Air and the Housing Question', was subsequently published as Fabian Tract 109, *Cottage Plans and Common Sense*. In these presentations Unwin argued not just that municipalities should provide housing, but that the housing they provided should be of a new and quite different sort, based on the Unwin-Carpenter notion of a rational cottage answering to the real needs of 'the simple life'.

In keeping with his argument that pragmatic policies could be justified only by success, Unwin approached the question of municipal housing in a resolutely practical way. Most local authorities acting to relieve the housing shortage, he said, would have to build neither in town nor country, but in the 'great suburban districts' in between, 'where, after all, the majority of working folk are housed'.[93] This meant that densities could scarcely be reduced below 24 to 36 houses per acre. Since under the system of local authority finance the capital cost of construction would be repaid over a long period, anything that was built should be the 'very best that is known', in other words 'based upon the permanent and essential conditions of life and health, not on passing fashions or conventions established by the speculative builder'.[94] This argument, linking Carpenter's distinction between convention and real needs to the demands of local authority finance, was later to figure prominently in Unwin's contribution to the post-war debate on standards for state housing.

The design of the municipal house, Unwin wrote, 'had to be thought out from the beginning, as though no custom in connection with such buildings had ever grown up'.[95] The needs of the

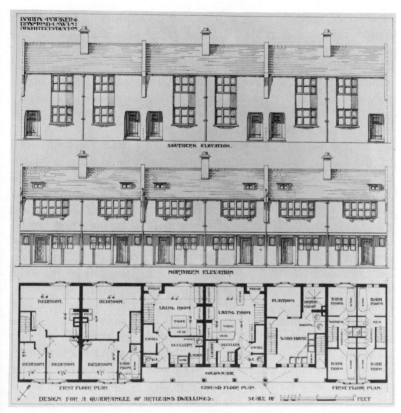

5.7 Parker and Unwin: design for a quadrangle of artisans' cottages, plans of dwellings and communal units (from *Cottage Plans and Common Sense*, 1902). The plans shown are (left) dwellings, first floor; (centre) dwellings, ground floor; (right) communal units, ground and first floor. The communal provision comprised, on the ground floor, wash-house with drying-closet and playroom adjoining; on the first floor, male and female bathrooms, with separate staircase access

occupants were of three sorts. First, their needs with respect to nature: essentially sun, light and air. This meant abandoning 'the convention that a cottage should face to the street'[96] and arranging the layout of roads and houses according to aspect and prospect, eliminating backyards and back-projections in the process. Second, their needs as members of a family. This meant ensuring a large and workable living-room, a scullery, larder, coalstore, WC/EC, and bedrooms, but not a parlour (not 'necessary to health or family life') nor a separate chamber for the entrance and stairs ('an extreme instance of valuable room and air space sacrificed to thoughtless custom and foolish pride').[97] Third, there were the needs of the occupants as members of a community. These were to be met by the provision of communal centres in the corner of each quadrangle, which would provide those facilities that were otherwise available only to the wealthy (laundries, reading-rooms and if necessary baths) and would foster the growth of the 'co-operative spirit', as befitted a municipal undertaking (Fig. 5.7).[98]

The publication of Unwin's lecture as a Fabian Tract was seen by the Fabian Society (which Unwin had joined only in March 1901)[99] as 'a new departure, both in respect of the introduction of plans and sketches . . . and in the subject matter, which is only indirectly political'. Nonetheless the Society was pleased to report that the tract 'has been very widely noticed in the Press, and a very unusual number of orders for single copies have been received'.[100] In retrospect the interest provoked by *Cottage Plans and Common Sense* does not seem surprising, for it has come to be seen widely as a turning-point in architectural thinking about housing design.

In the final sentence of *Cottage Plans and Common Sense* Unwin spoke of the 'simple dignity and beauty in the cottage' that was necessary to 'the proper growth of the gentler and finer instincts of men'. Throughout his writings of the period 1901–04, reference was made to the indispensability of art in housing and urban layout. Nowhere was the 'claim of beauty or art' more important, Parker and Unwin wrote in 1903, than in the 'transforming of open fields into dwelling places'.[101] In 1906 in a lecture on city planning at Cambridge, Unwin argued that

> the introduction of civic art, of the due consideration of the element of beauty, was the most important and most urgently required reform in town affairs at the present time.[102]

This emphasis on the role of art in the building of houses and towns was explicit in the title of Parker and Unwin's book, *The Art of Building a Home*. It was also evident in the original title proposed for the book that Unwin wrote to coincide with the town planning legislation of 1909: until shortly before publication this was to have been called, not *Town Planning in Practice*, but *The Art of Town Planning*.[103]

What did Unwin understand by 'art' in this context? A number of ideas contributed to his conception of art, but the most important in regard to the city was the Ruskinian idea of art as expression and particularly Carpenter's transcendentalist notion of art as the expression of life. One of the quotations from Carpenter cherished by Unwin was the following:

Art is expression: expression of that which is else inexpressible. In all true art, whenever we see beauty, something passes to us, some touch of that which is infinite: something from a kindred soul to ours. [104]

The notion that above all art was the expression of life was impressed on Unwin by Carpenter at an early stage of their relationship:

One early difference I recall, as the incident has significance.

When he was just in Millthorpe, we coming down the hill from Freebirch, I felt that the slate roof did not quite belong in that lovely valley.

He felt I had not understood his aim. Essentially seeking expression: not decoration. In building Millthorpe E.C. sought expression of life . . . . [105]

In dealing both with the house and the city Unwin employed this notion of art as the expression of the life of the inhabitants. In regard to the house, we have seen that in *The Art of Building a Home* Parker and Unwin insisted that expression be given to the individuality of the occupants. Likewise Unwin regarded the city as a work of art in which the collective life was expressed:

fine city building is an art. The city is a form in which the life of its people expresses itself.

It was therefore subject to the same rules as any other art.

In this art, as in any other, success depends on there being something fine to express and upon it being finely rendered. [106]

The role of the designer or town planner was to act as the medium in this process, like a brush in the making of a painting. Unwin's notes for a lecture in 1908 on 'town planning' (the term came into general use in 1906) made the point succinctly:

Demand for Town Planning [the] result of common life seeking expression. Essentially a Civic Art, designer being channel through which it expresses itself – the brush with which they paint.[107]

For the characterisation of the art that the designer was to realise, Unwin drew on Lethaby and the notion of art as the 'well-doing of what needs doing'. The common life of the community would find expression not at the expense of the practical needs of the people, but by meeting those needs with 'that small margin of generosity and imaginative treatment that constitutes it *well done*'.[108] It was this that gave city planning its value.

It is just the little margin of imaginative treatment which transforms our work from the building of clean stables for animals into the building of homes for human beings, which is of value; for it is just this which appeals to and influences the inner heart of man.[109]

The city could be reclaimed for art in this way only if the community took for itself the necessary powers over the control and ownership of land. In the middle ages, Unwin believed, the land had belonged to the people: the history of the land since then was simply 'a history of the confiscation of the people's rights'.[110] These rights had to be restored, through the collective ownership of land, if the community was to be in a position to determine the form taken by the town. In the garden city land was owned collectively; similar 'powers to purchase and hold land around the town should also be obtained for our municipalities'.[111] For only by the municipal control of land could the claims of beauty be made to tell.

So long as we leave individual landowners to develop their own plots of land in their own way, our towns must continue to grow in their present haphazard manner. But if their development is arranged and controlled by some central authority, it becomes at once easy to consider the possibilities of the site, to preserve features of beauty and interest, to keep open distant views, and to arrange roads with proper regard for convenience and beauty.[112]

Thus, while proposing a role for the state which Ruskin would have found hard to accept, Unwin's work in housing and city planning conformed fully to the goals of art as defined by Ruskin. Unwin was extending the borders of the category of art as defined by Ruskin to include the city, giving the city a place alongside the painting, the work of sculpture and the work of architecture as something capable of expressing, and speaking to, the human spirit.

In the end, then, Unwin belongs to the Ruskinian tradition, but in a much less direct way than the other figures studied in this book. Between Unwin and the tradition based on 'The Nature of Gothic' lay the cultural and political distance that separated the north from Oxford and London; between Unwin and Ruskin stood Carpenter. In the period of Unwin's intellectual formation Ruskin was a significant but remote influence. To a socialist activist of the 1880s, Ruskin was an ambiguous, if not downright reactionary, figure, with what Unwin called his 'onslaught onto Democracy, especially in *Fors Clavigera*'; in 1885 the prospect of addressing a group of Ruskinites, 'who are Christian socialists but opposed to organisation',[113] made Unwin decidedly nervous. Moreover while generally sympathetic to Ruskin's social and ethical teaching, Unwin had too much of Carpenter's positive attitude to the labour-saving potential of machinery to agree with Ruskin's proscription of the machine: the Ruskinian ideal, he wrote in 1885, was

> a very good one in the main though as to his theories of machinery probably we cannot send the clock of time back again . . . .[114]

It was in Morris that Unwin found the most persuasive presentation of the Ruskinian notions. Unwin recalled:

> Underlying and partly promoting Ruskin's love of Gothic architecture, this point of view emerged more clearly in the words of William Morris. It became indeed one of the moving impulses of his life. To Morris, art was the expression of man's joy in his work; and his life was spent in exploring the endless possibilities of such enjoyment, and was completed in a desperate attempt to secure for all men the kind of work in

which some gladness may be found, and the conditions of labour in which it may be enjoyed.[115]

Under Morris's influence Unwin for a time became an advocate of the view that free and joyful labour should form the basis of socialism, arguing the point at length in a lecture given at Sheffield in 1897, 'Gladdening v. Shortening the Hours of Labour'.[116] Within the pages of *The Art of Building a Home* Unwin reiterated the lesson of Gothic architecture as originally drawn by Ruskin:

> In fact, we read in these old buildings, as in an open book, of a simple workman who was something of an artist, one who could take pleasure in his work, finding joy in the perfection of what he created, and delight in its comeliness.
>
> Whenever we again raise up such an army of builders, working at their trades with the pleasure of artists, then will all buildings become as beautiful as . . . our old cathedrals and abbeys.[117]

And throughout his life he continued periodically to pay obeisance to this view. At the Lethaby evening at the RIBA in 1932 Unwin referred to the belief underlying

> the joy which Lethaby and William Morris took in Gothic art: that is, their belief that it gave great opportunities for enjoyment to the workman . . . .

and affirmed

> I still retain the conviction that some day we shall again find a style of building which will afford an opportunity for joy to all the workmen who are engaged on it

although he admitted that 'we do not seem to be approaching much nearer at the present time'.[118]

In practice however the notion of 'joy in labour' was peripheral to Unwin's thought. The most telling effect that Morris had on Unwin's architectural thought was his medievalism: under Morris's influence Unwin abandoned the antipathy to the middle ages evident in his 1886 lecture on the theory of surplus value, and in *The Art of Building a Home* and the other writings of the early 1900s argued for the middle ages as the architectural model for socially progressive building. Morris may also have been responsible for leading Unwin away from his initial interest in the 'scientific basis' to socialism given by Marx and represented in English socialist politics by Hyndman. In 1902 Unwin, recalling the 'revolutionary' days of the mid-1880s, depicted Hyndman and Morris as alternative faces of socialism, offering respectively the materialist and the ethical view. There was Hyndman, with 'his top hat, frock coat and general air of respectability':

> We admired his ability, we respected his pioneer work, we felt that the Marxian theories were great, though we did not presume to understand them . . . . Then, too, how we loved our Morris when he came to us sharing our illusions, full of life and joy, caring as little for the value theory as we did, but very much in earnest . . . .[119]

In general however Morris's effective influence on Unwin was limited by the political and geographical distance that separated them. Although his Oxford home and school days gave Unwin a bridge with the southern tradition, his intellectual formation took place in the north, where industry rather than crafts prevailed and – particularly among the factory districts of West Yorkshire – the labour movement was strong. Here the working class looked to self-organisation in trade unions and to the power of the state in order to gain better conditions of life and work, and had little time for the policy of abstention that appealed so strongly in the south. The northern socialists also showed a longstanding interest in socialist colonies as a way of delivering immediately some of the benefits of socialism. The result was that by the early 1900s Unwin looked to colonies such as Letchworth and even more to municipal initiatives in housing and town planning as the basis for his architectural prescriptions, accepting what Bruce Glasier termed 'the municipal and political Labour way' as the best means of socialist advance.

In the industrial north the belief in labour as the major source of human satisfaction had less appeal than in the non-industrial south. Rather, as Unwin put it in 1888, what people wanted was 'to produce enough wealth to keep us in comfort with as little labour as possible'[120] – something much closer to the Fabian view. Hence for the most part Unwin followed Carpenter in seeing socialism in terms of the reduction of toil, enabling 'each man to produce in the easiest way known',[121] and he looked forward to 'the increased leisure which only Socialism can make possible'.[122] This attitude to pleasure and labour was fundamentally at odds with that of the tradition based on 'The Nature of Gothic'.

6

A. J. Penty and the Building Guilds

The building guilds which flourished in Britain for a short period just after the First World War can be seen as the culmination of the tradition derived from Ruskin and 'The Nature of Gothic'. Like their immediate political parent, the guild socialist movement, the building guilds came of a mixed ancestry, and bore traces of most of the varieties of socialism that had flourished in Britain in the previous fifty years. The central notion in the building guilds nonetheless was the Ruskinian belief that by doing away with a system of production based on profit the guilds would restore the joy of labour and level of craftsmanship associated with the middle ages. 'Every word' of Ruskin, said the London Guild of Builders in its inaugural prospectus, regarding the 'joy of self-expression in free service, finds its echo here'.[1]

Nowhere was the Ruskinian basis clearer than in the writings of A. J. Penty (1875–1937). Penty had made his name as an architect while still a young man in York in the late 1890s, but a move to London in 1902 proved adverse to his career and architecturally he disappeared into obscurity. In direct contrast was the trajectory of his reputation as a social thinker. His book *The Restoration of the Gild System*, published in 1906, earned him the title of founder of the guild socialist movement. His fame abroad was even greater than at home: his books on the guild movement were well known in America and were translated into German, Italian, Chinese and Japanese.

Penty's thought proceeded from Ruskin. The 1906 book, according to the preface, was an attempt to give practical form to the idea, presented 'in the writings of John Ruskin', of 'restoring the Gild system as a solution to the problems presented by modern industrialism'.[2] The key text for Penty was 'The Nature of Gothic', which contained the 'greatest discovery of the nineteenth century', the aesthetic and sociological truth that 'the artist and craftsman must be one'.[3]

6.1 A. J. Penty, photographed c1914

At the end of the First World War, Penty based his call for building guilds on the Ruskinian belief in healing the division of labour by getting 'back to the medieval builder, who understood at the same time how to build and how to design'. Other writers in the architectural world saw the guilds in similarly Ruskinian terms, as a way of returning to 'the collective building enterprise of the Middle Ages'.[4] When the building guilds collapsed in the winter of 1922–23, faith in that vision could no longer be sustained, and what might have been the triumph of the Ruskinian tradition turned out instead to mark its demise.

Within the guild movement, it must be stated, Penty was regarded as something of an eccentric. His notion of the guilds was far more medieval than that of other guild socialist theorists; and in 1920, in the debates over Russian communism that split the guild socialist movement, Penty was described as 'the "diehard" of the extreme right'.[5] As in Ruskin, there was in Penty a mixture of radicalism and extreme conservatism, deriving from the precarious position of the small producers and craftsmen whose interests he espoused. After the collapse of both the building guilds and the guild socialist movement in 1923, Penty moved first into the right-wing circle around T. S. Eliot and the *Criterion*, and then into a position of overt support for the Fascism of Mussolini and Mosley. His unpublished autobiography of 1934, presenting the 'central ideas of a social theory, upon which the author has been working for thirty-two years' was entitled 'Industrialism, Guilds and Fascism' and described Fascism as the 'completion' of that theory.[6] While this was not the only possible destination for a thinker based on Ruskin, it does indicate the distance between the Ruskinian tradition and orthodox socialism, and recalls the description of his political position that Ruskin gave in 1886: 'Of course I am a Socialist – of the most stern sort – but I am also a Tory of the sternest sort'.[7]

THE RESTORATION OF THE GILD SYSTEM

To Margaret Cole Penty was a 'shaggy, stammering architect'; to Hobson, 'a genius who had lost his way'.[8] A. J. Penty was born in 1875, the eldest son of a successful architect in York, and at the age of about 13 left school to be apprenticed in his father's office. By the age of twenty he had designed his first major work, a country house near York in the Old English style of Norman Shaw; three years later (1899) he was a junior partner in the Penty firm responsible for design and detail. At this period Penty was in close contact with the fashionable art architecture of the day (in his surviving sketchbook for 1896 Henry Wilson, Voysey, Townsend and Mackintosh figure prominently) and he collaborated with the Glasgow architect and designer George Walton, who opened premises in York in 1898. By 1900 young Penty was making a name for himself as the architect of houses and restaurants 'conceived and executed in the latest evolution of English art'.[9] Coverage in the national press (the *British Architect, Builders' Journal and Architectural Record,* and *Building News*) was followed by inclusion in Muthesius' *Das Englische Haus* of 1904, where the Penty firm figured among the 'fine talents in the provincial cities of England'.[10]

At the time that he made his name, Penty was 'an enthusiastic disciple of Ruskin and Morris' and was 'nearly as much concerned with the ethics of production as the aesthetics of production'.[11] Through Morris he was attracted to socialism and in 1898 joined the York branch of the Fabian Society.[12] Penty started to move among intellectual circles in Leeds – which around the turn of the century was enjoying something of a cultural renaissance – joining the Young Man's Self-Improvement Society, the Theosophical Society and, in 1900, the Plato Group, a forum set up by the local intellectual luminaries A. R. Orage and Holbrook Jackson. Shortly thereafter Orage, Jackson and Penty formed the Leeds Arts Club as an airing ground for their favourite subjects – idealist philosophy, Nietzsche, theosophy, the arts and crafts and socialism.[13]

In 1902, shortly after his father's death, Penty gave up the York practice and moved to London. As a career move, this proved disastrous. In London he attempted to establish a practice by exhibiting at the Royal Academy and entering competitions, but to little avail. In 1905 with fellow Fabian Charles Spooner, the furniture teacher at Lethaby's Central School, he set up a furniture workshop in Hammersmith, producing 'well-designed and well-made furniture at a moderate price'.[14] This was a characteristic arts and crafts venture which received enthusiastic reviews but went bankrupt after a year.

After a spell in the United States working in New York for a furniture retailer, Penty returned to London and was forced to seek a job as an architectural assistant. In March 1908, after several months without work, he joined Raymond Unwin's office at

Hampstead Garden Suburb, remaining there until 1914, when Unwin 'had no more work left for me to do'.[15] Penty was responsible for some of the most celebrated items in the office's output, including the twin buildings at the Finchley Road entrance to the suburb, although as assistant he received no public credit for the work (Fig. 6.2). During the First World War Penty was further reduced to seeking employment in what he regarded as the lowest form of practice – a public office (at the LCC and subsequently at the London Underground and the Coal Control) – but marriage in 1916 to the wealthy American Fabian Violet Pike brought relief to his financial position.

The rise and fall of Penty's architectural reputation, according to his own testimony, provided the impetus for his interest in social and economic questions. In 1934 he reminisced about his early days:

> By profession I am an architect, and as a young man I met with a great deal of success. Opportunities came to me when I was barely out of my teens; illustrations of my work appeared in the architectural papers, and I came to be regarded as one of the coming men in my profession. Then after several years of prosperity my fortune changed. The ground slipped away under my feet. Commissions ceased to come my way, and from being somebody I fell to the position of being nobody; and this not because of anything I had done or failed to do, but because of a combination of circumstances, chief among which was that economic changes had destroyed the prosperity of that section of the middle class who had been accustomed to give me work. In such circumstances my mind naturally turned to economics . . . .[16]

Indeed Penty stated that it was his own personal experience – especially as an arts and crafts man whose business had been destroyed by 'large organisations and financiers'[17] – that formed the raw material for his 1906 book, *The Restoration of the Gild System*.

According to his autobiography, Penty began work on his guild theory in 1902. The origin of his interest in guilds lay in English sources, specifically in Ruskin, 'with whom we supposed the idea to have originated', nothing being known about the work done along similar lines by the European Catholic socialists.[18] Penty's book was above all an attack on Fabian collectivism and it was as

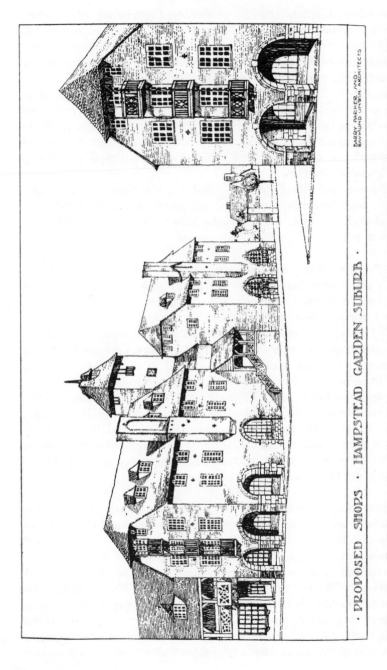

6.2 A. J. Penty (for Parker and Unwin): the twin entrance buildings to Hampstead Garden Suburb (1909) (from R. Unwin, *Town Planning in Practice*, 1909)

an anti-Fabian manifesto that the book acquired its reputation.[19] Penty recalled that the impetus for the work had come from an architectural exchange, 'a conversation I had with the then secretary of the Fabian Society, Mr E. R. Pease, one day in July 1902' about the newly completed building for the London School of Economics:

> The new building of the School of Economics in Clare Market had just been completed, and as the scheme had been promoted by Mr Sidney Webb the Fabians surveyed it with a sense of possession. 'What do you think of our new building' said Mr Pease to me. Knowing it to be a piece of very incompetent architecture I hesitated for a moment . . . . He did not wait for me to reply, but went on 'I suppose you are thinking about the architecture. Well, we didn't take much trouble about that. We got our architect through a competition which we decided on the statistical method'. 'What!' I exclaimed. 'Well' he continued 'we invited three architects to compete. Dr Garnett and I measured up the floor areas of each of the designs and we selected the one with the greatest area in the class rooms'.

To Penty this was inexcusable.

> That did it. I had been attracted to socialism by the writings of Morris, and I had somehow managed to persuade myself that the socialism of Morris and that of the Fabian Society had something in common. But any illusions I might have [had] were now entirely dispelled. I saw that the principles of Morris and Fabianism were opposed, and that by no possible means could Fabian policy eventuate in the Utopia of Morris.[20]

In the book Penty claimed that collectivism had established itself as the only popular alternative to the existing social system: but that in proposing to replace individual competition by nationalisation, collectivism would leave untouched the fundamental evil, which was the search for profit. Indeed, he believed that nationalisation would only make things worse by abolishing the private patrons of the arts and instituting what he regarded as the bad taste of the mass as the arbiter of what was produced. The weakness in collectivist doctrine, he asserted, was its unwitting acceptance of the political economists' interest in people not as producers, but

as consumers: against this, Penty counterposed Ruskin's insistence
that 'man' must be considered first and foremost as a producer if
spiritual harmony was to be restored.

> From this standpoint a man's health, mental and moral, must
> depend upon the amount of pleasure he can take in his work
> . . . . To unite these warring forces in man and to make him
> once more simple, harmonious and whole, he must again be
> regarded first and foremost in his capacity as producer.[21]

In place of the existing economic system based on industrialism
and world trade, Penty advocated a return to the system that had
prevailed in the middle ages, when, he claimed, beauty not profit
had been the motive of enterprise, and production had taken place
in small workshops under masters subject to the controls and
regulations of the guilds. (To describe this system, Penty quoted
at length from Morris's lecture on 'Architecture, Industry and
Wealth' and Lethaby's paper on 'Education in Building'.) The
proper locus for reform was not the political but the industrial
sphere. Trade unions needed to revert to guilds: this meant putting
the craftsman not the financier in control. The arts and crafts
movement needed to join 'hands with other reform movements'
and persuade the public of the need for moral and spiritual reform:
for only by 'the regeneration of the spiritual life of the people'
would a return to the guild system become possible.[22]

Between the publication of *The Restoration of the Gild System* in
1906 and the outbreak of the First World War Penty produced a
stream of articles and reviews. Two main themes emerge from
these writings; first, Penty's insistence on architecture as a fine art
and on himself as an artist, his socialist sympathies notwithstanding; and second, his continuing emphasis on artisanal or
crafts production as the only valid system both of work and of art.

The architect differed from the painter or sculptor, Penty wrote
in 1907, in that the architect had to deal on a daily basis with the
public and 'battle with ignorance and stupidity as other artists
need not'.[23] The architect therefore daily had to defend his artistic
liberty from the interference of the client. The architecture departments of the public authorities offered no haven: the housing
schemes built to date by municipalities were, with few exceptions,
'simply vile', because in public departments artistic ability was

squeezed out by bureaucracy and architects subjected to Borough Engineers.[24] An architect with any artistic sensibility therefore had no choice but to rely on private clients, taking comfort in the fact that 'fine aesthetic perceptions' were still to be found among a small élite of patrons.[25]

This meant a contradiction between the demands of art and the dictates of politics. Art, Penty declared, depended on aristocracy, not on democracy, and anything done to harm the economic position of the wealthy would mean the end of art.[26] For the architect 'who still persists in taking his art seriously', even 'though a Socialist in sympathies', the only source of work was from wealthy individuals commissioning private houses. That, said Penty, 'is why there are so few architects in the Socialist movement': but for himself, Penty declared, 'I am accustomed to call myself a Socialist, and shall continue to do so'.[27]

The second theme was Penty's insistence on the necessity of small-scale production. Penty stood for the petty producers against both the large capitalist and the proletariat. The arts and crafts movement, in his view, had been killed by the power exercised over the independent craftsmen by the financiers and big companies. Liberty, he said, could be secured only when the individual had the capacity to 'stand on his own feet, which in practice means that he is able to set up in business on his own account'.[28] Only if the producer was allowed to give rein to his individuality in his work did either the work or the product have any value; otherwise 'he becomes a machine and the work will cease to interest him and us on that account'.[29] Machinery itself, which Penty defined as 'a barrier to expression', was to be avoided.[30] If socialism was to achieve its objectives, therefore, it would need to restore the 'system of industrial organisation under which our cathedrals were built'.[31]

GUILD SOCIALISM

The main vehicle for Penty's writings in the years between the publication of *The Restoration of the Gild System* and the outbreak of the First World War was *The New Age*, the socialist weekly edited from 1907 onwards by Penty's friend from Leeds, A. R. Orage. When Orage came to London he and Penty lived together for a time, and in June 1906, shortly after the publication of Penty's book, they formed the 'Gilds Restoration League', with the declared aims of creating 'a common understanding between the Arts and Crafts Movement and Trades Unionism' and promoting the guild system in the crafts, as a preliminary to the eventual transformation of trade unions into guilds.[32] But although it attracted a certain amount of interest, Penty's agitation for a restoration of craft guilds was of limited appeal and Orage was not prepared to make *The New Age* into its propaganda organ. Orage and Penty had some kind of break late in 1907, after Penty's return from the USA, and it was not until 1911 that Penty again started to write regularly for *The New Age*.

Guild socialism emerged as a major political force in 1912 in a form very different from that of its inception under Penty in 1906–7. Guild socialism in 1912 was primarily a response by socialist intellectuals to the great industrial struggles of the immediate pre-war years. Political and parliamentary action of the sort favoured by the Fabians was discredited by the failure of the hopes aroused by the election victory of 1906; in contrast, industrial struggle, with the inspiration of both French syndicalism and the American 'One Big Union' movement, offered the prospect not just of short-term success but also of imminent advance to socialism. In 1912 the South Wales miners, in the pamphlet 'The Miners' Next Step', rejected the official union policy of nationalisation and called instead for direct control of the mines by the mineworkers, to be achieved by militant industrial action.[33]

As a political theory guild socialism was primarily a British product: essentially it reworked the collectivist parliamentary formula in the light of the changed industrial situation. Like industrial unionism and the war-time shop stewards' movement, its basis lay in the pre-war and war economy when, as Europe first prepared for and then undertook a 'total war', unemployment fell and a severe 'labour famine' developed, giving the labour movement considerable industrial power. In these conditions industrial action appeared to offer the shortest route to socialism. This remained the case until the plausibility of direct political action was revived by the Russian Revolution of October 1917, and, more decisively, the industrial strength of the labour movement was undermined by the slump of 1920–21.

French syndicalism provided the impetus for the formation of the theory of guild socialism. Penty later recalled that

Orage seized the opportunity which this new labour creed presented of reviving the Guild idea. But this time the partnership was not with me but with Mr S. G. Hobson, who formulated the theory known as Guild Socialism or National Guilds . . . .[34]

Hobson's guild idea differed substantially from Penty's, with none of the medievalism or arts and crafts attachment of the latter. Whereas Penty left production in the hands of small master craftsmen and gave the guilds a merely regulative role, Hobson's guilds were more like American 'Big Unions'. Hobson's great theme was the abolition of the wage system, or 'wagery': instead of labour being treated as a commodity, under the guild system workers would be given a new status based on the control of production and a guaranteed livelihood.

Hobson came from the mainstream of the English socialist movement, with an ancestry that included the Fabian Society, the Independent Labour Party, the Labour Church, and even Letchworth Garden City. In his own view, Hobson was independent and critical alike of Fabianism, ethical socialism and marxism: he stood with Marx against Jevons on the theory of value, but opposed Marx on the materialist view of history, insisting on the ethical and voluntarist aspects of socialism. Thus in his programme of 1912 he demanded that labour should determine 'no longer to sell its work on a commodity valuation, but to seek a new *status*', which would bring the class struggle to an end.[35]

Hobson's ideas were published as articles in *The New Age* in 1912 and as a book, *National Guilds*, in 1914. But Hobson was abroad for most of the war and in his absence leadership of the guild movement was assumed by a group of young Oxford intellectuals – principally G. D. H. Cole, William Mellor and M. B. Reckitt – who in 1915 set up the National Guilds League. The goal of the League was to 'define and spread the ideas and ideals of guild Socialism among the organised workers': in this way trade unionism would be infused with socialist principles and socialism would be rejuvenated by its contact with trade unionism.[36] The League constituted the institutional basis of the guild socialist movement until the collapse of the movement in 1923.

Within the guild movement Penty was regarded as, in his own words, 'a bit of a heretic – something of an enigma'.[37] His book was recognised as the first to advance guilds as a solution to the social crisis, but on many substantial points his thinking departed from orthodox guild socialist theory. In an article in *The New Age* in February 1914 Penty contrasted his ideas with those of Hobson and Orage. Whereas he approached the question from the point of view of 'architecture and the crafts', Penty stated, their approach was from the point of view of democracy. He had a number of criticisms of the Hobson scheme. The reform of morals and thinking had to precede any reform of institutions. To attempt to establish guilds immediately, without a prior moral and spiritual revolution, would be at best fruitless and at worst disastrous: rather than proceeding by strikes, Penty wanted centres of co-operation to be established in the form of small workshops. Nor was he persuaded by Hobson's attack on 'wagery': the problem was not wages as such, but large organisations and factories.[38]

When the National Guilds League was formed, Penty remained apart; as he put it, national guilds were not guilds 'in my sense of the word, but . . . Syndicalism plus the State'.[39] But the war led him to believe that the take-over of industry by the workers in the manner envisaged by the National Guilds League might prove the best route to the eventual goal of local guilds. While making no attempt to conceal his reservations, in 1917 he joined the League, setting up a Hammersmith branch which met at his house.[40] In 1920 he stood for and was elected to the executive of the League, where he figured as one of the leaders of the anti-Communist group in the split in the League over Russia. In December 1920, at a special conference held to debate this issue, Penty's group were defeated and he together with five others resigned from the executive, although not from the League, of which he seems to have remained a member until the end.[41]

Penty spelled out his intellectual differences with Marx and Communism in an article in *The New Age* in 1918, entitled 'National Guilds v. The Class War'. The question, he said, was whether to take 'a purely materialist or . . . a spiritual conception of the nature of the problem that confronts us'.

> Marx fell into contradictions because as he was a materialist he was blind to the fact that the relationship of material things is one of reciprocity and not of causality. It is the attempt to invest a material force with the authority of final causality that leads materialist thinkers into contradictions. On the other hand, consistency of statement is only possible on the

assumption that final causality is sought for in the realm of the spirit; accepting phenomena as the manifestation of the spirit in the material universe.[42]

Penty further developed this critique in *A Guildsman's Interpretation of History* (1920), which was intended specifically to counter the 'materialist conception of history'.[43]

THE BUILDING GUILDS

In 1920, somewhat to its surprise, the guild socialist movement found itself the sponsor 'not only of a theory of social reconstruction, but also of a practical attempt to put workers' control of industry into operation within the framework of the capitalist system'.[44] The building industry offered exceptionally favourable conditions for the practical implementation of guild theory. Compared to other industries, the labour content in building was high, and the level of fixed capital low. As Cole pointed out, in most industries any attempt at guild production would have to be preceded by the expropriation of the owners of the means of production (whether factories, mines, or railway stock), but in the building industry the workers had only to set themselves up as a guild, hire the relatively modest amount of equipment and machinery that was needed, and they would be able to start producing.[45]

The factor that turned the building guild from a hypothetical possibility into a reality at the end of the First World War was the urgent demand by the state for building for social purposes, particularly social housing. An opponent of the building guilds within the guild socialist movement put the point bluntly in 1920:

> What the 'Building Guild' amounts to simply is that in the present peculiar conditions of that part of an industry (housebuilding), in which the capitalist cannot get an economic return for his outlay, it may be possible for the trade unions concerned to persuade public bodies who are being forced by social pressure to provide houses, to employ labour through a joint trade union committee, instead of through a contractor.[46]

In Britain from 1917 onwards the government made promises about its plans for a post-war housing drive and after the armistice committed itself to building half a million houses in three years. This meant that the building industry, seriously depleted by four years of war, was being asked to meet not just normal annual demand, but also the backlog of construction and repair work that had accumulated during the war, the demand generated by the intense boom in the commercial market, and, on top of that, the government's housing campaign. Any organisation that could supply the major component needed for building – labour – was in a powerful position in relation both to private builders and to the state, which might not have approved of the political ambitions of a guild but which was under an overwhelming political imperative to get the houses built.

These unusual conditions existed not just in Britain but in many countries that had taken part in the war. It is not surprising therefore that building guilds or similar bodies appeared in many countries at this time. A survey in 1922 reported that

> The other European countries in which the guild movement is in action are Austria, Hungary, Germany, Holland, France and Ireland, all of whom owe their inspiration to the example of the British building workers.[47]

Building guilds became particularly important in Italy, where they emerged from the producers' co-operatives into a national building guild in 1920; in Vienna, where they were involved in the anti-urban settlement movement of the post-Armistice years; in Amsterdam, where they undertook some of the city's major housing contracts; and above all in Germany, where the building guilds developed in the 1920s as a major element of municipal housing provision, especially in Berlin.[48] In the United States, despite the efforts of the Anglophile group around C. H. Whitaker and the *Journal of the American Institute of Architects*, neither a post-war housing programme nor a building guild movement got underway, although this did not stop Whitaker and his friends from extolling the virtues of the British guilds.

Penty was one of the first to see the possibilities for building guilds in post-war conditions. In a letter to the *Architects' and Builders' Journal* in April 1918, he spoke of the 'changed social and economic conditions of society' that would prevail after the end of the war:

Though public bodies could never be persuaded to give commissions to individual architects, practising on their own account, it would be different if architects were organised with the workers into guilds . . . .[49]

A year later he published an article in the *Journal of the American Institute of Architects* entitled 'Towards a National Building Guild'. Under the existing system of building production, Penty asserted, both architects and building workers were no more than slaves under the tyranny of the big departments: the 'workers in the building trades must make common cause with the architects to overthrow this tyranny by organising themselves into a National Building Guild'. Penty envisaged a guild which would hold a monopoly of labour and to which the state would delegate control of the industry. With profit replaced by responsibility as the motive of production, the guild would not only regulate apprenticeship and training but also

would be completely responsible for the erection and mainten-ance in repair of all buildings, whether required by individuals, other guilds or the state.

Membership of the guild would be extended not only to workers, salaried staff and architects but also (a clear departure from national guild orthodoxy) to contractors, on the grounds that they were 'more akin to medieval master masons than [to] employers in other industries'. The 'Government Housing Scheme' offered a unique opportunity: through the co-operation of architects and builders in the guild, the isolation and self-consciousness of the professional architect would disappear; the workers would recover 'that sponta-neity and joy of creation which was the heritage of the medieval craftsman'; and architecture would again become as it had been in the middle ages 'a communal tradition of design', as natural and common as speech.[50]

Penty was not the only person calling for a building guild. Within the building industry moves towards some sort of corporate or guild system dated back to 1914, when the London lock-out prompted one of the employers, the Christian socialist Malcolm Sparkes, to seek ways of ending the class war in the industry. During the war Sparkes developed the idea both of a Builders' Parliament and a National Guild of Builders, which he discussed with G. D. H. Cole in September 1918. Sparkes' suggestion of a Builders' Parliament was taken up in the Whitley scheme of industrial councils in 1918, thereby, according to Penty, pointing the way towards a guild system. From the Builders' Parliament came in August 1919 a proposal for a limitation of the rate of profit in the industry, and it was the rejection of this by the employers that in Penty's view 'led immediately to the organisation of the Building Guilds'.[51]

While Sparkes led in developing the idea of the building guild, the first guild was actually formed by Hobson. Hobson returned to England in 1917 and at the time of the armistice was working for the Ministry of Labour in Manchester; this gave him an *entrée* to the building unions and particularly to Richard Coppock, an official of the Operative Bricklayers Society and the National Federation of Building Trade Operatives. Hobson won Coppock over to the idea of forming a building guild based on the regional organisation of the NFBTO, and in a series of meetings held throughout Lancashire and the north-west in the latter part of 1919 gained the support of the rank and file. In January 1920 a large gathering in Manchester announced the formation of the Manchester Building Guild.

Coppock was on Manchester City Council, which like all other local authorities at the time was finding great difficulty in implementing the housing programme due to the labour shortage. The Council therefore took seriously the Guild's tender for 100 houses because, as Hobson put it, even though the guild had neither premises nor plant and only £200 in the bank, it had the labour to build the houses.[52] The Ministry of Health, the government department responsible for the housing programme, also looked favourably on the guild's proposal, for it believed that collusion by building contractors was a major factor in the catastrophic rise in prices that was threatening to bring down the housing campaign. It was probably this consideration, rather than (as Hobson later suggested) the sympathy for guild socialism of Unwin as chief architect and Addison as Minister that led the Ministry to enter negotiations with the Guild to find a suitable form of contract. The negotiations, started in January 1920, were extremely protracted: not until June 1920 was agreement reached and not until August was the Model Contract issued.[53]

News of the formation of the Manchester guild was enthusiastically received by building workers in London, where Sparkes had been in discussion with the local union leadership about a possible guild for some months. In February 1920 a meeting to publicise the Manchester scheme was organised, and in Walthamstow and Greenwich building workers set up guild committees on the Manchester example and opened negotiations with their local authorities over housing contracts.[54] In May 1920 Malcolm Sparkes, as secretary of the Guild of Builders (London) Ltd, issued the guild's prospectus.

According to Sparkes there were three essential features of a building guild.[55] First, control by the rank and file. This meant not just operatives, but also technicians and architects, for a guild, as distinct from a trade union, had to include all workers in a given industry, professional and managerial as well as manual. Second, continuous pay. Ever since Hobson's onslaught on 'wagery' in *The New Age*, it had been central to the guild idea that labour should cease to be a commodity 'to be purchased or not as required'. Accordingly the guildsman was guaranteed his pay for life, 'in sickness or accident, in bad weather or in good, at work or in reserve'.[56] Third, no dividends. Public service, not financial gain, was the motive for production; any surplus would 'under no circumstances be distributed as dividends' but would be 'used for the improvement of the service'. It was this principle of 'working at cost price and admitting no profit of any kind' that distinguished the English building guilds both from earlier ventures in co-operative production and from the building guilds set up in Germany at this time.

From these three essentials was to spring a revival of the craft spirit and the standards of craft work of the middle ages. 'We shall do work worthy of the Middle Ages', declared the London guild.[57] The guild system, said Sparkes, would 'revive craftsmanship to an extent which had not been seen since the Middle Ages'.[58] The aim of the guilds, wrote one observer in 1921, was to

> revive the true craft spirit of the Middle Ages. The modern Guild organisation is to provide scope for the craftsman which no industrial order has provided since the Middle Ages.[59]

An independent investigation into the guilds undertaken in 1921 found that these notions of good workmanship were realised to a large extent. The guild workforce was self-selected, with building

6.3 London Guild of Builders: housing at the Higham Hill estate, Walthamstow (1920)

workers volunteering for guild service and waiting to be 'called up':

> It is not to be expected that all the men who volunteer for the Guild are enthusiastic guildsmen. But Guild enthusiasts set the pace, and this is bound to affect all who are engaged on the job . . . .
> There is a notable absence of the lethargic movements which one is accustomed to see on all kinds of building work. Everybody appears to be working with a will . . . .
> Every guildsman I talked to appeared proud of the work the guild was doing . . . .[60]

The result was not just a high rate of output and consequent low cost, but also a high standard of finished work. 'Experts are virtually unanimous in the opinion that the workmanship of the Guildsmen, as regards quality, is markedly superior to that of workers on private contracts', wrote another investigator in 1922.[61] According to a Ministry of Health official, the work of the Manchester guildsmen was 'the best in England and Wales'.[62]

The largest of the guild contracts was at Walthamstow, which accounted for nearly 400 out of the total of approximately 1500 houses built by the guilds (Fig. 6.3). The London guild also built for Greenwich (190 houses) and Enfield (50 houses). The Manchester guild stated in December 1920 that it was carrying out contracts at Manchester (100 houses), Worsley (261), Bedwelty (100), Tredegar (100), Wigan (135), Rotherham (200), Wilmslow (100) and Halifax (200). The Ministry of Health had agreed to an initial limit of 20 contracts, with the understanding that more would follow if they proved successful. But the slump starting in the winter of 1920–21 put the employers on the offensive, with first the guild experiment and then the housing programme itself coming under attack, and in 1921 the Ministry called a halt to both.[63]

It was with a fine disregard for these events that in July 1921, only days after the Minister of Health had announced the suspension of the housing programme, the Manchester and London guilds combined to form the National Building Guild. Without public housing contracts the guilds were in a virtually impossible position. The attempt to find private contracts, which led the London guild to construct a factory in Paddington to supply the necessary joinery, proved largely unsuccessful. The guilds turned to the building unions for support, but with a steep rise in unemployment and wage cuts threatened, the unions were in no position to underwrite the guilds, and there were moreover substantial doubts about the probity of Hobson's financial management of the Manchester and national guilds.[64] In November 1922 the crunch came and the Manchester guild went bankrupt. The London guild managed to disentangle itself from the national guild and struggled on until 1924; but by January 1923 it was evident that the building guild movement had failed.[65] Discredited by the ignominious collapse of the building guilds, the guild socialists decided to 'wind up the movement rather than await its gradual dissolution', and by the end of 1923 the guild socialist movement was also dead.[66]

What was Penty's position in the building guilds? In accordance with guild theory, architects, surveyors and technicians had been invited to join the London guild: on local guild committees a seat was reserved for an architects' representative, and the board of the London guild included a representative of the 'Architects' and Surveyors' Guild Group', a support group formed by the Architects' and Surveyors' Assistants Professional Union. At the first national convention of the ASAPU in 1920 Penty was elected union president and he became the Group's representative on the London board.[67] In this capacity he shared in the collective responsibility for the direction of the London guild, although not (contrary to the impression given by one American report) in its day-to-day management.[68]

The problem with the involvement of architects in the guild was that in practice there was not much for them to do, since in the housing contracts the guilds were operating as contractors, and design and supervision rested with the local authority. Nonetheless Penty was confident in 1920 that this would not remain the case indefinitely and that, when the guilds moved on to schemes other than housing contracts, architects would become as important an element of the guild in practice as they were in theory. Following the suspension of the state housing programme the search for private contracts appeared to encourage this belief: in 1922 the National Building Guild published a book of plans for private houses, with designs contributed by 'a group of Architects who are interested in Guild development and are represented on the London Regional Council'.[69] As well as Penty, half-a-dozen younger architects from the garden city movement contributed, including J. C. S. Soutar (from 1915 the consulting architect to Hampstead Garden Suburb), Charles Cowles-Voysey, and Hennell & James. But the collapse of the guild shortly afterwards brought this initiative to an end.

Within the architectural world, Penty was the most substantial advocate of the building guilds. In a published lecture at the Architectural Association in April 1920 he explained how the guilds would lead to a full-scale revival of medieval conditions, with the division of labour ended by the integration of the architect with the builder.[70] In a lecture written for the American Institute of Architects later in the year, Penty expressed his confidence in the building guild movement, and looked forward to the 'guildization of other industries' as they too became unworkable on a capitalist basis. At present, he conceded, the guilds had to 'conform to modern practice' and 'use the most up-to-date machinery': but once victorious they would abandon modern practices and 'tend increasingly to approximate to the medieval type'.[71] The guilds, he wrote in the *Journal* of the AIA in 1920, were the answer to the 'crisis in architecture'.[72]

While publicly giving support to the guilds, Penty's own thought was moving in a rather different direction. If the building guilds followed the line of Penty's 1906 book in regarding the advance to socialism and the revival of artistic labour as intimately connected, the tendency in Penty's own thought was towards a separation of the social and economic from the artistic, at least so far as immediate practical policy was concerned. Penty's interest focused increasingly on the question of currency, and he started to see guilds less as an end in themselves than as a consequence of changing the way in which prices were determined. Penty wanted prices to be settled by moral rather than market force. 'Let us just insist on the Just price and the Guilds will follow in its train', he wrote in 1920.[73] This change to the 'just price' now appeared to him as the key in changing from production for profit to production for need, and hence as the answer to the various economic questions of agriculture, machinery, credit and world trade. This notion was first advanced in *Guilds, Trade and Agriculture*, published in 1921, and was further developed in later writings of the 1920s and 1930s.[74]

Penty's 1923 lecture to the National Guilds Council, 'A Guildsman's Criticism of Guild Socialism', both gave his conclusions on the building guild experiment and indicated the direction in which his thought was tending. The comparison of 'Guilds as they existed in the Middle Ages and as they were advocated by National Guildsmen & given practical application in the Building Guilds' revealed the basic difference that the modern guilds 'are democratic through and through, while the Medieval Guilds are aristocratic and democratic at the same time'. Both the democratic and the aristocratic principles were needed (they were 'the warp and woof of which all true societies are woven'); without the aristocratic principle, 'mastership' became impossible, and from this arose the failure of the building guilds. Attempting to be only democratic, their administration had quickly become lost in a maze of committees, and they had been unable to accept the difference in status between salaried staff and the rank and file, undermining co-operation between the two groups and leading to demoralisation.[75] If the guild movement was to be re-built, Penty stated, it would have to avoid this basic mistake by adopting the principle of mastership, emphasising the regulative rather than the productive role of the guilds, and seeking the replacement of the economic by the just price.[76] While the bulk of these ideas (particularly the concept of regulative guilds and the belief in aristocracy) derived from his pre-war thinking, the greater emphasis on mastership and control was clearly indicative of Penty's subsequent support for Mussolini's Fascism.[77]

7

Ruskin and the Moderns

If the collapse of the building guild experiment meant the demise of the Ruskinian tradition *per se*, it did not mark the end of Ruskinian influence on architectural thought. On the contrary, Ruskinian ideas continued to play a major part in twentieth-century thought. In particular, modernism, which has been widely seen as the dominant strand in architectural thought between the 1920s and the 1960s, drew to a significant extent on the Ruskinian tradition, developing partly in reaction to, but also partly in continuation of, the main postulates of the Ruskinian position.

It would be unnecessary to make this point were it not for the widely held belief that modernism owed nothing to Ruskin. It is indeed a curiosity that while the role played in the development of modernism by others in the Ruskinian tradition (most obviously William Morris) has been emphasised, if not exaggerated, the case with Ruskin himself has been the opposite, and it is widely thought that modernism arose from a caesura with Ruskinian thought.

The prevalence of this view can be attributed to the way that the history of modernist thought was presented in two highly influential studies: Nikolaus Pevsner's *Pioneers of the Modern Movement* and Reyner Banham's *Theory and Design in the First Machine Age*. Written respectively in the 1930s and the 1950s, both are still in print (Pevsner in the revised 1960 version, renamed *Pioneers of Modern Design*; Banham in the 1980 edition), and both continue to be used widely as textbooks in schools of architecture and design. Successive generations of architects and designers, particularly in Britain, have been raised on these books, which are widely regarded as the authoritative studies of modern architectural thought. And while Banham's interpretation differed in several key respects from Pevsner's (and was indeed conceived as a deliberate revision of the Pevsnerian view), in one important respect Pevsner and Banham were at one: both excised Ruskin from modern architectural thought.

Pevsner's *Pioneers of the Modern Movement*, based on work done in Germany in 1930–32 but published in Britain in 1936, was a book with a theorem, presenting the 'Modern Movement' (a term popularised by Pevsner) as a much-needed revolt against the Victorian mania for elaborate and useless decoration. Pevsner's thesis was that the 'Modern Movement' was 'a synthesis of the Morris Movement, the development of steel building, and Art Nouveau'.[1] For Pevsner William Morris was a hero ('without William Morris . . . no Modern Movement would have started on the Continent')[2] and Ruskin was, if not a villain, at least not far from it. For in Pevsner's eyes Ruskin was the archetypal Victorian theorist of decoration, and therefore the figure ultimately responsible for the 'comedy' of the nineteenth-century 'Battle of the Styles' against which, according to Pevsner, the efforts of Morris and after him the 'Modern Movement' were directed.[3] While the deference accorded to Ruskin by Morris made Pevsner stop short of attacking Ruskin outright, the implied criticism was clear, and in Pevsner's account of the origins of modernism Ruskin was left on the sidelines, given no more than a passing mention as a mentor of Morris and excluded from Pevsner's roll of honour of modernist 'pioneers'.

Although Reyner Banham was a Ph.D student of Pevsner's at the Courtauld Institute in the 1950s, Pevsner's antipathy to Ruskin was one of the few Pevsnerian elements discernible in Banham's study. Banham's thesis, published in 1960 as *Theory and Design in the First Machine Age*, was the product of the faith in technology of the late 1950s and early 1960s – a faith of which Banham regarded himself as the prophet. The thrust of Banham's interpretation was that modernist architectural theory, in the form in which it coalesced in Europe during and immediately after the First World War, was Futurist in origin and, latently, in nature; from this Banham was able to go on to castigate the modernists of the 1920s for departing from the technological orientation of their 'original' Futurist inspiration. To cement this view of the Futurist basis of modernist thought, Banham proposed that there was one element on which all the modernist thinkers, whatever their other differences, were agreed: the rejection of Ruskin.

> Men whose means of moving ideas from place to place had been revolutionised at their writing desks by the type-writer and the telephone, could no longer treat the world of technology with hostility or indifference, and if there is a test that divides the men from the boys in say, 1912, it is their attitude

to Ruskin. Men whose view of the aims of art and the function of design were as diverse as could be, nevertheless united in their hatred of *ce déplorable Ruskin*.[4]

Banham's book has had and continues to have enormous influence over the understanding of modern architectural thought. Yet the suggestion that modernism arose from a complete rupture with Ruskin was misleading. On the contrary, not only did modernism develop historically from a basis in Ruskinian thought, but there remained within modernist thinking powerful legacies of the Ruskinian system. This is not to say, of course, that modernism is reducible to Ruskinianism, or to imply that there was nothing 'new' about modernism: but if we are to get both modernism and the Ruskinian tradition into perspective, regard must be given to the continuities as well as the differences between them.

The position can be clarified if we look briefly, not at those thinkers generally regarded as part of the twentieth-century Ruskinian strand, such as Unwin or Geddes in Britain or Mumford in the USA, but at three figures who in virtually every account are seen as central to the development of modernism: Le Corbusier, Walter Gropius and Frank Lloyd Wright. A brief examination of the impact of Ruskinian ideas on the development of modernist thought in, respectively, France, Germany and the USA, is perhaps the best way to counter the notion that Ruskin 'had nothing to do' with modernism.

Any understanding of the development of European architectural thought in the first thirty years of this century must take cognisance of the vogue for Ruskin that swept Europe around the turn of the century. Largely unknown until then outside the English-speaking world – in part as a result of his perverse refusal to allow his books to be translated – Ruskin was seized upon in the latter half of the 1890s, primarily as the apostle of the artistic concerns of the *fin de siècle* – the symbolic, the primitive and the natural – but also as the theorist of the English arts and crafts and as a Christian social thinker. Coming at the height of this interest in his work, Ruskin's death in 1900 removed his perverse embargo on translations and unleashed in Europe a flood of Ruskinian issues, both exegetical works and translations of the major texts. By 1905 books by and on Ruskin had appeared *in extenso* in French, German, Spanish and Italian, and also in Dutch, Danish, Catalan, Polish, Hungarian and Russian. It was in this situation that many of the figures who

in the 1920s were to be the leaders of European modernism came
to maturity, including Le Corbusier (born in 1887 in French
Switzerland) and Walter Gropius (born in 1883 in Berlin).
In France Ruskin's art criticism had created a ripple of interest
in the 1860s but thereafter had been ignored. In mid-nineteenth-
century France Ruskin's emphasis on the morality and intellectual
content of art, rather than on invention and technique, was seen
as provincial and ill-informed. In the artistic climate of the *fin de
siècle* in contrast these same characteristics exerted a powerful
fascination, with the result that, as Marcel Autret has shown,
Ruskin became celebrated in the artistic and intellectual circles of
the French-speaking world. Revived initially as the theorist of the
English decorative arts (by G. O. Destrée, *Les Préraphaelites. Notes
sur l'art decorative et la peinture en Angleterre*, 1894), in the second
half of the 1890s Ruskin was heralded as the originator of the
movement in art away from the rational and the classical towards
the symbolic and the primitive. In *Ruskin et la Religion de la Beauté*
(1897) Robert de la Sizeranne hailed Ruskin as 'the Prophet
of Beauty', announced himself a convert to this religion and
propounded the idea of 'pilgrimages', in the steps of the prophet,
to the locations immortalised in Ruskin's writings – an idea soon
taken up by Proust. Ruskin was also regarded with favour by the
Catholics of the *Ralliement* as a writer who addressed social
problems from a religious standpoint, and extracts from his work
were translated by *Le Sillon* and the *Union pour l'Action Morale*. The
leading figure in the latter, Paul Desjardins, was Marcel Proust's
professor, and in Proust's celebration of Ruskin these various
strands – *fin-de-siècle* aestheticism, Catholic reformism, anti-
rationalism – came together: for Proust (who on Ruskin's death
claimed to know the *Seven Lamps*, *Bible of Amiens*, *Val d'Arno* and
Praeterita by heart), the significance of Ruskin was that he made
beauty, morality and poetry all one. Works of exegesis in French
in the decade after 1895 were accompanied by translations of
extracts from Ruskin's works and, after 1900, by translations of the
major works, including *The Seven Lamps of Architecture* (1900), *Unto
this Last* (1902), *The Bible of Amiens* (1904, translated by Proust),
Mornings in Florence (1906), *The Stones of Venice* (1906, in the abridged
version), *Sesame and Lilies* (1906, also translated by Proust), and *The
Nature of Gothic* (1907).[5]
     The art school at La Chaux-de-Fonds, under Charles L'Eplattenier,
shared in this Ruskinian enthusiasm: L'Eplattenier stocked the

7.1 Le Corbusier: Ducal Palace, Venice, window detail (1907)

school's library with French translations of Ruskin and instituted a scheme of instruction based on Ruskin's precept of studying nature. It was this school that Le Corbusier entered in 1900 to study his father's craft of watchcase-engraving, and his attendance there until 1907 constituted the main element in his formal education. Not only did Le Corbusier study under this Ruskinian regime, but he imbibed from L'Eplattenier the devotion to Ruskin; as Le Corbusier later recalled, both of them 'passionately admired Ruskin'.[6] In 1907, on leaving the school, Le Corbusier went on a visit to Italy with Ruskin's *Les Matins à Florence* in hand, and in Italy saw, and drew, like Ruskin (Fig. 7.1).

As Paul Turner has shown, the Italian trip of 1907 marked the high point of Le Corbusier's deference to both Ruskin and L'Eplattenier. From the time of his entry into the office of Auguste Perret in 1908 his thought developed in both a rationalist and a technocratic direction, culminating in the 1920s in his enthusiasm for Fordism. Nonetheless his admiration for Ruskin remained. In *L'Art decoratif d'aujord'hui* (1925) he accorded Ruskin first place in the revival of the decorative arts, stating 'Our childhood was encouraged by Ruskin' and recounting enthusiastically the episode from *The Stones of Venice* in which Ruskin revealed the 'mendacity' of the tomb of Doge Andrea Vendramin. Le Corbusier concluded

> That was how Ruskin with his profound exhortations shook our youthful understanding.[7]

In 1941, assessing the contribution to the revival of architecture made by various countries, Le Corbusier again paid tribute to Ruskin:

> It was the English who preached the first aesthetic crusade; after the dawn of the machine age, the voice of Ruskin was heard. Painters, craftsmen, architects brought to life the Ruskin aesthetic. The new garden suburbs surrounded London with a measure of architectural revival. But the thought of Ruskin alone was an insufficient base.[8]

Notwithstanding this reservation, the overall conception of architecture that Le Corbusier had learned in his early days stayed with him: architecture remained for Le Corbusier, as it had been for Ruskin and L'Eplattenier, an affair of the spirit. In *Vers une architecture* (1923) (translated into English as *Towards a New Architecture*, 1927), Le Corbusier gave his famous definition of architecture:

> ARCHITECTURE is a thing of art, a phenomenon of the emotions, lying outside questions of construction and beyond them. The purpose of construction is TO MAKE THINGS HOLD TOGETHER; of architecture TO MOVE US . . . . Architecture is a matter of 'harmonies', it is 'a pure creation of the spirit'.[9]

This definition, drawing a clear distinction between architecture and building, relegating material concerns to the latter and locating architecture solely in the realm of the spirit, was entirely consistent with the definition given by Ruskin at the start of *The Seven Lamps of Architecture* (see above, p. 16). For, as Le Corbusier succinctly put it, 'It is of spirituality that Ruskin spoke'.[10]

Within German culture the take-up of Ruskin's ideas at the turn of the century was scarcely less dramatic than in the French. Germany was emerging from the most rapid process of industrialisation yet seen in Europe, and a major artistic concern there was to reconcile the new industrial society with the established ideas about art inherited from the great age of German Romanticism. Above all it was for a lead on this question that the Germans looked to Ruskin.

Ruskin was published as extensively in Germany as in France. In 1898 Heitz of Strasburg launched the 'Selected Works of Ruskin' in German translation; by 1903 fifteen volumes had been published, including four volumes of selected writings on art (including 'The Nature of Gothic'), *The Stones of Venice* (abridged version, in two volumes), *Mornings in Florence*, *Queen of the Air*, *The Eagle's Nest* and *Praeterita*. In the same years exegetical works were published by Fechheimer (1898), Sänger (1901) and von Bunsen (1903).

One of the leading German promoters of Ruskin was Hermann Muthesius, who in 1907 was to set up the Deutsche Werkbund to unite art and industry in mass production. From 1896 to 1903 Muthesius was attached to the German embassy in London, investigating English architecture and design: from London he sent reports on English subjects for publication in German magazines, including 'John Ruskin' (1900) and 'Ruskin in German Translation' (1901), and on his return published the monumental *Das Englische Haus* (3 vols, 1904–5), which included a succinct summary of Ruskin's thought. Ruskin was 'a prophet of . . . enormous importance to art':

> To the England of his day he was the prophet of a new artistic culture . . . . Ruskin was the first to reach the point of calling in question machine civilisation as a whole. He maintained that it made man himself a machine since it forced him to spend his whole life performing a single mechanical operation and was thus literally death to the worker's spiritual and material wellbeing.[11]

In 1914 the Werkbund was riven by the 'individualism versus standardisation' debate. In this famous controversy, Muthesius's emphasis on the needs of mass production was challenged by those who sided with Henry van de Velde in placing the emphasis on individual artistry. In this debate one of the supporters of van de Velde was Walter Gropius. Surprisingly little has been written about Gropius's intellectual development, although Hitchcock tells us that in the 1900s Gropius found in Ruskin's works the same sort of inspiration that van de Velde, the 'Belgian "Ruskinian"', had found a decade before.[12] Gropius's thought was marked by an attachment both to the new machine world of German industry and to the Romantic belief in the importance of the spirit. As he stated on his arrival in the USA in 1937:

> My ideas are often interpreted as the peak of rationalization and mechanization. This gives quite a wrong picture of my endeavours. I have always emphasized that the other aspect, the satisfaction of the human soul, is just as important . . . .[13]

Gropius's reputation rests largely on the Bauhaus, founded at Weimar in 1919: the teaching method developed there was subsequently replicated by Gropius in America (at Harvard, from 1937) and has been adopted for architectural and design education throughout the world. The Bauhaus was set up in the period immediately after the First World War when Gropius's thought was strongly coloured by 'Ruskinian romanticism'.[14] The goal of the Bauhaus as defined by Gropius in 1919 was to heal the split which had developed both within the individual and within society by reuniting the heart with the hand, the artist with the craftsman, and the thinker with the maker. In the famous Foundation Manifesto of April 1919 Gropius declared that artists and architects were to stop being mere brain-workers and become hand-workers as well: 'Architects, sculptors, painters, we must all return to the crafts!'.[15] The model for Gropius was the Gothic cathedral of the middle ages (depicted on the cover of the Bauhaus proclamation in a woodcut by Feininger) and the social organisation that had created it, the guild. The Bauhaus was to be a 'new guild of craftsmen', complete with guild statutes and the guild titles of master, journeyman and apprentice.[16]

After 1921, as the millenarianism that marked German thought of the immediate post-war years receded, Gropius gave renewed emphasis to 'the machine' as an inalienable fact of 'the age'. Even so, both the notion of the Bauhaus as the equivalent of the medieval guild and the ambition of healing the social rupture by integrating art and production remained. He stated in 1922 that 'the fragmentation of existence' was to be overcome by the 'new unity' provided by the Bauhaus;[17] but that, if the present age was to find expression in the way that 'the Gothic cathedral was the expression of its age', it was necessary to make use of the machine.[18] It was thus appropriate that in his major statement on the Bauhaus, 'The Theory and Organisation of the Bauhaus' (1923), Gropius should have cited Ruskin as the first of those who sought and found 'the basis of a reunion between creative artists and the industrial world'.[19]

With both Le Corbusier and Gropius, we can see the effect of the European interest in Ruskin of the early 1900s on the thought of two of those who were to be hailed in the 1920s as 'masters of modern architecture'. When we look at the development of architectural thought in the USA, we see a different picture: an absorption of Ruskinian ideas that was both earlier and, in the case of Frank Lloyd Wright, even more long-lasting.

The popularity achieved by and the importance attached to Ruskin in nineteenth-century America was, if anything, even greater than in Britain. The adoption of Ruskin's thought in the United States was, as both Roger B. Stein and H.-R. Hitchcock have noted, remarkable both for its speed and its extent – all the more so since the subject of Ruskin's first book, J. M. W. Turner, was scarcely known in the USA. In 1847 Ruskin's first book, *Modern Painters* I, was published in a pirated edition by John Wiley of New York, and its success was so great that it ensured American publication for Ruskin's subsequent *oeuvre*, all (until the change in copyright law in 1891) in pirated editions. Wiley issued volume II of *Modern Painters* in 1848 and the subsequent three volumes shortly after their English publication in 1856 and 1860, and published *The Seven Lamps of Architecture* within months of its London edition in 1849. Even minor Ruskinia, such as the early 'Poetry of Architecture' of 1837 and the polemical *Construction of Sheepfolds* were given American editions (the former very successfully). The only hiccup in the story was the first volume of *The Stones of Venice* (1851), which America found too technical; in consequence there was a gap of several years between the English (1853) and American (1860) publication of volumes II and III, although thereafter the work in its three-volume Wiley edition enjoyed wide popularity.[20]

The result of all this was that Ruskin became a major influence not just on specifically artistic thought and activity in nineteenth-century America but also on American thought more generally. Ruskin issues in the United States reached a peak in the 1880s, when they were purchased on a large scale by the new public libraries. *The Seven Lamps of Architecture* and the *Lectures on Architecture and Painting* were issued annually between 1884 and 1886, *The Two Paths* annually between 1883 and 1888, and *The Stones of Venice* annually between 1880 and 1890. In addition in 1884 Wiley started an edition of the 'Works of Ruskin', which was followed the next year by a rival from another New York publisher and, in 1891, by the authorised 'Brantwood' edition, with introductions by Ruskin's American disciple, the professor of art history at Harvard, Charles Eliot Norton.

Why did Ruskin's writings on art go down so well in the United States? Roger B. Stein has argued persuasively that Ruskin appealed to Americans essentially because he told them what they wanted to hear: that the world of art, which in nineteenth-century America was regarded as important but somewhat suspect, could be subjected to the same rules as the worlds of morality and nature, with which Americans felt thoroughly at home. Ruskin's artistic doctrine of 'truth to Nature' not only echoed the transcendentalist ideas of Emerson and his followers but had an attraction in the United States additional to any that it had in Europe and Britain: for in the American context, where 'Nature' meant native resource as against the 'Culture' of Europe, Ruskin's advice to 'go to Nature' also meant turning to indigenous America rather than the foreign European heritage.[21]

Nowhere was the chauvinistic appeal of 'going to Nature' stronger than in the Mid-West. The phenomenal growth of Chicago from the 1870s gave rise in succeeding decades to intense political and economic rivalry with the older-established East Coast (particularly New York), and in this process 'Nature' was identified with Mid-West agricultural virtue, as against the financial and cultural cosmopolitanism of the East Coast.

> We of the Middle West are living on the prairie. The prairie has a beauty of its own and we should recognize and accentuate this natural beauty . . . .[22]

The author here was Frank Lloyd Wright. Born in 1869, Wright came from a Welsh Unitarian family that had settled on the prairie in Wisconsin in the 1840s. The family values were the Bible, work and

> that ruthless but harmonious order I was taught to call nature. I was more than familiar with it on the farm.[23]

All these were values that young Wright (who his mother had determined should be an architect) found reiterated in Ruskin. As a teenager in the 1880s he was given by his school-teacher aunts the *Seven Lamps* and the *Stones of Venice*, and in addition to these he also read *Modern Painters* and *Fors Clavigera*.[24] Ruskinian precepts were reinforced by the years he spent in the office of Louis Sullivan, who followed Ruskin in seeing architecture as a spiritual affair for which the motifs were to be drawn from nature.

Ruskinian principles accordingly formed the basis of Wright's theory of 'organic architecture'. In one major area alone did Wright not follow Ruskin: in the specific concerns about industrial production and the division of labour that had culminated in 'The Nature of Gothic'. This can be seen most clearly in the question of 'the machine'. Whereas for Ruskin, contemplating the results in the 1840s of the first industrial revolution, 'the machine' meant the factory – and hence the 'division of men' and the fragmentation of society – for Wright in the 1880s and 1890s 'the machine' meant the agricultural machinery of his uncle's farm on the prairie, and hence implied harmony and natural order rather than the opposite. For Wright Ruskin's concern with the need to overcome the division of labour in architecture, and his proscription of machinery, made no sense.

For the rest, however, as John D. Rosenberg observed, the architectural notions propounded by Wright from the 1890s to the 1950s corresponded to the major points of Ruskinian theory.[25] For Wright, as for Ruskin in the *Seven Lamps*, spirit was the active force in architecture ('Architecture I know to be a Great Spirit . . .', as Wright put it in 1939)[26] and it was on this basis that architecture was

> to be distinguished from mere building. Mere building may not know spirit at all.[27]

Hence for Wright, as for Ruskin, architecture was subject to the laws of morality, and beauty was inseparable from goodness and truth. As Wright stated in the 1910 Berlin edition of his works, 'We feel the good, true and beautiful to be one with our own souls in any last analysis'.[28] Equally, for Wright as for Ruskin, harmony in art could be achieved only with harmony in individual and social life: 'we cannot have an organic architecture unless we achieve an organic society'.[29]

In this way of thinking the basis of art could be found only in nature. In the first volume of *The Stones of Venice* Ruskin stated that for architecture there were 'more valuable lessons to be learned in the school of nature than in that of Vitruvius'. From the turn of the century until his death in 1959 Wright reiterated again and again this conviction. In 1908 he declared that

> Nature furnished the materials for architectural motifs . . . her wealth of suggestion is inexhaustible . . . there is no source so fertile, so suggestive, so helpful aesthetically for the architect as a comprehension of natural law . . . [whereas] Vignola and Vitruvius fail, as they must always fail.[30]

In 1953 the message was the same.

> You must read the book of nature. What we must know in organic architecture is not found in books. It is necessary to have recourse to Nature with a capital N in order to get an education. Necessary to learn from trees, flowers, shells . . . .[31]

Without actually saying so (he was notoriously unwilling to acknowledge indebtedness to anyone), Wright was thereby reiterating the doctrine of the dependence of architecture on nature that Ruskin had made famous a hundred years before.

Conclusion

This book has been primarily concerned to give an historical account of the Ruskinian tradition; that is, to explain why these thinkers thought about architecture as they did. In the course of doing so, we have seen that this entire tradition stood rather closer to both German Romanticism and philosophical idealism, and rather further from both historical materialism and the orthodox socialist movement, than has generally been thought. In conclusion I want to move away from a primarily historical to a primarily critical concern, and ask how we should evaluate the legacy of the Ruskinian tradition today. The question to be answered is this: has this tradition, stemming as it did from Romantic ideas of nearly two hundred years ago, anything valid or useful to offer us as we approach the end of the twentieth century?

On one point, it seems to me, the Ruskinian tradition does have something useful to offer us: its recognition of the social character of architecture and architectural experience. To Ruskin and his followers, architecture was a product of society as a whole, and could not be treated in isolation from it: architectural experience was no more the exclusive preserve of one individual, whether architect or observer, than an historic building was the exclusive property of the individual who owned it. After Ruskin's death this notion of the shared character of architecture formed the currency of architectural thought during the period of the hegemony of modernism, but recently it has been under attack. Postmodernism, with its emphasis on the market and the commodity character of architecture, has tended to restore the rights of the individual proprietor as against those of society as a whole; while the New Right has emphasised the a-social individuality of both the architect as creator and the spectator as connoisseur.[1] Against both of these tendencies the Ruskinian tradition forms a useful bulwark.

For the rest, however, it seems to me that Ruskin and his followers have been responsible for introducing a number of unnecessary complications into architectural thought, and that today we ought to reject their legacy. For the sake of brevity I will focus on three concepts which are central to this tradition and which seem today to be highly problematic. These are the Ruskinian concept of work; the Ruskinian concept of production; and the Ruskinian concept of architecture as the means to social regeneration.

The Ruskinian concept of work can be objected to on three counts. The first is its essentially *rentier* character. The Ruskinian concept of work was an image of manual work as it appeared to a group or class (Ruskin, Morris, Carpenter *et al.*) who, unlike those they observed, did not have to work for a living and who were therefore able to indulge in fantasies about both the supposed pleasures of labour and the supposed attributes of the labourer. The joys and expressive potential ascribed to manual labour by the tradition based on 'The Nature of Gothic' were attributes imagined by those who never had to depend on manual labour for their livelihood, just as the object of the 'worker-worship' of this tradition was the manual workers as observed and imagined by others, not manual workers as seen by themselves.[2] To this misconception of work, the proper answer was Unwin's: we work not in search of joy or expression, but 'to produce enough wealth to keep us in comfort with as little labour as possible'.[3]

The second objection to the Ruskinian concept of work is that it arbitrarily gives value to one type of work over and against all others. Out of all the many different forms of labour in which people are involved – in farms, mines, factories, workshops, offices, schools, hospitals and so on – the Ruskinian tradition declares that only one, artisanal hand-work, is of value. Other forms of work, in which the hand is not involved or in which it is guided by something other than the heart, are declared inferior or invalid. While we can understand the historical circumstances in the nineteenth century that led to the formulation of this view, there is no reason to allow what was essentially a reaction against the down-grading of craftwork by industrialisation to remain a central ingredient of our thought.

The final objection to the Ruskinian concept of work is that it confines the term to male productive labour, and omits altogether female reproductive labour. For Ruskin and his followers, work is work only if it results in physical objects, that is, material products in which the spirit of the maker is embodied; work that results not in objects but in people – in other words, the work done by women in raising children and looking after families – is simply not seen. Hence it is no accident that women figure so little in this story, and that they do so only as consorts or when they abandon reproductive work in favour of productive work, and become makers of things.[4] Again, we can understand the historical circumstances that led to this theoretical blindness to reproductive work, but that is no reason to retain it today.

One of the hallmarks of the Ruskinian tradition was its concern with the relationship between architecture and its producers. It could obviously be objected that this is one-sided, in that it discounts the consumers of architecture, and that the test of the pudding lies in the eating, not the making (essentially Unwin's view). But even if we leave this aside, and take the emphasis on production on its own terms, it has to be stated that the Ruskinian concept of the production of architecture is inadequate. For the Ruskinians the production of architecture is always the production of art as conceived by the Romantics, an affair purely of the spirit in which the impetus comes from the maker seeking 'material in which to breathe his spirit' and thereby communicate with another spirit[5] – which is scarcely the motive for most of those who work in architecture and building. Even when dealing with their own times, the producer of architecture for the Ruskinians was always the descendant of Goethe's Master Erwin, not any actual carpenter, plasterer or surveyor of the nineteenth century. Major developments in nineteenth-century building – changes within the building site, the growth of monopoly contractors, the reorganisation of the craft unions, the development of the building professions – therefore do not figure in the scope of Ruskinian theory, because it has no way of relating material conditions of this sort to its notion of the production of architecture as a spiritual affair. There is no reason to think that Ruskin had ever visited a building site, let alone understood and analysed what was happening there, when he wrote 'The Nature of Gothic', and the deficiency was by no means remedied by those of his followers, notably Webb and Lethaby, who as architectural practitioners came into contact with the building industry in their daily work. When Lethaby encountered the palpably material reality of the London building trade unions at the Technical Education Board, his response, as we have seen, was merely to urge them to take up the Ruskinian task of injecting art into production by turning themselves into guilds.

The third of the central concepts of Ruskinian theory with which we should take issue is its millenarian conception of architecture – a conception that was particularly important in that it was taken over wholesale by modernism. When architecture was finally achieved, the Ruskinians believed, mankind would be reintegrated with itself and with the world and would become whole and complete once more. For the achieving of architecture (in Morris's definition, 'the turning of necessary articles of daily use into works of art') would mean the overthrow of the division of labour and with it, as Ruskin said, the division of men and the division of society.[6] Mankind would thereby become, to quote Penty, 'simple, harmonious and whole' once more.[7]

The most telling response to this was made in 1900, when the European vogue for Ruskin was at its height, by the Viennese architect and critic Adolf Loos. As an anglophile, Loos was well acquainted with Ruskinian theory through the English arts and crafts. His essay 'The Poor Little Rich Man' was a fairy story about a man who, in the manner of Ruskin or Morris, wanted to reintegrate life and art.

Loos's story concerned a happy and successful businessman, who decided one day to bring 'Art' into his life. He went to a famous architect who designed and had built for him a house that was a wonder-work of art.

> The rich man was overjoyed. Overjoyed, he walked through his new rooms. Wherever he cast his glance was Art, Art in each and everything. He grasped Art when he took hold of a door handle; he sat on Art when he settled into an armchair; he buried his head in Art when, tired, he laid it down on a pillow; he sank his feet into Art when he trod on a carpet.[8]

His achievement was lauded and the art critics were 'full of praise for the man who had opened up a new field with his "art in the utilitarian object"'.

But the attempt to render daily life into an art-work was not without its problems. The company responsible for the buses that passed in front of the rich man's door turned down his suggestion that, in place of their nonsensical ringing, its vehicles should adopt the bell-motif from *Parsifal*. The rich man himself found it rather oppressive to actually reside in art and 'preferred to be home as little as possible'.

> After all, one also wants to take a rest now and then from so much art. Or could you live in a picture gallery? Or sit through *Tristan und Isolde* for months on end?

Finally the rich man's birthday came and he was given many presents by his family and children: but all were banished by the architect as impermissible intrusions on the canvas of his art.

Then a transformation took place in the rich man. The happy man suddenly felt deeply, deeply unhappy. He imagined his future life. No one was allowed to give him pleasure . . . . None of his dear ones was permitted to give him a picture. For him there were to be no more painters, no more artists, no more craftsmen. He was precluded from all future living and striving, developing and desiring. He thought, this is what it means to learn to go about life with one's own corpse. Yes indeed. He is finished. *He is complete.*

The moral of Loos's story was that the only 'completeness' that could be achieved by turning life into art was the completeness of oblivion. As such it constitutes the epitaph of the Ruskinian dream.

Notes and References

ABBREVIATIONS

BAL	British Architectural Library
BL	British Library
CSAC	Central School of Arts and Crafts
FGCHM	First Garden City Heritage Museum, Letchworth
GLRO	Greater London Record Office
IISH	International Institute for Social History, Amsterdam
NCO	Nuffield College, Oxford
NDA	North Devon Athenaeum, Barnstaple
PC	private collection
RIBA	Royal Institute of British Architects
SPAB	Society for the Protection of Ancient Buildings
UMDAP	University of Manchester Department of Architecture and Planning
WLHL	Walthamstow Local History Library
V & A	Victoria and Albert Museum
WMG	William Morris Gallery, Walthamstow
Ruskin Works	E. T. Cook and A. Wedderburn (eds), *The Works of John Ruskin* (39 vols, 1903–12)
Morris Letters	P. Henderson (ed.), *The Letters of William Morris to his Family and Friends* (1950)
Morris Works	M. Morris (ed.), *The Collected Works of William Morris* (24 vols, 1910–15)
WMAWS	M. Morris, *William Morris: Artist, Writer, Socialist* (2 vols, Oxford, 1936)

Place of publication is London except where indicated.

INTRODUCTION

1. The main existing studies of the Ruskinian tradition are R. Macleod, *Style and Society. Architectural Ideology in Britain 1835–1914* (1971); and A. Saint, *The Image of the Architect* (1983) ch. 2, 'Myth and the Medieval Architect'.
2. D. Watkin, *Morality and Architecture. The Development of a Theme in Architectural History and Theory from the Gothic Revival to the Modern Movement* (Oxford, 1977); R. Scruton, *The Aesthetics of Architecture* (1979); M. Tafuri and F. Dal Co, *Modern Architecture* (Italian original 1976; English translation 1980); M. Tafuri, *Vienna Rossa. La Politica residenziale nella Vienna socialistica 1918–1933* (Milan, 1980).

3. Among others see 'Social Housing in the Weimar Republic' (special issue) *Architectural Association Quarterly*, 11, 1 (1979); 'Revising Modernist History: The Architecture of the 1920s and 1930s', (special issue) *Art Journal*, 43, 2 (1983); B. D. Finnimore, 'The Industrialisation of Building: Building Systems and Social Housing in Welfare Britain, 1942–75' (University of London PhD, 1986); A. Saint, *Towards a Social Architecture. The Role of School Building in Post-War England* (1987).
4. E. Gombrich, *In Search of Cultural History* (Oxford, 1969); E. Gombrich, 'Hegel and Art History', *Architectural Design*, 51 (1981) pp. 3–10; also M. Podro, *The Critical Historians of Art* (1982).
5. P. V. Turner, *The Education of Le Corbusier: A Study of the Development of Le Corbusier's Thought 1900–1920* (Harvard University D.Phil, 1971; New York, 1977).
6. F. Engels, 'Socialism: Utopian and Scientific' (1880), in K. Marx and F. Engels, *Selected Works* (3 vols, Moscow, 1969–70) 3, p. 132.
7. See for example R. Wittkower, *Architectural Principles in the Age of Humanism* (1949; 1973); P. Collins, *Changing Ideals in Modern Architecture 1750–1950* (1965).
8. See L. B. Walker, 'E. S. Prior, 1852–1932' (University of London PhD, 1978); A. Crawford, *C. R. Ashbee. Architect, Designer and Romantic Socialist* (1985); S. Beattie, *A Revolution in London Housing. The LCC Housing Architects & their Work 1893–1914* (1980).
9. WMG J126 Morris to J. Bruce Glasier, 15 Aug [1888/1890].

1   RUSKIN AND 'THE NATURE OF GOTHIC'

1. 'To B. R. Haydon' (1815), in E. de Selincourt and H. Darbishire (eds), *The Poetical Works of William Wordsworth* (Oxford, 1947 and 1954) p. 21. On Ruskin and Wordsworth, see Ruskin to Furnivall, 3 April 1855, in Ruskin Works, 5, p. 429.
2. For this section I have drawn on P. Frankl, *The Gothic. Literary Sources and Interpretations through Eight Centuries* (Princeton, NJ, 1960); W. D. Robson-Scott, *The Literary Background of the Gothic Revival in Germany. A Chapter in the History of Taste* (Oxford, 1965); and W. Vaughan, *German Romanticism and English Art* (1979). Also useful are F. Ewen, *The Prestige of Schiller in England 1788–1859* (New York, 1932) and C. von Klenze, *From Goethe to Hauptmann. Studies in a Changing Culture* (New York, 1926 and 1966).
3. J. W. von Goethe, *Von Deutscher Baukunst* (1772), in E. G. Holt, *A Documentary History of Art* (2 vols, New York, 1958) 2, p. 365.
4. Ibid., p. 367.
5. Ibid., p. 366.
6. Quoted in Robson-Scott, *The Literary Background*, p. 222.
7. Goethe, in Holt, *Documentary History*, p. 364.
8. Robson-Scott, *The Literary Background*, p. 90.
9. I. Kant, *Critique of Judgement* (1790), in B. Bosanquet, *A History of Aesthetic* (1892) pp. 260–1.

10. G. W. F. Hegel (trans. T. M. Knox), *Aesthetics. Lectures on Fine Art* (2 vols, Oxford, 1975) 1, pp. 60–3.
11. Quoted in Bosanquet, *History of Aesthetic*, p. 319.
12. *Principles of Gothic Architecture*, in F. von Schlegel (trans. E. J. Millington), *The Aesthetic and Miscellaneous Works of Friedrich von Schlegel* (1849) p. 175.
13. Ibid., p. 174.
14. Hegel, *Aesthetics*, 1, p. 12.
15. T. Carlyle, *Critical and Miscellaneous Essays* (5 vols, 1840) 1, p. 69.
16. Principal references are as follows: RIO – Ruskin to J. J. Ruskin, 15 February 1852, in J. L. Bradley (ed.), *Ruskin's Letters from Venice 1851–1852* (1955) p. 179; KUGLER – *The Stones of Venice* III (1853), in Ruskin Works 11, p. 360; PUGIN – *The Stones of Venice* I (1851), in Ruskin Works 9, p. 438; JAMESON – *Modern Painters* I (1843), in Ruskin Works 3, p. 150, and *Praeterita* (1885–89), in Ruskin Works 35, p. 373; EASTLAKE – entry for 29 July 1847, in J. Evans and J. H. Whitehouse (eds), *The Diaries of John Ruskin* (3 vols, 1956–59) 1, p. 351, and *The Seven Lamps of Architecture*, in Ruskin Works 8, p. 119; LINDSAY – review by Ruskin in the *Quarterly Review* (1847), in Ruskin Works 12, pp. 169–248. See also A. D. Holcomb, 'Anna Jameson: the first professional English art historian', *Art History*, 6, 2 (1983) pp. 171–87; and J. Steegman, 'Lord Lindsay's *History of Christian Art*', *Journal of the Warburg and Courtauld Institutes*, 10 (1947) pp. 123–31.
17. *Modern Painters* II (1846), in Ruskin Works 4, p. 57. On Ruskin's debt to German thought, see W. G. Collingwood, *The Art Teaching of John Ruskin* (1891) pp. 16–17 and Bosanquet, *History of Aesthetic*, pp. 441–2.
18. *Modern Painters* II (1846), in Ruskin Works 4, pp. 121 and 215–18; letter of 7 February 1852, in Bradley, *Ruskin's Letters*, pp. 166–7.
19. *Modern Painters* I (1843), in Ruskin Works 3, p. 624. For Ruskin's thought see J. D. Rosenberg, *The Darkening Glass: A Portrait of John Ruskin's Genius* (New York, 1961; 1963); G. F. Landau, *The Aesthetic and Critical Theories of John Ruskin* (Princeton, NJ, 1971); and K. O. Garrigan, *Ruskin on Architecture: his Thought and Influence* (Madison, Wisc., 1973).
20. *Modern Painters* I (1843), in Ruskin Works 3, p. 87.
21. Ibid., p. 95.
22. *The Stones of Venice* III (1853), in Ruskin Works 11, p. 201.
23. Ruskin to J. J. Ruskin, 10 July 1845, in Ruskin Works 4, p. xxxiv.
24. A.-F. Rio *De la poésie Chrétienne dans son principe, dans sa matière et dans ses formes* (Paris, 1836) pp. 190–4 and 538.
25. Ruskin to J. J. Ruskin, 15 February 1852, in Bradley, *Ruskin's Letters*, p.179.
26. 1855 Preface to *The Seven Lamps of Architecture*, in Ruskin Works 8, p. 11.
27. *The Stones of Venice* I (1851), in Ruskin Works 9, p. 438; *Modern Painters* III (1856), in Ruskin Works 5, p. 428. See also Garrigan, *Ruskin on Architecture*, pp. 18–28.

28. *Parliamentary Debates*, 5 & 6 Vict. 65, col. 1224 (T. Duncombe, 10 August 1842).
29. T. Carlyle, *Chartism* (1839), in A. Shelston (ed.), *Thomas Carlyle: Selected Writings* (Harmondsworth, 1971) pp. 152–3.
30. J. J. Ruskin to W. H. Harrison, 29 May 1849, in Ruskin Works 8, p. xxvi.
31. E. T. Cook, *The Life of John Ruskin* (2 vols, 1911) 1, p. 175.
32. Ruskin to M. R. Mitford, 21 April 1848, in G. A. Cate (ed.), *The Correspondence of Thomas Carlyle and John Ruskin* (1982) p. 12.
33. *Modern Painters* III (1856), in Ruskin Works 5, p. 428; see also Cate, *Correspondence of Carlyle and Ruskin*, pp. 1–3.
34. Ruskin, unpublished letter to *The Times*, 9 March 1852, in Ruskin Works 12, p. 593.
35. *Lectures on Architecture and Painting* (1854), in Ruskin Works 12, pp. 100–1.
36. Appendix on the Manuscript of *The Seven Lamps of Architecture*, in Ruskin Works 8, p. 278. See also Ruskin Works 8, pp. xix–xxxvi; and W. G. Collingwood, *The Life of John Ruskin* (1900) pp. 108–10.
37. *The Seven Lamps of Architecture* (1849), in Ruskin Works 8, p 28.
38. Ibid., p. 248.
39. Ibid., p. 136.
40. 'Explanatory Note to the Venetian Index', *The Stones of Venice* III (1853), in Ruskin Works 11, pp. 356–7. See also Ruskin Works 11, p. xvi.
41. *The Stones of Venice* I (1851), in Ruskin Works 9, pp. 47 and 57–8.
42. *Modern Painters* I (1843), in Ruskin Works 3, p. 93.
43. Ibid., p. 94.
44. Ibid.
45. *The Seven Lamps of Architecture* (1849), in Ruskin Works 8, p. 46.
46. Ibid., p. 82.
47. Ibid., p. 119; C. Eastlake, *Contributions to the Literature of the Fine Arts* (1848) pp. 351–96.
48. *The Seven Lamps of Architecture* (1849), in Ruskin Works 8, pp. 190–1.
49. Ibid., p. 218.
50. *The Stones of Venice* I (1851), in Ruskin Works 9, p. 291.
51. Ibid., p. 291.
52. Ruskin to J. J. Ruskin, 22 February 1852, in Ruskin Works 10, p. 180.
53. According to Cook, the definition in terms of the forms of Gothic dated from 1849; Ruskin Works 10, p. liii.
54. *The Stones of Venice* II (1853), in Ruskin Works 10, p. 188.
55. Ibid., p. 190.
56. Ibid., pp. 191–2.
57. Ibid., p. 192.
58. Ibid., p. 193. Cf. Carlyle, *Past and Present* (1843), in *Thomas Carlyle's Works. The Standard Edition* 3 (18 vols, 1906) pp. 178–9.
59. Carlyle, *Past and Present*, p. 157.
60. Ibid., p. 129.
61. *The Stones of Venice* II (1853), in Ruskin Works 10, pp. 193–4.
62. Ibid., p. 196.

63. Ibid.
64. Ibid., p. 201.
65. Ibid.
66. Ibid., p. 204.
67. Ibid., p. 267.
68. Ruskin to J. J. Ruskin, 1 August 1853, in Ruskin Works 10, p. lix.
69. *Lectures on Architecture and Painting* (1854), in Ruskin Works 12, pp. 100–1.
70. *Daily News* (4 April 1899), in Ruskin Works 10, p. lx.

2 PHILIP WEBB: ARCHITECTURE AND SOCIALISM IN THE 1880s

1. M. Girouard, *The Victorian Country House* (Oxford, 1971; expanded edn, 1979) p. 79. The main secondary studies of Webb are J. Brandon-Jones, 'Philip Webb' in P. Ferriday (ed.), *Victorian Architecture* (1963) and R. J. Curry and S. Kirk, *Philip Webb in the North* (Middlesbrough, 1984).
2. W. R. Lethaby, *Philip Webb and his Work* (Oxford, 1935; expanded edn with introduction by G. Rubens, 1979) p. 116. All references are to the 1979 edition.
3. Investigation of the clients of the 49 'more important' buildings by Webb (Lethaby, *Philip Webb*, pp. 269–74) gives the following results: commissioned by artists, 5; commissioned by art-patrons, 19; commissioned by friends or relatives of artists or art-patrons, 19; commissioned by friends of friends of artpatrons, 1; unclassified, 5.
4. D. Cherry, 'The Hogarth Club: 1858–1861', *Burlington Magazine*, 122 (1980) pp. 238–42; also N. Pevsner, 'Colonel Gillum and the Pre-Raphaelites', *Burlington Magazine*, 95 (1953) pp. 78 and 81.
5. Ruskin to W. Hale White, 27 October 1867, in D. V. White, *The Groombridge Diary* (1924) pp. 40–1.
6. E. P. Thompson, *William Morris: Romantic to Revolutionary* (1955; revised edn, 1977) pp. 109 and 172.
7. BL Add MSS 45354 f38–39 Webb to Boyce nd [1871].
8. BAL LeW/2/6.
9. Webb to Major Godman, 10 December 1879, in J. Brandon-Jones, 'Notes on the Building of Smeaton Manor', *Architectural History*, 1 (1958) p. 56.
10. Webb to C. L. Eastlake, 14 March 1870, in J. Brandon-Jones, 'Letters of Philip Webb and his Contemporaries', *Architectural History*, 8 (1965) p. 66.
11. V & A 86 TT 13 Webb to Morris, 3 October 1892 and 6 June 1893. See also Lethaby, *Philip Webb*, pp. 124–5.
12. BAL Begley papers B10 Box 1 no 2002, C. C. Winmill to W. W. Begley, nd. On Winmill, see J. Winmill, *Charles Canning Winmill. An Architect's Life by His Daughter* (1946).

13. BAL LeW/2/5.
14. BAL LeW/1/15. See also LeW/2/5 Webb to Cockerell, 16 December 1902.
15. Thompson, *Romantic to Revolutionary*, p. 25.
16. BAL LeW/2/6.
17. BL Add MSS 45354 f34–35 Webb to Boyce, 14 April 1871; f93–94 Webb to Boyce, 17 March 1877; f231 Webb to Boyce, 18 August 1885; BAL LeW/1/6, L. Bell to Webb 13 April 1900.
18. BAL LeW/2/5. On Robson see D. E. B. Weiner, 'The Institution of Popular Education: Architectural Form and Social Policy in the London Board Schools 1870–1904' (Princeton University PhD, 1984) p. 187.
19. See Shaw's comment on Street in Lethaby, *Philip Webb*, p. 75; also D. B. Brownlee, *The Law Courts. The Architecture of George Edmund Street* (1984) pp. 269–73.
20. SPAB Webb Papers, Webb to *Stratford-on-Avon Herald*, 28 July 1887.
21. Lethaby, *Philip Webb*, p. 118.
22. PC, Webb to Estcourt, 25 January and 3 February 1882.
23. 'Artists' Homes. No 8: Mr Val C. Prinsep's House, Kensington', *Building News*, 39 (29 October 1880) p. 511.
24. BL Add MSS 45354 f89 Webb to Boyce, nd [15 February 1877]; also f71–2 Webb to Boyce, 13 August 1885.
25. Lethaby, *Philip Webb*, p. 27.
26. Morris to Andreas Scheu, 5 September 1883, in *Morris Letters*, p. 186.
27. G. Burne-Jones (ed.), *Memorials of Edward Burne-Jones* (2 vols, 1904) 1, p. 277.
28. BL Add MSS 45354 f15–16 Webb to Boyce, 14 September 1869.
29. Lethaby, *Philip Webb*, p. 136.
30. BAL LeW/2/1 Webb to C. Astley, 26 May 1904.
31. BL Add MSS 45354 f83 Webb to Boyce, 10 September 1976. See also Curry and Kirk, *Webb in the North*, pp. 18–20.
32. G. Howard, 10 May 1906, quoted in A. Penn, *The Building of Saint Martin's Church, Brampton* (Brampton, 1972) p. 19.
33. G. A. Grey, 30 August 1879, quoted in Penn, *Saint Martin's Church*, p. 15.
34. Webb to W. Weir, 1 March 1902, quoted in Penn, *Saint Martin's Church*, p. 21.
35. PC, P. Wyndham to Webb, 28 April 1883.
36. PC, P. Wyndham to Webb, 15 January 1886.
37. PC, P. Wyndham to Webb, 18 July 1886.
38. PC, P. Wyndham to Webb, 13 November 1893; Webb to Wyndham, nd [November 1893].
39. 'On Philip Webb's Town Work', *Architectural Review*, 2 (1897) pp. 199–208.
40. H. Ricardo, 'The House in the Country', *Magazine of Art* (1900) p. 110.
41. J. Rae (1891) quoted in S. Yeo, 'A New Life: the Religion of Socialism in Britain, 1883–1896', *History Workshop*, 4 (1977) p. 7. For this section I have drawn also on Thompson, *Romantic to Revolutionary* and

S. Pierson, *Marxism and the Origins of British Socialism. The Struggle for a New Consciousness* (1973).

42. *Commonweal*, 6, 238 (2 August 1890) p. 246 and 6, 253 (15 November 1890) pp. 361–2.
43. Lethaby, *Philip Webb*, pp. 240–1; BAL LeW/1/6 Webb to Boyce, nd [autumn 1871 and 1872].
44. BL Add MSS 45354 f93–94 Webb to Boyce, 17 March 1877.
45. BL Add MSS 45354 f95 Webb to Boyce, nd [14 April 1877].
46. Lethaby, *Philip Webb*, p. 242.
47. V & A 86 TT 13 Webb to Morris, 3 February 1885.
48. V & A 86 TT 13 Webb to K. Faulkner, 28 March 1885.
49. Faulkner suffered an incapacitating stroke in 1888 and died in 1892; Morris's health collapsed in 1891 and he died five years later.
50. IISH Socialist League papers 525a Bloomsbury Branch, List of members; 3459 (3) Bloomsbury Branch, 'Free Lectures' (January 1886); Lethaby, *Philip Webb*, p. 241; RIBA LeW/2/1 Webb to K. Faulkner, 17 February 1886.
51. BAL LeW/2/1 Webb to C. Faulkner, 9 October 1885.
52. IISH Socialist League Papers 114 Auditors' Report, 5 December 1885.
53. IISH Socialist League Papers 70 Council Meeting, Agenda, 1 February 1886; Socialist League Papers 102a Council Attendance Book, 1886–1888.
54. Socialist League *Report of the Third Annual Conference of the Socialist League* (1887) p. 3; IISH Socialist League Papers 3185 Webb to Sparling, June 1886.
55. IISH Socialist League Papers 54 General Meetings of London Members, Agendas, June–December 1886.
56. *Commonweal*, 2, 24 (26 June 1886) p. 104; 2, 35 (11 September 1886) p. 192.
57. 'Town and Gown', *Commonweal*, 2, 47 (4 December 1886) pp. 284–5.
58. BL Add MSS 45354 f240–241 Webb to Boyce, 17 October 1886.
59. BL add MSS 45354 f242–243 Webb to Boyce, 4 January 1887.
60. IISH Socialist League Papers 3180 Webb to Barker, 19 September 1887.
61. BL Add MSS 45354 f245–246 Webb to Boyce, 11 October 1887.
62. BL Add MSS 45354 Webb to Boyce, 8 May 1888; IISH Socialist League Papers 3182 Webb to F. Charles, 31 July–8 September 1888.
63. WMG J111 Morris to J. Bruce Glasier, nd [May 1888].
64. IISH Socialist League Papers 3182 Webb to Charles, 10 and 24 August 1888; 3183 Webb to Charles, September 1888; 3184 Webb to Charles, October–November 1888; 318 Ledger, Commonweal Accounts, 7 July–29 September 1888.
65. V & A 86 TT 13 Webb to Morris, 25 November 1890.
66. BL Add MSS 45893 Hammersmith Socialist Society, Minutes 1890–96.
67. V & A 86 TT 13 Webb to Morris, 18 January 1895.
68. WMG J181 Webb to Mackail, 12 August 1898.
69. BAL LeW/1/15.
70. Lethaby, *Philip Webb*, p. 242.

71. In both spheres Webb was handicapped by his lack of foreign languages, notably French.
72. Lethaby, *Philip Webb*, p. 235.
73. Webb to Lethaby, 1903, in Lethaby, *Philip Webb*, p. 132.
74. SPAB *Thirteenth Annual Meeting of the Society, Report of the Committee and Paper read thereat by Rev W Cunningham DD, June 1890* (1890) pp. 20 and 8.
75. Ibid., p. 18.
76. Ibid.
77. Ibid., p. 20.
78. Ibid.
79. Ibid., p. 10.
80. Ibid.
81. Ibid., p. 11.
82. SPAB Webb Papers, Webb to Dean and Chapter of Peterborough Cathedral, 24 March 1883; Webb to Rev. Newman, 7 August 1883; 'Note on the Steeple of Irthlingborough Church' (19 June 1884).
83. SPAB *Thirteenth Annual Meeting of the Society*, p. 12.
84. SPAB Webb Papers, Webb to Rev. Canon Greenwall, 6 July 1882.
85. SPAB Webb Papers, Webb to J. H. Metcalfe, 19 August 1887.
86. SPAB *Thirteenth Annual Meeting of the Society*, p. 20.
87. Webb to Eastlake, 14 March 1870, in Brandon-Jones, 'Letters of Webb', p. 66.
88. PC, Webb to Wyndham, nd [November 1893]. 'Mr Ellicott' is presumed to be W. B. Ellicott (1853–1944), a Philadelphia-trained domestic architect who later practised in Baltimore.
89. Webb to Lethaby, 1903, in Lethaby, *Philip Webb*, p. 132.
90. BAL LeW/2/1 Webb to C. Astley, 10 February 1904.
91. V & A 86 TT 13 Webb to Morris, 3 February 1885.
92. Lethaby, *Philip Webb*, p. 243.
93. BAL LeW/2/5.
94. BAL LeW/1/15.
95. RIBA Drawings Collection V 16/34/.
96. Lethaby, *Philip Webb*, p. 243.
97. PC, Note by Webb on 'Motion to consider whether Commonweal shd be dropped or continued', nd [December 1889].
98. *Seed Time* (October 1890) in W. H. G. Armytage, *Heavens Below. Utopian Experiments in England 1560–1960* (1961) p. 334.
99. Lethaby, *Philip Webb*, p. 252.
100. PC, Webb to A. Powell, 21 April 1904.
101. BAL LeW/2/1 Webb to C. Astley, 13 May 1905.
102. Pierson, *Marxism and British Socialism*, p. 220.

3   THE ARCHITECTURAL THEORY OF WILLIAM MORRIS

1. 'The Beauty of Life' (1880), in Morris Works 22, p. 61.
2. Published as 'The Lesser Arts' (1877), in Morris Works 22, p. 5. The original title of the lecture was 'The Decorative Arts'.

3. Preface to 'The Nature of Gothic', in WMAWS 1, p. 292.
4. Morris to A. Scheu, 5 September 1883, in Morris Letters, p. 187.
5. Morris to C. E. Maurice, 22 June 1883, in Morris Letters, p. 174.
6. G. Hough, *The Last Romantics* (1949) p. 93; P. Meier, *William Morris: the Marxist Dreamer* (2 vols, Hassocks, 1978) 1, p. 134.
7. Evidence to Royal Commission on Technical Instruction, 17 March 1882, in WMAWS 1, p. 206; Morris to G. Burne-Jones, 1 June 1884, in Morris Letters, p. 198.
8. Morris to A. Scheu, 5 September 1883, in Morris Letters, pp. 185–6.
9. Morris to E. S. Morris, 11 November 1855, in N. Kelvin (ed.), *The Collected Letters of William Morris* (Princeton, NJ, 1984–) 1, p. 25.
10. Morris to the *Manchester Examiner*, 14 March 1883, in Morris Letters, p. 166.
11. J. W. Mackail, *The Life of William Morris* (2 vols, 1899; one volume edn, 1922) 1, p. 49. In this section I have drawn on M. Grennan, *William Morris: Medievalist and Revolutionary* (New York, 1945) and Meier, *Marxist Dreamer*.
12. M. Morris, introduction to Morris Works 22, p. xxxi.
13. Mackail, *Life of Morris*, p. 83.
14. *Oxford and Cambridge Magazine*, 7 (July 1856) p. 446.
15. G. Burne-Jones (ed.), *Memorials of Edward Burne-Jones* (2 vols, 1904) 1, p. 99.
16. M. Morris, introduction to Morris Works 22, pp. xxxi–xxxii.
17. Morris to the *Athenaeum*, 5 March 1877, in WMAWS 1, p. 106.
18. Morris to A. Scheu, 5 September 1883, in Morris Letters, p. 185.
19. *Oxford and Cambridge Magazine*, 4 (April 1856) p. 194.
20. SPAB Cockerell Papers, Diary, entry for 2 August 1891, p. 7. See also Meier, *Marxist Dreamer*, 1, p. 109.
21. Grennan, *Medievalist and Revolutionary*, p. 52.
22. SPAB *The Second Annual Meeting of the Society. Report of the Committee thereat read, 28 June 1879* (1879) pp. 30–1.
23. CSAC Lethaby Papers, Lethaby Notebook.
24. WMG J189, 'Canon Dixon's Memoir of "the Set" at Oxford' (nd). On Godwin see A. King, 'Another Blow for Life: George Godwin and the Reform of Working Class Housing', *Architectural Review*, 136 (December 1964) pp. 448–52. For further information on Godwin and design rationalism I am indebted to Ruth Richardson of the *Builder* Index project.
25. *Journal of Design and Manufacture* 4, p. 14ff, in N. Pevsner, *Some Architectural Writers of the Nineteenth Century* (Oxford, 1972) p. 158.
26. WMG J189, 'Canon Dixon's Memoir'.
27. 'Some Hints on Pattern Designing' (1881), in Morris Works 22, pp. 181–2 and 195; see also P. Floud, 'William Morris as an Artist: A New View', *Listener* (7 October 1954) pp. 562–4.
28. 'The History of Pattern Designing' (1879), in Morris Works 22, p. 229. On Viollet see R. D. Middleton, 'Viollet-le-Duc's Influence in Nineteenth-Century England', *Art History*, 4, 2 (1981) pp. 213–19.
29. Morris to Jenny Morris, 29 November [1877], in Kelvin, *Collected Letters*, 1, p. 415.

30. Morris to G. Burne-Jones, 10 August 1880, in Kelvin, *Collected Letters*, 1, p. 579.
31. 'The Art of the People' (1879), in Morris Works 22, p. 42.
32. 'The Prospects of Architecture in Civilization' (1881), in Morris Works 22, p. 139.
33. Morris to Ruskin, 10 July 1877, in Kelvin, *Collected Letters*, 1, p. 383.
34. 'The Beauty of Life' (1880), in Morris Works 22, p. 59.
35. 'The Prospects of Architecture in Civilization' (1881), in Morris Works 22, p. 140.
36. 'Art under Plutocracy' (1883), in Morris Works 23, p. 173.
37. 'The Aims of Art' (1886), in Morris Works 23, p. 84.
38. 'The Lesser Arts' (1877), in Morris Works 22, p. 6.
39. Ibid., p. 4.
40. 'Some Hints on Pattern Designing' (1881), in Morris Works 22, pp. 177–8.
41. Ibid., p. 181.
42. 'The Lesser Arts' (1877), in Morris Works 22, p. 5.
43. 'Prospects' (1881), in Morris Works 22, p. 144.
44. 'The Art of the People' (1879), in Morris Works 22, pp. 40–1.
45. 'The Beauty of Life' (1880), in Morris Works 22, p. 66.
46. 'The History of Pattern Designing' (1879), in Morris Works 22, p. 211.
47. Ibid., p. 220.
48. Ibid., p. 229.
49. Ibid., pp. 229 and 208.
50. *The Seven Lamps of Architecture* (1849), in Ruskin Works 8, p. 63; *The Stones of Venice* I (1851), in Ruskin Works 9, p. 35. For the French view of Byzantine see R. D. Middleton, 'The Rationalist Interpretations of Classicism of Léonce Reynaud and Viollet-le-Duc', *AA Files*, 11 (1986) pp. 29–48.
51. 'The Beauty of Life' (1880), in Morris Works 22, p. 55.
52. Ibid., p. 57.
53. 'The Prospects of Architecture in Civilization' (1881), in Morris Works 22, pp. 133–4; 'Making the Best of It' (1880), in Morris Works 22, p. 85.
54. 'How I became a Socialist' (1894), in Morris Works 23, p. 280. For this section I have drawn on S. Yeo, 'A New Life: the Religion of Socialism in Britain, 1883–1896', *History Workshop*, 4 (1977) pp. 5–56; E. P. Thompson, *William Morris: Romantic to Revolutionary* (1955; revised edn, 1977); S. Pierson, *Marxism and the Origins of British Socialism. The Struggle for a New Consciousness* (1973); Meier, *Marxist Dreamer*; and K. Willis, 'The Introduction and Critical Reception of Marxist Thought in Britain 1850–1900', *Historical Journal*, 20, 2 (1977) pp. 417–59.
55. Morris to T. Wardle, 8 March 1878, in Kelvin, *Collected Letters*, 1, p. 454.
56. Morris to G. Burne-Jones, 1 January 1881, in Morris Letters, p. 143.
57. 'How I became a Socialist' (1894), in Morris Works 23, p. 277.

58. Morris to Jane Morris, 10 February [1881], in WMAWS 2, p. 581. See also Thompson, *Romantic to Revolutionary*, pp. 261–5.
59. 'How I became a Socialist' (1894), in Morris Works 23, p. 279.
60. Ibid., p. 278; see also Meier, *Marxist Dreamer*, 1, p. 172.
61. Morris to W. B. Scott, September 1886, in Morris Letters, p. 259.
62. Morris to unknown correspondent, 28 February [1885], in Thompson, *Romantic to Revolutionary*, p. 761.
63. *Cassell's Saturday Magazine* (18 October 1890) p. 81.
64. 'How I became a Socialist' (1894), in Morris Works, 23, p. 277.
65. Mackail, *Life of Morris*, 2, p. 104. See also Sotheby, Wilkinson & Hodge, *Catalogue of a Portion of the Valuable Collection of Manuscripts, Early Printed Books, &c. of the late William Morris* (1898) p. 68.
66. 'How I became a Socialist' (1894), in Morris Works 23, p. 278.
67. Morris to R. Thompson (24 July 1884), in Morris Letters, p. 205.
68. T. J. Cobden-Sanderson, *The Journals of Thomas James Cobden-Sanderson 1879–1922* (2 vols, 1926) 1, p. 385.
69. Published in twenty-one parts in *Commonweal*, 2, 18 (15 May 1886) to 3, 82 (6 August 1887).
70. Pierson, *Marxism and British Socialism*, pp. 63–4. See also Meier, *Marxist Dreamer*, 1, pp. 221–3.
71. WMG J536 Morris to C. J. Faulkner, 23 October 1883.
72. *Cassell's Saturday Journal* (18 October 1890) p. 81.
73. Morris to C. E. Maurice, 1 July 1883, in Morris Letters, p. 175.
74. 'The Revival of Handicraft' (1888), in Morris Works 22, p. 334.
75. Morris to R. Thompson, 24 July 1884, in Morris Letters, p. 206.
76. CSAC Lethaby Papers, Lethaby Notebook; 'A Factory as It Might Be' (1884), in WMAWS 2, pp. 130–40; 'Art and Socialism' (1885), in Morris Works 23, p. 206.
77. Morris to G. Bainton, 4 April 1888, in Morris Letters, p. 285.
78. Ibid.
79. Morris to C. E. Maurice, 1 July 1883, in Morris Letters, p. 176.
80. Morris to T. C. Horsfall, 25 October 1883, in Morris Letters, p. 190.
81. Morris to G. Bainton, 2 April 1888, in Morris Letters, p. 283; Morris to R. Thompson, 24 July 1884, in Morris Letters, p. 207.
82. Morris to G. Bainton, 2 and 10 April 1884, in Morris Letters, pp. 284 and 287.
83. G. Bernard Shaw, 'Morris as I knew him', in WMAWS 2, pp. ix–x.
84. F. Boos (ed.), *William Morris's Socialist Diary* (1985) p. 32.
85. WMG J94 Morris to J. Bruce Glasier, 18 March 1887.
86. WMG J536 Morris to C. J. Faulkner, 17 October 1883.
87. WMG J88 Morris to J. Bruce Glasier, 1 December 1886.
88. Thompson, *Romantic to Revolutionary*, pp. 578–9.
89. Morris to unknown correspondent, 4 September [1882], in WMAWS 2, p. 584.
90. Morris to R. Thompson, 24 July 1884, in Morris Letters, p. 204.
91. *Commonweal*, 2, 18 (15 May 1886) p. 50.
92. *Commonweal*, 2, 25 (3 July 1886) p. 109.
93. 'Art under Plutocracy' (1883), in Morris Works 23, p. 173.
94. 'The Gothic Revival II' (1884), in E. D. Lemire (ed.), *The Unpublished*

Lectures of William Morris (Detroit, 1969) p. 77; 'The Revival of Architecture' (1888), in Morris Works 22, p. 323.

95. Morris to *Pall Mall Gazette* nd (1885), in Morris Works 22, p. xij.
96. 'Architecture and History' (1884), in Morris Works 22, p. 299.
97. Ibid., p. 311.
98. Ibid., p. 305.
99. Ibid., p. 309.
100. Ibid., p. 313.
101. Morris to G. Burne-Jones, August 1888, in Morris Letters, p. 294.
102. 'The Exhibition of the Royal Academy' (1884), in WMAWS 1, pp. 239–40.
103. 'Gothic Architecture' (1889), in WMAWS 1, pp. 268 and 285.
104. Ibid., p. 275.
105. 'The Influence of Building Materials upon Architecture' (1891), in Morris Works 22, p. 391.
106. 'Gothic Architecture' (1889), in WMAWS 1, p. 270.
107. 'The Arts and Crafts of Today' (1889), in Morris Works 22, pp. 363–4; 'Art and Industry in the Fourteenth Century' (1890), in Morris Works 22, p. 376.
108. CSAC Lethaby Papers, Lethaby Notebook, entry for 11 February 1893.
109. B. Bosanquet, *A History of Aesthetic* (1892) p. 457; see also pp. 306 and 448.
110. Bosanquet, *History of Aesthetic*, p. xiii. See also J. Muirhead, *Bernard Bosanquet and his Friends* (1935) p. 20.
111. 'The Revival of Architecture' (1888), in Morris Works 22, p. 319.
112. Ibid., pp. 322–3.
113. Ibid., pp. 326–7.
114. Ibid., pp. 328–9.
115. Ibid., p. 323.
116. Ibid., p. 330.

4   W. R. LETHABY AND THE FABIANS

1. The British Museum was conveniently close both to the Shaw office at 29 Bloomsbury Square and to Lethaby's lodgings nearby. Lethaby later recalled that he was at the 'British Museum constantly from 29 Bloom. Sq.', particularly in the evenings and at lunchtimes and in the periods (as in 1885) when there was a 'lull in work' and he was 'at the office for only 3 days a week for a few months': CSAC Lethaby Papers, Lethaby Notebook.
2. 'English and French Renaissance', *The Architect*, 29 (30 June 1883) p. 434. The major study of Lethaby is G. Rubens, *William Richard Lethaby: His Life and Work 1857–1931* (1986).
3. R. Schultz Weir, *William Richard Lethaby* (1932; 1938) p. 7.
4. NDA Lethaby Papers, Lethaby Sketchbook, 1885/1.

5. 'Of the "Motive" in Architectural Design', *Architectural Association Notes*, 4, 32 (November 1889) p. 24; 'Cast Iron and Its Treatment for Artistic Purposes', *Journal of the Society of Arts*, 38 (14 February 1890) pp. 272–82.

6. 'Cast Iron', p. 282.

7. 'Modern Building Design', *Builder*, 69 (2 November 1895) pp. 312–13.

8. *The Art of England* (1884), in Ruskin Works 33, pp. 287–303.

9. 'Expression in Architecture', in J. D. Sedding, *Art and Handicraft* (1893) pp. 160–1. See also H. Wilson, *A Memorial to the late J. D. Sedding* (1892) pp. 5–7. For the arts and crafts, see G. Naylor, *The Arts and Crafts Movement: a study of its sources, ideals and influences on design theory* (1971); P. Davey, *Arts and Crafts Architecture: the Search for Earthly Paradise* (1980); and M. Richardson, *Architects of the Arts and Crafts Movement* (1983).

10. NDA Lethaby Papers, Lethaby Sketchbook 1885/1; J. D. Sedding, 'Architecture: Old and New', *British Architect*, 15 (17 June 1881) p. 299.

11. *Westminster Abbey Re-examined* (1925) pp. 82–3.

12. 'De la construction des édifices religieux en France depuis le commencement du Christianisme jusqu'au XVIe siècle', *Annales Archaéologiques*, 3 (1845) p. 325, quoted in R. D. Middleton, 'Viollet-le-Duc' in Adolf K. Placzek (editor-in-chief), *Macmillan Encyclopaedia of Architects* (4 vols, New York, 1982) 4, p. 326. See also R. D. Middleton, 'Viollet-le-Duc's Influence in Nineteenth-Century England', *Art History*, 4, 2 (1981) pp. 203–19.

13. E. E. Viollet-le-Duc (trans. G. M. Huss), *Rational Building* (New York, 1895) p. 9.

14. *Leadwork, Old and Ornamental, and for the most part English* (1893), title page. Lethaby also read Prosper Mérimée and Auguste Choisy.

15. *Philip Webb and His Work* (Oxford, 1935; expanded edn with introduction by G. Rubens, 1979) p. 242.

16. CSAC Lethaby Papers, Lethaby Notebook; NDA Lethaby Papers, Lethaby Sketchbooks 1885/1 and 1886.

17. Schultz Weir, *Lethaby*, pp. 7–8.

18. CSAC Lethaby Papers, Lethaby Notebook.

19. *Morris as Work-Master* (Birmingham, 1901). Lethaby's sympathies were Tolstoyan: see Lethaby to Cockerell, 25 September 1905, in V. Meynell (ed.), *Friends of a Lifetime. Letters to Sydney Carlyle Cockerell* (1940) p. 129.

20. 'Ernest Gimson's London Days', in *Ernest Gimson, His Life and Work* (1924) pp. 2 and 7.

21. G. Rubens, 'The Life and Work of William Richard Lethaby' (University of London PhD, 1977) p. 102.

22. 'Modern Building Design', *Builder* (1895) p. 312.

23. 'The Builder's Art and the Craftsman', in R. N. Shaw and T. G. Jackson (eds), *Architecture. A Profession or an Art. Thirteen Essays on the Qualifications and Training of Architects* (1892) p. 151.

24. Ibid., p. 153.

25. NDA Lethaby Papers, Lethaby Sketchbook 1884–85; *The Stones of*

Venice II, in Ruskin Works 10, p. 253. Lethaby read 'The Nature of Gothic' in the 1873–74 edition of *The Stones of Venice*.

26. NDA Lethaby Papers, Lethaby Sketchbook 1884–85; *St Mark's Rest*, in Ruskin Works 24, pp. 280–1.

27. (with H. Swainson) *The Church of Sancta Sophia, Constantinople. A Study of Byzantine Building* (1894) p. 223–4. See also 'The Royal Gold Medal: Presentation to M. Auguste Choisy, 20th June 1904', *RIBA Journal*, 3rd ser., 11 (1904) p. 451 and R. Middleton, 'Auguste Choisy, Historian: 1841–1909', *International Architect*, 5, 1, issue 5 (1981) pp. 37–42.

28. *The Church of Sancta Sophia*, p. 208.

29. Ibid., p. 199.

30. Ibid., p. 253.

31. Ibid., preface, np.

32. By creating a separate Board (rather than a normal committee) for technical education, Webb was able to incorporate representatives from bodies such as the London School Board that otherwise might have objected to his plans, and to free himself of the bureaucratic restrictions that prevailed within the LCC and thereby to assume an exceptional degree of personal control over the Board's activities. As well as being chairman of the Board (a position to which he was re-elected annually every year until 1898), he was also chairman of the Board's sub-committee on the teaching of art and technology. See B. Webb, *Our Partnership* (1948) p. 82.

33. A. M. McBriar, *Fabian Socialism and English Politics 1884–1918* (1962; 1966) p. 30. See also N. and J. Mackenzie, *The First Fabians* (1977; 1979) p. 64. For this section I have also drawn on B. Simon, *Education and the Labour Movement 1870–1920* (1965); S. Maclure, *One hundred years of London education 1870–1970* (1970); E. J. T. Brennan (ed.), *Education for National Efficiency: the Contribution of Sidney and Beatrice Webb* (1975).

34. Fabian Tract 70, quoted in McBriar, *Fabian Socialism*, p. 98.

35. G. B. Shaw (ed.), *Fabian Essays in Socialism* (1889) pp. 47–8.

36. Ibid., p. 35.

37. G. Stedman Jones, *Outcast London. A Study in the Relationship between Classes in Victorian Society* (Oxford, 1971; Harmondsworth, 1976), introduction and chs 1 and 7; N. B. Dearle, *Problems of Unemployment in the London Building Trades* (1908) pp. 48–50.

38. London County Council, *Report to the Special Committee on Technical Education, Being the result of an Inquiry into the needs of London with regard to Technical Education, the existing provision for such education, and the best means to be taken by the London County Council for improving that provision, under the Technical Instruction Acts, 1889 and 1891, and the Local Taxation (Customs and Excise) Act 1890, by H. Llewellyn Smith, MA, BSc, Secretary of The Committee* (1892), p. 35.

39. Ibid., p. 13.

40. Ibid.

41. Ibid., p. 36.

42. Ibid., p. 35.

43. Ibid., p. 16.

44. E. R. Taylor (1838–1912), the head of the Birmingham School and a

disciple of Ruskin and admirer of Morris and Burne-Jones, advised Llewellyn Smith on the section of his report dealing with art education. On Birmingham see A. Crawford, *By Hammer and Hand: The Arts and Crafts Movement in Birmingham* (Birmingham, 1984) pp. 27–39.

45. *Report on Technical Education*, pp. 25 and 76.
46. BL Add MSS 52730 f6–7 Lethaby to Cockerell, nd [22 October 1894]. See also 'W. R. Lethaby: An Impression and a Tribute', *RIBA Journal*, 39, 8 (20 February 1932) p. 310.
47. Following Lethaby's appointment, this support took more practical form: in 1895 lectures were given for the TEB by Walker, Cobden-Sanderson and Morris himself; and gifts were made to the Central School by the Morris estate, by Burne-Jones and by Mrs Jane Morris. May Morris taught at the School. When Frampton resigned in 1898, Catterson-Smith, a former Morris assistant, was appointed in his place.
48. GLRO HC2 TEB Minutes, 19 November 1894, p. 444.
49. B. M. Allen, *Down the Stream of Life* (1948) p. 61.
50. GLRO HC3 TEB Minutes, 17 June 1895, 'Report on Architecture and Allied Arts by W. R. Lethaby', p. 145.
51. Ibid., p. 146.
52. GLRO HC3 TEB Minutes, 15 July 1895, p. 141.
53. 'Mr Lethaby's Architectural Gospel', *Builder*, 69 (9 November 1895) p. 326. For the lectures see 'Modern Building Design', *Builder*, 69 (2 November 1895) pp. 312–13, and 69 (9 November 1895) pp. 334–5.
54. GLRO HC4 TEB Minutes, 18 May 1896, pp. 156–7, Memorandum by Webb.
55. Ibid., p. 156.
56. GLRO HC4 TEB Minutes, 18 May 1896, pp. 157–8, Reports by Frampton and Lethaby on 'Works submitted for scholarships and the need for schools of practical art' and 'Central School for Artistic Crafts'.
57. London County Council Technical Education Board, *Prospectus and Time Table of the Central School of Arts and Crafts, 316 Regent Street, London W, December 20 1896* (1896), p. 3.
58. N. Pevsner, 'Post-War Tendencies in German Art Schools', *Journal of the Royal Society of Arts*, 84 (17 January 1936) p. 249. See also GLRO HC11 TEB Minutes, 23 November 1903, p. 822.
59. W. Augustus Steward, 'Technical Schools and their Work', *The Watchmaker, Jeweller, Silversmith and Optician*, Special Home and Colonial Number (1907) p. 96.
60. GLRO HC11 TEB Minutes, 2 March 1903, p. 112.
61. London County Council, *Report of the Technical Education Board for the year 1896–97* (1897) p. 15.
62. H. Ricardo, 'Architecture as taught at the London County Council Central School of Arts and Crafts', *Architectural Review*, 15 (1904) p. 113.
63. LCC, *Report on Technical Education*, p. 13; see also *Report of the TEB for 1896–97*, p. 3.
64. London County Council, *Technical Education Gazette*, 1, 12 (October 1895) p. 313. See also GLRO HC6 TEB Minutes, 24 January 1898, p. 8.

65. 'Arts and the Function of Guilds', *The Quest* (1896), reprinted in Lethaby, *Form in Civilization* (1922) p. 205.
66. GLRO HC19, 'Report of the Special Sub-Committee on the Building Trades' (1899) p. vii.
67. Ibid., p. xii.
68. GLRO HC5 TEB Minutes, 17 May 1897, p. 167.
69. 'Education in Building', *RIBA Journal*, 3rd ser., 8 (22 June 1901) p. 387.
70. Ibid., p. 391.
71. Ibid., pp. 392–3.
72. GLRO HC11 TEB Minutes, 23 November 1903, p. 812.
73. GLRO HC12 TEB Minutes, 8 February 1904, p. 43.
74. London County Council School of Building, *Prospectus and Time Table for the Third Session 1905–6* (1905) p. 4.
75. London County Council, *The First Fifty Years. History of the Brixton School of Building 1904–1954* (1954) p. 7.
76. 'W. R. Lethaby', *RIBA Journal*, 1932, p. 309.
77. *Medieval Art: from the Peace of the Church to the Eve of the Renaissance 312–1350* (1904) p. 142.
78. Ibid., pp. 1–2.
79. Ibid., pp. 136 and 142.
80. N. Pevsner, *An Outline of European Architecture* (Harmondsworth, 1943; 1968) pp. 10–11.

5   RAYMOND UNWIN: THE EDUCATION OF AN URBANIST

1. 'The Architect's Contribution. The Inaugural Address by the President, Dr Raymond Unwin, read before the RIBA on Monday 2 November 1931', *RIBA Journal*, 3rd ser., 39, 1 (November 1931) p. 9. On Unwin see M. K. Miller, 'To Speak of Planning is to Speak of Unwin. The Contribution of Sir Raymond Unwin (1863–1940) to the Evolution of British Town Planning' (University of Birmingham PhD, 1981), which largely supersedes the published studies: W. Creese, *The Search for Environment. The Garden City: Before and After* (1966); M. G. Day, 'The Contribution of Sir Raymond Unwin (1863–1940) and R. Barry Parker (1867–1947) to the development of site planning theory and practice, c. 1890–1918', in A. Sutcliffe (ed.), *British Town Planning: the formative years* (Leicester, 1981) pp. 156–99; and F. Jackson, *Sir Raymond Unwin. Architect, Planner, Visionary* (1985).
2. 'The Royal Gold Medal. Presentation to Sir Raymond Unwin', *RIBA Journal*, 3rd ser., 44, 12 (April 1937) p. 582. See also UMDAP Unwin Papers, 'Notes for speech to London Society' (nd); 'Founder's Day Ceremony: Sir Raymond Unwin and Planning', *Manchester Guardian* (16 May 1935) p. 13.
3. *Architectural Review*, 163, 976 (June 1978), 'The Garden City Idea'

(special issue); M. Swenarton, 'Rationality and Rationalism: the theory and practice of site planning in modern architecture, 1905–1933', *AA Files*, 4 (1983) pp. 49–59.

4. 'Edward Carpenter and "Towards Democracy"', in G. Beith (ed.), *Edward Carpenter. In Appreciation* (1931) p. 234.
5. *Daily Independent* (Sheffield) (5 December 1932) p. 6; Miller, 'Unwin', p. 53.
6. 'The Prince and his Hand', *Commonweal*, 5, 157 (12 January 1889) p. 10.
7. 'Co-operation and Competition', *Commonweal*, 2, 26 (10 July 1886) p. 114.
8. 'Edward Carpenter and "Towards Democracy"', p. 234.
9. PC, Unwin to Ethel Parker, 4 May [1884].
10. 'Edward Carpenter and "Towards Democracy"', p. 235.
11. PC, Unwin to Ethel Parker, 10 January 1891. In the surviving seventeen letters from the period 1884–1891, Carpenter figures in ten.
12. 'Edward Carpenter and "Towards Democracy"', pp. 234–5.
13. UMDAP Unwin Paper, Notes for lecture on Carpenter, 3 July 1939.
14. 'Edward Carpenter and "Towards Democracy"', pp. 234–6.
15. UMDAP Unwin Papers, Notes for lecture on Carpenter, 3 July 1939.
16. UMDAP Unwin Papers, 1887 Diary, entry for 12 August. The Diary, comprising entries addressed to Ethel Parker, substituted for correspondence between them, which had been prohibited by her father.
17. E. Carpenter, *My Days and Dreams* (1916; 3rd edn 1921) pp. 139–40 and p. 114.
18. PC, Unwin to Ethel Parker, nd [3 May 1885]; UMDAP Unwin papers, 1887 Diary, entry for 11 September.
19. PC, Unwin to Ethel Parker, nd [3 May 1885].
20. BAL Unwin Papers UN 15/2 'The Dawn of a Happier Day' (January 1886) p. 26.
21. 'Socialist Tactics. A Third Course', *To-Day*, ns 7, 49 (December 1887) p. 185; UMDAP Unwin Papers, 1887 Diary, entry for 19 May.
22. 'The Question of Political Policy. The Movement Past and Present', *Labour Leader* (18 January 1902) p. 21.
23. PC, Unwin to Ethel Parker, nd [31 January 1885].
24. IISH Socialist League Papers 3031, Unwin to the Secretary, 21 August 1885.
25. IISH Socialist League papers 606, Monthly Reports October 1885–March 1886.
26. IISH Socialist League papers 3042, Unwin to the Secretary, 27 June 1886.
27. *Commonweal*, 2, 44 (13 November 1886) p. 264; E. P. Thompson, *William Morris: Romantic to Revolutionary* (1955; revised edn, 1977) p. 414.
28. UMDAP Unwin Papers, 1887 Diary, entry for 16 May.
29. IISH Socialist League Papers 3042, Unwin to the Secretary (27 June 1886).

30. IISH Socialist League Papers 3042, Unwin to the Secretary (4 July 1886).
31. 'The Axe is Laid unto the Root', *Commonweal*, 2, 31 (14 August 1886) p. 155.
32. PC, Unwin to Ethel Parker, 10 January and 20 January 1891.
33. UMDAP Unwin Papers, 1887 Diary, entry for 18 September.
34. C. Tsuzuki, *Edward Carpenter 1844–1929. Prophet of Human Fellowship* (Cambridge, 1980) p. 66.
35. Ibid.
36. Carpenter, *My Days and Dreams*, pp. 131–2.
37. Tsuzuki, *Edward Carpenter*, p. 96.
38. PC, Unwin to Ethel Parker, 26 January 1891.
39. J. L. Mahon, quoted in Thompson, *Romantic to Revolutionary*, p. 473.
40. UMDAP Unwin Papers, 1887 diary, entry for 6 June.
41. *Commonweal*, 3, 80 (23 July 1887) p. 240.
42. UMDAP Unwin papers, 1887 Diary, entry for 2 August.
43. IISH Socialist League Papers 3046, Unwin to the Secretary, 18 September 1887.
44. 'Socialist Tactics. A Third Course', *To-Day*, ns 7, 49 (December 1887) pp. 180–6.
45. 'Westward Ho!', *Commonweal*, 6, 227 (10 May 1890) p. 151.
46. UMDAP Unwin Papers, 1887 Diary, entry for 16 August.
47. UMDAP Unwin Papers, 1887 Diary, entry for 2 August.
48. PC, Unwin to Ethel Parker, 4 May [1884].
49. UMDAP Unwin papers, 1887 Diary, entry for 3 August.
50. UMDAP Unwin papers, 1887 Diary, entry for 21 August.
51. UMDAP Unwin Papers, 1887 Diary, entry for 22 May.
52. UMDAP Unwin Papers, 1887 Diary, entry for 23 August.
53. UMDAP Unwin papers, 1887 Diary, entries for 5 May to 15 June, passim; 'Positivism and Socialism', *Commonweal*, 3, 80 (23 July 1887) p. 235.
54. PC, Unwin to Ethel Parker, 10 January [1891].
55. PC, Unwin to Ethel Parker, 24 April 1891.
56. PC, Unwin to Ethel Parker, 9 August 1891.
57. *Labour Leader* (18 January 1902) p. 21.
58. *Labour Annual* (1897) p. 245.
59. *Labour Prophet*, 6, 74 (February 1898) p. 159; B. Parker, 'Memoir of Sir Raymond Unwin', *RIBA Journal*, 3rd ser., 47, 9 (15 July 1940) p. 209.
60. 'The Place of the Labour Church', *Labour Prophet and Labour Church Record*, 6, 75 (March 1898) pp. 161–2.
61. Parker, 'Unwin', p. 209.
62. UMDAP Unwin Papers, Notes for lecture on Hinton, nd [1905–6].
63. 'Early Communal Life and What It Teaches. Pt V', *Commonweal*, 3, 70 (14 May 1887) p. 157.
64. BAL Unwin Papers UN 15/4, 'Gladdening v. Shortening the Hours of Labour', pp. 15–16.
65. 'The Passing of Sir Raymond Unwin', *Labour's Northern Voice* (August 1940) p. 2.

66. (with B. Parker) *The Art of Building a Home* (1901) p. 61.
67. 'The Art of Building a Home', *Architects' Magazine*, 1, 12 (October 1901) p. 224.
68. *Art of Building a Home*, p. 1.
69. Ibid., p. 111.
70. *Cottage Plans and Common Sense* (Fabian Tract 109, 1902) p. 3.
71. *Art of Building a Home*, p. 114.
72. Ibid., p. 64.
73. Ibid., p. 66.
74. *Architects' Magazine*, 1, 4 (February 1901) p. 68.
75. *Art of Building a Home*, p. 132.
76. UMDAP Unwin Papers, 1887 Diary, entry for 21 August.
77. 'Sutton Hall', *Commonweal*, 5, 179 (15 June 1889) p. 190.
78. *Labour Prophet and Labour Church Record*, 6, 63 (March 1897) p. 46. See also W. H. G. Armytage, *Heavens Below. Utopian Experiments in England 1560–1960* (1961) ch. 6 and S. Pierson, *Marxism and the Origins of British Socialism. The Struggle for a New Consciousness* (1973) p. 221.
79. C. Lee, 'From a Letchworth Diary', *Town and Country Planning*, 21, 113 (September 1953) pp. 435–6. For Unwin's appointment as architect at Letchworth Garden City, see Miller, 'Unwin', pp. 232–42.
80. 'Co-operation in Building', *Architects' Magazine*, 1, 2 (December 1900) p. 20, and 1, 3 (January 1901) pp. 37–8.
81. BAL Unwin Papers UN 15/2, 'The Dawn of a Happier Day' (1886) pp. 1–3.
82. *Art of Building a Home*, p. 92.
83. Ibid., p. 100.
84. Ibid., p. 104.
85. 'The Houses our Forefathers lived in', *Architects' Magazine*, 1, 3 (January 1901) p. 44.
86. *Art of Building a Home*, pp. 104–5.
87. 'Of the Building of Houses in Garden City', *The Garden City Conference at Bourneville. Report of Proceedings* (1901) p. 72.
88. FGCHM, 'The Improvement of Towns. A Paper read at the Conference of the National Union of Women Workers of Great Britain and Ireland, November 8th 1904, by Mr Raymond Unwin' (offprint, 1904) p. 8.
89. *Labour Chronicle* (Leeds), 1 (May 1893) p. 7. On the ILP see Pierson, *Marxism and British Socialism*, pp. 268–71.
90. 'The Question of Political Policy. The Movement Past and Present', *ILP News*, 5, 58 (January 1902) pp. 1–2.
91. *ILP News*, 5, 58 (January 1902) p. 4.
92. 'The Question of Political Policy. The Movement Past and Present', *Labour Leader* (18 January 1902) p. 21; *Archives of the Independent Labour Party. Series III. The Frances Johnson Correspondence, 1888–1950. Part I 1888–1908* (Microfiche, Hassocks, 1980) Reel 5 (1902) 12A, Unwin to K. Hardie, 26 January 1902.
93. *Cottage Plans and Common Sense*, p. 4.
94. Ibid., p. 2. On Unwin and post-war housing see M. Swenarton,

Homes fit for Heroes. The Politics and Architecture of Early State Housing in Britain (1981) pp. 94–5.
95. *Cottage Plans and Common Sense*, p. 2.
96. Ibid., p. 3.
97. Ibid., p. 13.
98. Ibid., p. 15.
99. NCO Fabian Society Papers, Membership Record Cards, Raymond Unwin.
100. *Labour Annual* (1903) p. 79.
101. FGCHM, (with B. Parker) 'Cottages near a Town' (offprint, Northern Art Workers Guild, 1903) p. 12.
102. 'City Planning', *Cambridge Independent Press* (16 February 1906) p. 3.
103. Miller, 'Unwin', p. 184.
104. BAL Unwin Papers UN 15/5/4, Quotations from Carpenter transcribed by Unwin.
105. UMDAP Unwin Papers, Notes for lecture on Carpenter (3 July 1939).
106. 'City Planning', p. 3.
107. BAL Unwin Papers UN 2/1, Notes for lecture on Town Planning (28 February 1908).
108. 'The Improvement of Towns', pp. 2 and 15.
109. 'The Improvement of Towns', p. 8.
110. 'Early Communal Life and What It Teaches. Pt II', *Commonweal*, 3, 67 (23 April 1887) p. 135.
111. 'The Improvement of Towns', pp. 7–8.
112. 'The Improvement of Towns', p. 8.
113. UMDAP Unwin Papers, Notes for speech on Aristocracy and Democracy, nd; PC, Unwin to Ethel Parker, 5 December 1885.
114. PC, Unwin to Ethel Parker, nd [November 1885].
115. 'Looking Back and Forth. An Address to Students by the President, Dr Raymond Unwin', *RIBA Journal*, 39, 6 (January 1932) pp. 205–6.
116. BAL Unwin Papers UN 15/4, 'Gladdening v. Shortening the Hours of Labour' (1897).
117. *Art of Building a Home*, p. 88.
118. 'W. R. Lethaby: An Impression and a Tribute', *RIBA Journal*, 3rd ser., 39, 8 (20 February 1932) p. 304.
119. *Labour Leader* (18 January 1902) p. 21.
120. 'Some Objections Answered', *Commonweal*, 4, 126 (9 June 1888) p. 181.
121. 'The Saving of Labour', *Commonweal*, 4, 124 (26 May 1888) p. 163.
122. *Commonweal*, 4, 126 (9 June 1888) p. 181.

6 A. J. PENTY AND THE BUILDING GUILDS

1. *RIBA Journal*, 3rd ser., 27, 15 (12 June 1920) p. 386. The main study of Penty and the guilds (but from a non-architectural viewpoint) is by F. Matthews: 'The Building Guilds' in A. Briggs and J. Saville (eds), *Essays in Labour History 1886–1923* (1971) pp. 284–331; and 'The Ladder of Becoming: A. R. Orage, A. J. Penty and the Origins of

Guild Socialism in England' in D. E. Martin and D. Rubinstein (eds), *Ideology and the Labour Movement. Essays presented to John Saville* (1979) pp. 147–66.

2. A. J. Penty, *The Restoration of the Gild System* (1906) p. vii. For Penty's international reputation see O. Por (trans. E. Townshend), *Guilds and Co-operatives in Italy* (1923) p. 141; A. Goote, *Het Gilden-Socialisme in Engeland* (Baarn, 1926); E. J. Kiernan, *Arthur J. Penty: His Contribution to Social Thought* (Washington, DC, 1941); G. D. H. Cole, *A History of Socialist Thought. Vol. III The Second International 1889–1914* (2 vols, 1956; 1967) 2, p. 243.

3. 'Aestheticism and History', *New Age*, ns, 14, 22 (2 April 1914) p. 683. See also Penty, *Restoration of the Gild System*, p. 88.

4. 'Preparing for Peace', *Architects' and Builders' Journal*, 47, 1214 (10 April 1918) p. 166; T. S. Attlee, 'The Architect and the Guild', *Builder*, 120, 4090 (24 June 1921) pp. 796–7.

5. *Guildsman*, 42 (June 1920) p. 6.

6. PC, Penty Papers, 'Industrialism, Guilds and Fascism' (1934) pp. 1–2.

7. Ruskin to S. C. Cockerell, 26 March 1886, in V. Meynell (ed.), *Friends of a Lifetime. Letters to Sydney Carlyle Cockerell* (1940) p. 26.

8. M. Cole, 'Guild Socialism and the Labour Research Department', in A. Briggs and J. Saville (eds), *Essays in Labour History 1886–1923* (1971) p. 263; S. G. Hobson, *Pilgrim to the Left. Memoirs of a Revolutionist* (1938) pp. 176–7.

9. 'Men Who Build. No 61. Messrs Penty and Penty', *Builders' Journal and Architectural Record*, 300 (7 November 1900) p. 267.

10. H. Muthesius, *Das Englische Haus* (3 vols, Berlin, 1904); Eng. trans. (ed. D. Sharp, trans. J. Seligman) *The English House* (1979) p. 58. Also *British Architect*, 43 (26 April 1895) p. 289; *Builders' Journal and Architectural Record*, 12 (7 November 1900) pp. 267–73 *et seq.*; *Building News*, 84, 2511 (20 February 1903) pp. 262–3, and 85, 2532 (17 July 1903) pp. 67–8; *RIBA Journal*, 3rd ser., 44 (March 1937) p. 466.

11. Ibid.

12. NCO Fabian Society Papers, Membership Record Cards, A. J. Penty, and F85/1, Lists of Local Societies and Members (1893–94).

13. See P. Mairet, *A. R. Orage* (1936) pp. 16–30; J. Carswell, *Lives and Letters* (1978) pp. 23–4.

14. Elmdon & Co., *A Catalogue of Furniture made by Elmdon & Co. at 1 Ravenscourt Park, Hammersmith, London. From Designs by Charles Spooner and Arthur J. Penty* (nd, 1905) p. x.

15. PC, Penty Papers, Diary, entry for 2 March 1914 (I am indebted to B. Grafton Green for this reference).

16. PC, Penty Papers, 'Industrialism', p. 22.

17. 'Aestheticism and History', *New Age*, ns, 14, 22 (2 April 1914) p. 683. See also PC, Penty Papers, 'Industrialism', p. 26.

18. PC, Penty Papers, 'Industrialism', p. 8. See also F. S. Nitti, *Catholic Socialism* (Italian original 1895; English trans. 1911).

19. 'The Restoration of the Gild System', *Fabian News*, 16, 10 (September 1906) p. 2; C. Chesterton, 'Guilds and Utopia', *New Witness*, 4, 84 (11 June 1914) p. 176.

20. PC, Penty Papers, 'Industrialism', pp. 28–9.
21. Penty, *Restoration of the Gild System*, p. 11.
22. Ibid., pp. 84 and 95.
23. 'The Restoration of Beauty to Life', *New Age*, ns 1, 1 (9 May 1907) p. 5.
24. 'Book of the Week. Advice to Housing Reformers', *New Age*, ns, 2, 16 (15 February 1908) p. 313.
25. Penty to *New Age*, ns, 15, 3 (21 May 1914) p. 70.
26. 'Art and National Guilds', *New Age*, ns, 14, 16 (19 February 1914) p. 493.
27. PC, Penty Papers, letter to *New Age*, nd [1908–9].
28. 'The Machine Problem', *New Age*, ns, 14, 9 (1 January 1914) p. 269.
29. 'Back to Manchesterism', *New Age*, ns, 1, 9 (27 June 1907) p. 132.
30. 'The Machine Problem', p. 268; see also 'Art and Apprentices. What can be done by Trade Unions. Mr Penty Interviewed', *Daily News* (12 November 1909).
31. 'Back to Manchesterism', p. 133.
32. PC, Penty Papers, 'The Gilds Restoration League' (June 1906). See also W. Martin, *The New Age under Orage. Chapters in English Cultural History* (Manchester, 1967) pp. 23–4. The restoration of craft guilds also formed the programme of the misleadingly entitled Fabian Arts Group launched in 1907 by Holbrook Jackson.
33. Cole, *History of Socialist Thought*, 2, p. 240.
34. PC, Penty Papers, 'Industrialism', p. 58.
35. Hobson, *Pilgrim to the Left*, p. 172.
36. NCO Cole Papers B3/5/B no 53 file 13, 'A Guild Socialist League' (1915).
37. PC, Penty Papers, 'A Guildsman's Criticism of Guild Socialism' (March 1923) p. 1.
38. 'Art and National Guilds', *New Age*, ns, 14, 16 (19 February 1914) p. 493.
39. PC, Penty Papers, 'Industrialism', p. 61.
40. NCO Cole Papers B/3/5/B no 53 file 1, National Guilds League Annual Meeting (8 April 1917) pp. 10–14.
41. *Guildsman*, 49 (January 1921) pp. 4–5; NCO Cole Papers B/3/5/B no 53 file 16, Cole Notebook, 'NGL Annual and Special Conferences 1920. Annual Conference 1921', pp. 33, 43 and 59.
42. 'National Guilds v. The Class War', *New Age*, ns, 23, 16 (15 August 1918) pp. 250 and 252. In this critique of Marx, Penty drew heavily on the Spanish theorist Ramiro de Maetzu.
43. PC, Penty Papers, 'Industrialism', p. 188.
44. Cole, *History of Socialist Thought*, 2, p. 452.
45. *Guild Socialist*, 58 (October 1921) p. 9.
46. *Guildsman*, 41 (May 1920) p. 6.
47. J. T. Gunn, 'The Expansion of the Guild Movement', *Social Welfare* (September 1922) pp. 261–3. For British housing policy see M. Swenarton, *Homes fit for Heroes. The Politics and Architecture of Early State Housing in Britain* (1981) pp. 112–35; and for European building guilds see A. Ellinger, 'Socialization Schemes in the German Building Industry', *International Labour Review*, 1, 3 (March 1921) pp. 287–301.

48. Por, *Guilds in Italy*, pp. 60–2; K. Novy, 'The Rosenhügel Pioneers', *9H*, 6 (1983) pp. 45–51; H. Searing, 'With Red Flags Flying: politics and architecture in Amsterdam, 1915–23', in H. A. Millon and L. Nochlin (eds), *Art and Architecture in the Service of Politics* (Boston, 1978) p. 262; Ellinger, 'Socialization Schemes', pp. 287–301; 'Public Utility Building Guilds in Germany', *International Labour Review*, 7, 2–3 (February–March 1923) pp. 241–51; International Labour Office, *Housing Policy in Europe* (Geneva, 1930) pp. 375–6.
49. 'Preparing for Peace', *Architects' and Builders' Journal*, 47, 1214 (10 April 1918) p. 166.
50. 'Towards a National Building Guild', *Journal of the American Institute of Architects*, 7, 4 (April 1919) pp. 149–51.
51. PC, Penty Papers, 'Architecture and the Building Guilds', nd [1920] p. 9. See also NCO Cole Papers B3/5/B no 53 file 14, Sparkes to Cole, 26 September 1918; Matthews, 'Building Guilds', pp. 292–3; R. Postgate, *The Builders' History* (1923) pp. 440–8.
52. Hobson, *Pilgrim to the Left*, p. 222.
53. *Builder*, 118, 4036 (11 June 1920) p. 698; Matthews, 'Building Guilds', p. 303. See also Hobson, *Pilgrim to the Left*, p. 223 and Swenarton, *Homes fit for Heroes*, p. 126.
54. WLHL Walthamstow UDC Housing Committee Minutes, 6 April 1920; *Walthamstow Guardian* (12 November 1920) p. 4; NCO Bedford Papers Box 4 file 12, Greenwich Building Guild Committee to NGL, 2 March 1920, and Walthamstow Building Guild to NGL, 8 April 1920.
55. *Builder*, 120, 4077 (25 March 1921) p. 370.
56. Sparkes, 'The Coming of the Guild of Builders', *Guildsman*, 42 (June 1920) p. 3.
57. Guild of Builders (London) Ltd, *An Industry Cleared for Action*, nd [1920] p. 5.
58. *Builder*, 120, 4077 (25 March 1921) p. 370.
59. E. Selley, 'An Inquiry into the Working of the Building Guilds', *Garden Cities and Town Planning*, 11, 6 (June 1921) p. 134.
60. Selley, 'Working of the Guilds', pp. 138 and 140.
61. N. Carpenter, *Guild Socialism. An Historical and Critical Analysis* (New York, 1922) p. 335.
62. Selley, 'Working of the Guilds', p. 139.
63. *Guildsman*, 51 (March 1921) p. 1 and *Guild Socialist* 55 (July 1921) p. 7; Swenarton, *Homes fit for Heroes*, pp. 129–35.
64. NCO Bedford Papers Box 4 file 11, Verbatim Report of Conference (November 1922); Cole Papers B3/5/B no 53 file 3, Cole to B. Webb, 26 September 1939.
65. *Builder*, 123, 4169 (29 December 1922) p. 1014 and 124, 4173 (26 January 1923) p. 177.
66. G. D. H. Cole, *A History of Socialist Thought. Vol. IV Communism and Social Democracy, 1914–1931* (2 vols, 1958) 1, pp. 453–4. See also J. M. Winter, *Socialism and the Challenge of War. Ideas and Politics in Britain 1912–18* (1974) pp. 281–2.
67. *Guildsman*, 44 (August 1920) p. 5.
68. The statement in PC, Penty Papers, 'Industrialism', p. 66, is confirmed

by all available evidence; the contrary (incorrect) view originated with Carpenter, *Guild Socialism*, p. 118.

69. National Building Guild, *Labour-Saving Houses. A Book of Type Plans*, nd [1922] p. 6.
70. 'Architecture and the Guild Revival', *Architectural Association Journal*, 35, 399 (May 1920) p. 293.
71. PC, Penty Papers, 'Architecture and the Building Guilds', nd [1920].
72. 'The Crisis in Architecture. I. An Economic Forecast', *Journal of the American Institute of Architects*, 8, 2 (February 1920) p. 59.
73. *Guildsman*, 37 (January 1920) p. 4. See also PC, Penty Papers, Orage to Penty, 12 August 1919.
74. A. J. Penty, *Guilds, Trade and Agriculture* (1921). See also *Guild Socialist*, 56 (August 1921) p. 9; PC, Penty Papers, 'Industrialism', pp. 100–80.
75. PC, Penty Papers, 'A Guildsman's Criticism of Guild Socialism' (1923) pp. 5–6.
76. Ibid., p. 11.
77. PC, Penty Papers, 'Industrialism', pp. 1–5 and 210–64.

7 RUSKIN AND THE MODERNS

1. N. Pevsner, *Pioneers of the Modern Movement from William Morris to Walter Gropius* (London, 1936) p. 137.
2. N. Pevsner, 'Post-War Tendencies in German Art Schools', *Journal of the Royal Society of Arts*, 84 (17 January 1936) p. 248.
3. Pevsner, *Pioneers of the Modern Movement*, pp. 19–20; N. Pevsner, *Pioneers of Modern Design from William Morris to Walter Gropius* (Harmondsworth, 1960) pp. 19–20.
4. R. Banham, *Theory and Design in the First Machine Age* (1960) pp. 11–12.
5. J. Autret, *Ruskin and the French before Marcel Proust* (Geneva, 1965) pp. 11–37; J. Autret, *L'Influence de Ruskin sur la Vie, Les Idées et L'Oeuvre de Marcel Proust* (Geneva, 1955) pp. 16–17 and 169–70.
6. Le Corbusier (1944), quoted in P. V. Turner, *The Education of Le Corbusier: A Study of the Development of Le Corbusier's Thought 1900–1920* (Harvard University D.Phil, 1971; New York, 1977) p. 7.
7. Le Corbusier, *L'Art decoratif d'aujord'hui* (Paris, 1925) p. 134 (author's translation); *Stones of Venice* I, in Ruskin Works 9, pp. 49–52.
8. Le Corbusier, *The Four Routes* (French original, Paris, 1941; Eng. trans. 1947) pp. 127–8. I am indebted to Adrian Forty for this reference.
9. Le Corbusier (trans. F. Etchells), *Towards a New Architecture* (French original, Paris, 1923; Eng. trans. 1927) p. 23.
10. Le Corbusier, *L'Art decoratif*, p. 134. On Le Corbusier and Ruskin, see also M. P. M. Sekler, 'Le Corbusier, Ruskin, the Tree, and the Open Hand', in R. Walden (ed.), *The Open Hand. Essays on Le Corbusier* (Cambridge, Mass., 1977) pp. 42–95.
11. H. Muthesius, *Das Englische Haus* (3 vols, Berlin, 1904–1905); Eng. trans. (ed. D. Sharp, trans. J. Seligman), *The English House* (1979)

p. 13. See also S. Custoza, M. Vogliazzo, J. Posener, *Muthesius* (Milan, 1981) p. 128.
12. H.-R. Hitchcock, 'Ruskin and American Architecture, or Regeneration Long Delayed', in J. Summerson (ed.), *Concerning Architecture. Essays on Architectural Writers and Writing presented to Nikolaus Pevsner* (1968) pp. 167 and 206.
13. W. Gropius, 'Architecture at Harvard University', *Architectural Record*, 81, 5 (May 1937) p. 11.
14. B. Miller Lane, *Architecture and Politics in Germany 1918–1945* (Cambridge, Mass., 1968) p. 66. See also M. Franciscono, *Walter Gropius and the Creation of the Bauhaus in Weimar: The Ideals and Artistic Theories of its Founding Years* (Urbana, 1971) pp. 13–70.
15. Gropius, 'Programm des Staatlichen Bauhauses in Weimar' (1919), in H. M. Wingler, *The Bauhaus. Weimar, Dessau, Berlin, Chicago* (Cambridge, Mass., 1969 and 1976) p. 31.
16. Ibid., pp. 31–2.
17. Gropius (1922), quoted in Lane, *Architecture and Politics*, p. 67.
18. Gropius (1923), quoted in ibid., p. 67.
19. Gropius, 'The Theory and Organization of the Bauhaus' (1923), in H. Bayer, I. Gropius and W. Gropius (eds), *Bauhaus 1919–1928* (Boston, 1952) p. 21. Gropius made the same comment about Ruskin on his arrival at Harvard: Gropius, 'Education Toward Creative Design', *American Architect and Architecture*, 150, 2657 (May 1937) p. 27.
20. R. B. Stein, *John Ruskin and Aesthetic Thought in America, 1840–1900* (Cambridge, Mass., 1967) p. 80; Hitchcock, 'Ruskin and American Architecture', p. 172.
21. Stein, *Ruskin and America*, pp. 14 and 152.
22. Frank Lloyd Wright, 'In the Cause of Architecture', *Architectural Record*, 23, 3 (March 1908) p. 157.
23. Wright, *Ausgeführte Bauten und Entwürfe* (Berlin, 1910), in E. Kaufmann (ed.), *An American Architecture; Frank Lloyd Wright* (New York, 1955) p. 27.
24. Frank Lloyd Wright, *An Autobiography* (1932; New York, 1977) pp. 53 and 73. See also N. G. Menochal, *Architecture as Nature. The Transcendentalist Idea of Louis Sullivan* (Madison, Wisc., 1981) pp. 81–5.
25. J. D. Rosenberg, *The Darkening Glass. A Portrait of John Ruskin's Genius* (New York, 1961) pp. 71–6. But see K. O. Garrigan, *Ruskin on Architecture: His Thought and Influence* (Madison, Wisc., 1973) pp. 152–4 for the opposing view.
26. Wright, 'Organic Architecture' (1939), in Kaufmann, *Frank Lloyd Wright*, p. 18.
27. Wright, 'Architecture and Modern Life' (1937), in ibid., p. 20.
28. Wright, *Ausgeführte Bauten* (1910) in ibid., p. 26.
29. Frank Lloyd Wright, *An Organic Architecture. The Architecture of Democracy* (London, 1939 and 1970) p. 6.
30. Wright, 'In the Cause of Architecture', p. 155; *The Stones of Venice* I, in *Ruskin Works* 9, p. 85.

31. Wright, in the *New York Times* (1953) in Kaufmann, *Frank Lloyd Wright*, p. 260.

CONCLUSION

1. On this aspect of postmodernism, see P. Harries, A. Lipman, S. Purden, 'The marketing of meaning: aesthetics incorporated', *Environment and Planning B*, 9 (1982) pp. 457–66; also M. Swenarton, 'Post-Modern Quartet', *Building Design* (26 May 1985) pp. 24–31. The founding text of the New Right in architecture is D. Watkin, *Morality and Architecture. The Development of a Theme in Architectural History and Theory from the Gothic Revival to the Modern Movement* (Oxford, 1977).

2. The sexual fantasies about manual workers of Carpenter and Ashbee were the most extreme instance of this. See E. Carpenter (ed. D. Fernbach and N. Greig), *Selected Writings. Volume I. Sex* (1984); A. Crawford, *C. R. Ashbee. Architect, Designer and Romantic Socialist* (1985).

3. R. Unwin, 'Some Objections Answered', *Commonweal*, 4, 126 (9 June 1888) p. 181.

4. But see A. Callen, *Angel in the Studio: Women in the Arts and Crafts Movement* (1979).

5. J. W. von Goethe, 'Von Deutscher Baukunst' (1772), in E. G. Holt, *A Documentary History of Art* (2 vols, New York, 1958) 2, p. 367.

6. W. Morris, 'The Prospects of Architecture in Civilization' (1881), in Morris Works 22, p. 144; J. Ruskin, *The Stones of Venice* II (1855) in Ruskin Works 10, p. 196.

7. A. J. Penty, *The Restoration of the Gild System* (1906) p. 11. For this idea in modernist thought, see S. Giedion, *Space, Time and Architecture* (Cambridge, Mass., 1941 and 1980) p. vi and pp. 11–13 and 875–81.

8. A. Loos, 'The Poor Little Rich Man' (1900), in A. Loos, *Spoken into the Void. Collected Essays 1897–1900* (Cambridge, Mass., 1982) pp. 125–7. For a discussion of Loos and Ruskin, see E. Timms, 'Facade and Function: the alliance between Karl Kraus and Adolf Loos', *9H* 6 (1983) pp. 9–14.

Index

Figures in **bold** refer to illustrations